LEGAL ISSUES IN CLINICAL PRACTICE WITH VICTIMS OF VIOLENCE

LEGAL ISSUES IN CLINICAL PRACTICE WITH VICTIMS OF VIOLENCE

John E. B. Myers

THE GUILFORD PRESS
New York London

A Division of Guilford Publications, Inc.
370 Seventh Avenue, Suite 1200, New York, NY 10001
www.guilford.com

Printed in the United States of America

This book is printed on acid-free paper.

Last digit is print number: 9 8 7 6 5 4 3 2 1

Library of Congress Cataloging-in-Publication Data

Names: Myers, John E. B., author.
Title: Legal issues in clinical practice with victims of violence / John E. B. Myers.
Description: New York : The Guilford Press, 2017. | Includes bibliographical references and index.
Identifiers: LCCN 2016022261 | ISBN 9781462528592 (hardcover)
Subjects: LCSH: Victims of crimes—Legal status, laws, etc.—United States. | Family violence—Law and legislation—United States. | Evidence, Expert—United States. | Physicians—Malpractice—United States.
Classification: LCC KF9763 .M94 2017 | DDC 344.7303/28815—dc23
LC record available at https://lccn.loc.gov/2016022261

This book is dedicated to . . .

Lucy Berliner, a source of wisdom, humor, and guidance for many and me.

Don Bross, my first mentor, about 1,000 years ago.

Dave Corwin, my idea man and compassionate leader.

Howard Dubowitz, the co-keeper of our collective conscience.

Kathleen Coulborn Faller, the other co-keeper of our collective conscience.

Martin Finkel, a leading voice for children's medical and mental well-being.

David Finkelhor, a pioneer and colleague, who is so dang smart he makes me nervous.

Gail Goodman, the queen of child witness research—long live the queen.

Michael Lamb, "Oh, so that's how you are supposed to interview kids." Thanks, Michael.

Tom Lyon, the king of child witness research—long live the king.

Gary Melton, for important contributions—and, on a much smaller scale, for correcting my errant thinking more often than I like to admit.

Karen Saywitz, for her quiet compassion on the front lines of mental health care for victims.

Paul Stern, who has put more bad guys in jail than Detective Olivia Benson of *Law and Order: SVU.*

Anthony Urquiza, a leading researcher on treatment and my go-to person when a child needs the best help there is *right now*!

Charles Wilson and Donna Pence, the dynamic duo of child protection.

About the Author

John E. B. Myers, JD, is Professor of Law in the McGeorge School of Law at the University of the Pacific in Sacramento, California. An authority on legal and historical aspects of child maltreatment, intimate partner violence, stalking, sexual assault, elder abuse, and mental health, he has published 14 books and over 140 articles and chapters related to mental health and interpersonal violence and has given more than 400 presentations across the United States and internationally. His writing has been cited by more than 190 courts, including the U.S. Supreme Court.

Preface

On a cold February night, 3-week-old Mary died of hypothermia in the homeless camp where she and her mother, Rachel, had been living in a tent. Mary was clad only in a thin onesie and a urine-soaked diaper. She froze as her mother lay next to her in a methamphetamine-induced stupor. Rachel had been addicted to meth for years. Why didn't someone come to Mary's rescue before it was too late? What should happen to Rachel?

Rita came to the United States from Mexico on a student visa. While at college, she met Sam, who was just back from four tours of duty with the Army in Iraq and Afghanistan. Sam had posttraumatic stress disorder (PTSD) and mild traumatic brain injury. By his own admission, Sam was "lost." He spent most of his time skateboarding and drinking with friends. Rita and Sam's love affair was tumultuous, and Sam occasionally slapped Rita when he was drinking and angry. When their baby, Jasmine, was born, Sam paid little attention. When Jasmine was 3 months old, Rita was informed by immigration that her student visa was expired, and she had to leave the country. Believing Sam was not a "good father or partner," Rita returned to Mexico with Jasmine. She did not tell Sam. Once in Mexico, Rita hid. Meanwhile, Sam got treatment for his PTSD, quit partying, finished college, and "grew up." Sam started looking for Rita soon after she left, and after 2 years of trying, he found Rita and Jasmine in Mexico. What can Sam do? He wants a relationship with his daughter. What should Rita do? She is settled and working in Mexico, and she cannot return legally to the United States. What is best for Jasmine?

Priya is a psychotherapist. For 6 months, Priya provided treatment to Ted, who was experiencing depression related to a nasty divorce. At one point, Ted asked Priya out on a date. Priya responded appropriately (therapeutically and ethically), but Ted would not abandon his desire for a social relationship. Priya terminated therapy. Soon, Priya found flowers on her car windshield three or four times a week. Ted wrote frequent letters to Priya, explaining his love for her. Priya asked Ted to stop, but he wouldn't. Several times, Priya noticed Ted sitting in his car across the street from her office. One Saturday, Priya walked out the front door of her home, which is 40 miles from her office, to see Ted sitting in his parked car. Is Priya in danger? What can she do?

Not long ago, 90-year-old John lost his wife of 70 years. Since his wife died, he has been depressed. John's only child died a while back *of old age*! John has grand- and great-grandkids, but they live far away. Nine months ago, Mary Sue, the 40-year-old daughter of John's neighbor, offered to help John around the house. Mary Sue started paying John's bills and managing his affairs. Before long, Mary Sue was paying herself $1,000 a month from John's Social Security. Mary Sue also had her name placed on John's bank accounts. Finally, Mary Sue helped John draft a will that gives his home and money to her and leaves nothing to his family. When asked, John says, "Listen, I may be old, but my mind works just fine. The only one to offer me any help is Mary Sue. I know exactly what she's doing with my money, and I approve. I'm leaving everything to her because that's what I want, so mind your own business." Should anything be done about this situation? If so, what?

These and innumerable other cases raise complex clinical, ethical, moral, and legal issues. Often, there is no clear answer or resolution to those issues. As a professional clinician, you are equipped with clinical expertise, and your moral compass points you in the right direction. The purpose of this book is to address the legal and ethical dimensions of problems like these. Of course, the book won't necessarily offer easy answers; answers to complex human problems aren't supposed to be easy. Indeed, the answers may become more elusive as you deepen your understanding of both the law and ethics.

The law pervades our professional lives. This book will help equip mental health, social work, nursing, and medical professionals who treat victims of interpersonal violence, neglect, and abuse with the legal knowledge to improve practice. Melton, Petrila, Poythress, and Slobogin (2007) remind us of the importance of legal knowledge: "Whether legally or behaviorally trained, professionals whose practice takes them into interdisciplinary matters have an ethical obligation to learn enough to be able to function competently in such a context" (p. 6). Along similar lines, the American Psychological Association's (2013) "Specialty Guidelines for Forensic Psychology" emphasize that professionals who interact with the legal system appreciate "the importance of obtaining a fundamental and reasonable level of knowledge and understanding of the legal and professional standards, laws, rules, and precedents that govern their participation in legal proceedings" (Guideline 2.04, p. 9). In its "Guidelines for Child Custody Evaluations in Family Law

Proceedings," the American Psychological Association (2010b) again emphasizes the importance of legal knowledge, writing that custody evaluators "strive to remain familiar with applicable legal and regulatory standards, including laws governing child custody adjudication" (p. 864). For social workers, Slater and Finck (2012) provide a thorough analysis of legal issues.

The pages that follow discuss a broad range of subjects, including criminal law, family law, juvenile court, privilege, malpractice, testifying in court, coping with cross-examination, the duty to report child abuse, and other issues at the interface of law and clinical practice, especially practice with victims of interpersonal violence, neglect, and abuse. The first half of the book (Parts I–III) provides an overview of the criminal and civil justice systems, with a particular focus on federal and state laws, legal cases, and other facets of the legal system that are relevant to clinical professionals. The second half of the book (Parts IV–V) discusses practical and procedural legal issues you need to be savvy about when you are called as a witness in court and when you are seeing clients and patients in your office or the clinic. The book concludes with a discussion of how interpersonal violence, abuse, and neglect are proven in court and the vital roles clinicians play in offering such proof.

It is important to know what this book does *not* do. It does not tell clinical professionals how to do their jobs. It would be presumptuous for me, a lawyer, to tell you how to do psychotherapy, conduct a physical examination, interview a child, or conduct a risk assessment. What these pages do, I hope, is add to your understanding of the legal implications of your work.

Readers of this book are familiar with the *Diagnostic and Statistical Manual of Mental Disorders* (DSM-5; American Psychiatric Association, 2013). However, clinicians may wonder: Do judges and attorneys use the DSM? The answer is yes, all the time. Judges recognize DSM-5 as the leading authority on diagnosis. In the case of *Detention of New* (2014), for example, the Illinois Supreme Court spoke for itself and other courts when it wrote, "The manual, which is published by the American Psychiatric Association, provides an authoritative categorical classification of mental disorders" (p. 409). In a similar vein, the Mississippi Supreme Court wrote in *Chase v. State* (2015) that DSM-5 provides a clear standard to be used by courts to evaluate whether a person is intellectually disabled.

In the abstract, the law is often dry and tedious. It is when the law applies to real people that it comes alive. In this book, I periodically inject case studies—such as the ones just alluded to—to tell the stories of real people and to illustrate the enormous range of legal and ethical issues confronting clinicians.

A NOTE ON CITATION OF LEGAL CASES

Most likely, you are familiar with the literature in your discipline and with how books and articles are cited in it. But it's less likely that you are familiar with how legal cases are cited. This book discusses many legal cases, most of which are opinions from state and federal appellate courts. As you read this book, you will encounter numerous citations to appellate court cases. Citation to a case begins with the name of the case, followed by the year the case was decided [e.g., *Detention of New* (2014)]. If you want to read the court's decision, go to the References at the back of the book for the full citation to the case [e.g., *Detention of New*, 21 N.E.3d 406, 409 (Ill. 2014)]. The numbers and letters that follow the name of the case tell you where to find the court's decision. Let's take a moment to unlock the meaning of these numbers and letters.

Decisions by appellate courts are published in the National Reporter System by West Publishing. The Reporter System divides the states into seven regions: Atlantic (abbreviated A. or A.2d or A.3d for first, second, or third series) (CT, DE, DC, ME, MD, NH, NJ, PA, RI, VT); North East (abbreviated N.E. or N.E.2d, or N.E.3d) (IL, IN, MA, NY, OH); North West (abbreviated N.W. or N.W.2d or N.W.3d) (IA, MI, MN, NE, ND, SD, WI); South East (abbreviated S.E. or S.E.2d S.E.3d) (GA, NC, SC, VA, WV); South (abbreviated So. or S.2d or S.3d) (AL, FL, LA, MS); South West (abbreviated S.W. or S.W.2d or S.W.3d) (AR, KY, MO, TN, TX); and Pacific (abbreviated P or P.2d or P.3d) (AK, AZ, CA, CO, HI, ID, KS, MT, NV, NM, OK, OR, UT, WA, WY).

Federal cases have their own books in the Reporter System: United States Supreme Court Reports (abbreviated: U.S. or S. Ct.); federal circuit court of appeal decisions are published in the Federal Reporter (abbreviated F or F.2d or F.3d); federal district court decisions are published in the Federal Supplement (abbreviated F. Supp. or F. Supp. 2d or F. Supp. 3d); military cases are published in the Military Justice Reporter (abbreviated M.J).

Published appellate court decisions are listed by their citations. The first number after the name of the case is the volume in which the case appears. The volume number is followed by the Reporter that contains the full report of the court's decision, for example, N.E.3d. The number following the Reporter is the first page of the court's decision. Unlike citations in the psychological and medical literatures, legal citations contain only the first page, not inclusive pages. Next comes the state where the case was decided, and finally, the year of decision. Referring to *Detention of New*, 21 N.E.3d 406 (Ill. 2014), you can find this case in volume 21 of North East Reporter, third series, beginning at page 406, decided in 2014 by the Illinois Supreme Court. If you desire to read any of the court decisions cited in this book, you can find the decision by Googling the citation.

It is important to thank my primary editor at The Guilford Press, Jim Nageotte, who contributed substantially to the organization and content of the book. Many thanks too to Cathleen Mulloy-Gregson, my long-suffering assistant, without whose good humor and able assistance nothing gets done.

Shall we begin?

Contents

PART I. THE BASICS

1. The American Legal System 3
What Roles Will You Play in the Legal System? 3
Sources of Law 4
The United States Is a Common-Law Country 11
The Adversary System of Justice 12
The Right to Jury Trial 13
Ambivalence about Lawyers 14
Conclusion 15

PART II. THE CRIMINAL JUSTICE SYSTEM

2. Crimes and Defenses 19
Case Studies 19
The "Reasonable Person" Standard in Law 21
Crimes 22
Defenses to Crime 35
Case Studies Revisited 51
Conclusion 53

3. Criminal Investigation and Trial 54
Investigation of Crime 54
Trial of a Criminal Case 60
Sentencing 64
Conclusion 67

4. Hearsay 68

Exceptions to the Hearsay Rule 71
The Impact of the U.S. Constitution on Hearsay 75
A Final Note about Documentation 83

PART III. THE CIVIL JUSTICE SYSTEM

5. Family Law 87

Divorce 88
Establishing the Parent–Child Relationship: Parentage 90
Child Custody 90
The Hague Convention on Civil Aspects of International Child Abduction 102
Visitation 103
Conclusion 104

6. Child Protective Services and Juvenile Court 105

Child Protective Services 107
Juvenile Court 112
Abuse and Neglect: Dependency Proceedings in Juvenile Court 116
Conclusion 125

7. Voluntary and Involuntary Mental Health Treatment 127

A Short History of Involuntary Commitment 127
Short-Term Emergency Hospitalization 128
Legal Standards for Civil Commitment to Inpatient Treatment 129
Risk Assessment: Predicting Dangerousness 130
Legal Standards for Outpatient Commitment 131
The Right to Refuse Treatment 132
Periodic Review of Civil Commitment 132
Civil Commitment of Persons with Intellectual Disability 133
Civil Commitment of Children 133
Civil Commitment of Sex Offenders 134
Voluntary Hospitalization 136
Advance Directives 137
Conclusion 138

PART IV. CLINICIANS AND COURTS

8. Testifying in Court 143

Competence to Testify 143
How Testimony Unfolds 144
Secrets of Cross-Examination 149
Objections at Trial 154
Conclusion 157

9. Expert Testimony 158

Opinion Testimony from Lay Witnesses 159
Who May Provide Expert Testimony? 161
Bases for Expert Testimony 162
Opinions on Ultimate Issues 163
The Reasonable Certainty Standard for Expert Testimony 164
Scientific Evidence 167
Preparation Is the Key 169
Experts Are Educators, Not Advocates 170
Direct Examination of Expert Witnesses 170
Cross-Examination of Expert Witnesses 171
Case Study: Samantha 173
Should a Forensic Interviewer Do More Than Lay the Foundation for a CAC Interview? 182
Cross-Examination of the Forensic Interviewer 185
Cross-Examination Using a Learned Treatise 192
Conclusion 201

10. Confidentiality and Privilege 202

Case Studies 203
Confidentiality Defined 204
Sources of Confidentiality 205
Waiver, Forfeiture, and Inapplicability of Privileges 215
A Dangerous Patient 217
Confidentiality and Privilege in Forensic Evaluations 217
Confidentiality and Privilege in Couple, Family, and Group Therapy 219
Disclosure of Confidential and Privileged Information 220
Case Studies Revisited 224
Conclusion 225

11. Malpractice and Ethical Violations 226
Malpractice Liability for Psychotherapy 227
Clinical and Forensic Roles in Mental Health 228
Professional Boundaries 228
Dual Relationships 229
Informed Consent 232
Disclosure of Confidential and/or Privileged Matter 233
Suicide 234
The Duty to Protect Third Persons from a Dangerous Patient 237
Abandonment versus Termination of Treatment 243
The Duty to Report Child Abuse and Neglect 243
Civil Rights Violations 244
Court-Appointed Experts Have Immunity 245
Your Right to Be Safe 245
Conclusion 246

PART V. PROVING INTERPERSONAL VIOLENCE IN COURT

12. Proof in Court 249
Proof of Domestic Violence 249
Proof of Child Physical Abuse 250
Proof of Neglect 253
Proof of Child Sexual Abuse 254
A Final Case Study: Allegations of Child Sexual Abuse in Family Court—Systemic Dysfunction 263
Conclusion 276

13. Concluding Thoughts 277

References 283

Index 295

LEGAL ISSUES IN CLINICAL PRACTICE WITH VICTIMS OF VIOLENCE

Part I

The Basics

Part I, Chapter 1, provides fundamental information about the law and the American legal system. For clinicians whose last formal brush with the legal system was a course in high school or college, Chapter 1 should be enlightening, particularly the material on the court system. You can skip this chapter if you are well schooled in the fundamentals of the legal system.

1

The American Legal System

This chapter introduces the American legal system. What is meant by law? The U.S. Supreme Court has defined law as "the rules of action or conduct duly prescribed by controlling authority, and having binding legal force" (*United States Fidelity and Guaranty Co. v. Guenther,* 1930, p. 37).

WHAT ROLES WILL YOU PLAY IN THE LEGAL SYSTEM?

Mental health, medical, and social work professionals play key roles in society's response to interpersonal violence. Outside the legal arena, clinicians diagnose and treat victims and offenders of interpersonal violence. At the interface of law and clinical work, clinicians provide court-ordered evaluations and treatment. Victims often disclose abuse to clinicians, triggering the duty of clinicians to report. Clinicians are subpoenaed to testify in court to repeat victim disclosures, raising complex issues related to confidentiality, privileged communications, the validity of subpoenas, and hearsay evidence. Finally, in countless legal cases, clinicians provide expert testimony in court that is essential to the search for truth.

Examples of expert testimony abound. Consider what occurs in a typical courthouse. In a criminal trial alleging child sexual abuse, a mental health professional's testimony helps a jury understand that many sexually abused children delay disclosing abuse. Another mental health professional in the same trial critiques how the child was interviewed at a child advocacy center. A third expert may be a physician or nurse, who describes the results of a physical examination. In a child custody case in the next courtroom, a mental health professional describes the results of a custody evaluation. In yet another courtroom, a juvenile court judge, who is presiding over a child neglect case, listens to testimony from the child protection worker handling the case, as well as to testimony from a psychologist who evaluated the child and the parents. If the child is Native American, the juvenile court will solicit expert cultural advice from an expert on the child and parents' tribe. There are many more situations in which testimony from clinicians plays key roles in court.

If you work with victims or offenders of interpersonal violence, you will regularly interact with the legal system. A thorough understanding of the system can make you a better clinician. This chapter begins with the fundamentals of our system. Subsequent chapters discuss the complexities of the legal system in more depth.

SOURCES OF LAW

The laws that govern your life and impact your profession come from several sources. You may recall from your high school government class that the United States has a federal government and 50 state governments. Within each state are county, city, school district, and other governing bodies that have something to say about how you do your work.

Federal Government

The highest law of the land is the U.S. Constitution. The Preamble to the Constitution states: "We the people of the United States, in order to form a more perfect union, establish justice, insure domestic tranquility, provide for the common defense, promote the general welfare, and secure the blessings of liberty to ourselves and our posterity, do ordain and establish this Constitution for the United States of America." The Constitution is the legal bedrock of our society.

A Government of Limited Powers

Under the Constitution, the federal government is a government of limited, or delegated, powers. The federal government possesses only those powers delegated to it by the Constitution. Congress has delegated authority to pass laws to collect taxes, provide for the common defense, declare war, borrow money on the credit of the United States, and regulate commerce among the states.

To implement the powers delegated to the federal government by the Constitution, Article I, Section 8 of the Constitution gives Congress the power to "make all laws which shall be necessary and proper for carrying into execution" the delegated powers. The necessary and proper clause, as it is called, gives Congress broad authority to enact legislation designed to carry into effect the delegated powers.

Governmental powers that are not delegated to the federal government by the Constitution are reserved to state governments and to the people, according to the Tenth Amendment. The U.S. Supreme Court and lower courts continue the never-ending task of defining the extent and limits of federal delegated power.

The powers delegated to the federal government don't include giving Congress authority to pass laws that set policies regarding child maltreatment, intimate partner violence, elder abuse, stalking, or sexual assault. These matters are within the authority of the states. Yet, if you work in this field, you know that Congress plays a critical role in setting national policy regarding interpersonal violence and in funding programs. How does Congress set policy over matters that belong to the states, and over which Congress has no delegated authority? The answer is simple: money. As mentioned previously, the Constitution gives Congress the authority to collect taxes. Incident to the authority to collect money is the authority to spend it: Congress's so-called "spending power." Congress sends millions of dollars to the states, but the money comes with certain strings. Congress shapes national policy by telling states, in effect, if you want federal dollars, you must comply with Congress's policy agenda. Because states are usually starved for cash, they take the money *and* the policy strings.

Separation of Powers

The Constitution divides the federal government into three branches: legislative, executive, and judicial. The power to enact legislation is vested in the legislative branch, or Congress (Article I). Laws passed by Congress, and signed by the President, are statutes, and are compiled in the *United States Code* (U.S.C.). The annotated U.S.C. contains more than 350 volumes of statutory federal law.

The President is head of the executive branch (Article II). The executive branch is home to hundreds of federal agencies, including, to name a few, the Department of Health and Human Services (HHS), the Children's Bureau (CB), the Centers for Disease Control and Prevention

(CDC), the Department of Justice (DOJ), the Department of Defense (DOD), and the Food and Drug Administration (FDA).

Agencies of the executive branch have authority to promulgate regulations that are needed to implement statutes passed by Congress. Federal regulations are collected in the *Code of Federal Regulations* (CFR). Federal regulations, like statutes, are law.

The third branch of the federal government is the judicial branch (Article III), which consists of the U.S. Supreme Court and lower federal courts created by Congress. The federal judiciary has three levels: The Supreme Court is the nation's highest court. Below the Supreme Court are 13 judicial circuits, each presided over by a Federal Circuit Court of Appeals. For example, the Ninth Circuit Court of Appeals embraces Hawaii, Alaska, Washington, Oregon, California, Nevada, Montana, Idaho, and Arizona. The Fifth Circuit Court of Appeals covers Texas, Louisiana, and Mississippi.

The third level in the federal judicial system consists of federal district courts, or courts where trials are held. Federal trial judges are district court judges. Nearly all federal court cases begin in the district court. Federal courts have authority over matters involving federal civil and criminal law. As well, federal courts have what is commonly called "diversity jurisdiction," which allows a citizen of one state to sue a citizen of another state in federal court.

Of interest to readers of this book, there are federal criminal laws to punish interstate stalking (18 U.S.C. § 2261A), and domestic violence that crosses state lines (18 U.S.C. § 2261). The federal Violence Against Women Act can be enforced in federal court. Federal courts, as well as state courts, enforce civil rights laws.

The party who loses a case in the federal district court may appeal to the appropriate Federal Circuit Court of Appeals. The loser in the Court of Appeals may appeal to the U.S. Supreme Court. The Supreme Court has discretion regarding which appeals to accept, and accepts only a small fraction of appeals.

Lawsuits for divorce, spousal and child support, and child custody are not litigated in federal court. In *Ankenbrandt v. Richards* (1992), the U.S. Supreme Court ruled that the so-called "domestic relations exception" to the authority of federal courts divests federal courts of authority over matters of divorce, alimony, and child custody. Thus, family law matters are handled in state court.

There is one aspect of family law that can be litigated in federal court. The United States is a party to the Hague Convention on the Civil Aspects of International Child Abduction, an international treaty that facilitates the return of children wrongfully removed by parents from their home country. Cases under the Hague Convention can be litigated in federal or state court. The Hague Convention is discussed in Chapter 5.

Federal judges are nominated by the president and confirmed by the U.S. Senate. Federal judges serve for life. Judges of the district court, judges of the Court of Appeals, and justices of the Supreme Court are sometimes called Article III judges because their positions are articulated in Article III of the U.S. Constitution.

At the trial court level, in addition to district court judges, the federal judiciary consists of bankruptcy judges and magistrate judges. Federal magistrate judges are appointed by the district courts judges within a federal judicial district, and handle a broad range of legal matters.

The Supremacy Clause of the U.S. Constitution

What happens when a state law is inconsistent with the U.S. Constitution, a federal statute, or a federal regulation? The answer is supplied by Article VI of the U.S. Constitution—the so-called Supremacy Clause—which states that federal law "shall be the supreme law of the land." A state law that conflicts with federal law is unconstitutional. A famous example is *Cooper v. Aaron* (1958), decided by a unanimous U.S. Supreme Court in 1958. To understand *Cooper v. Aaron,* it is necessary to go back in time 4 years, to 1954, the year that the U.S. Supreme Court handed down the momentous decision in *Brown v. Board of Education* (1954), outlawing racial segregation in public schools. The *Brown* Court ruled that segregation violates the equal protection of the law guaranteed by the Fourteenth Amendment to the U.S. Constitution. Therefore, the Supreme Court ordered states to dismantle segregation "with all deliberate speed." Following *Brown,* the school board in Little Rock, Arkansas, proceeded with plans to integrate the city's public schools, starting with Central High School. However, the Arkansas Legislature passed laws attempting to nullify the Supreme Court's decision in *Brown,* and Governor Orval Faubus deployed the National Guard to block African American students from entering Central High. Due in part to the extreme hostility to integration, fueled by the legislature and the governor, the school board asked a federal district court judge to postpone integration for 2½ years. The judge granted the school board's request, finding that Central High was afflicted with "chaos, bedlam and turmoil" (*Cooper v. Aaron,* 1958, p. 12), and that threats had been made against school administrators and the nine African American students—the Little Rock Nine—brave enough to enroll at Central High.

When the case reached the U.S. Supreme Court, the Court ruled that the district court judge was wrong to postpone integration. The Supreme Court wrote:

> The constitutional rights of [African American children] are not to be sacrificed or yielded to the violence and disorder which have followed upon the actions of the Governor and Legislature. . . . The constitutional rights of children not to be discriminated against in school admission on grounds of race or color declared by this Court in the *Brown* case can neither be nullified openly and directly by state legislators or state executive or judicial officers, nor nullified indirectly by them through evasive schemes for segregation whether attempted ingeniously or ingenuously. (*Cooper v. Aaron,* 1958, p. 17)

Efforts by Arkansas legislators and the governor to nullify the Supreme Court's desegregation ruling in *Brown* ran afoul of the Supremacy Clause, and were not successful. The U.S. Constitution, as the "supreme law of the land," includes the right to equal protection of the law. The racist efforts of state officials failed.

State and Local Governments

Each state has its own constitution which, like the U.S. Constitution, divides government into three branches: legislative, executive, and judicial. The legislature passes statutes, which are collected in a state code.

The executive branch of each state is led by the state's governor. Agencies of the executive branch promulgate regulations. Like their federal counterparts in the CFR, state regulations have the force of law. Laws regulating clinical practice can be found in state codes and state regulations.

The state judiciary is made up of trial and appellate courts. The state supreme court is the highest appellate court, except in New York, where the Supreme Court is the trial court and the highest court is the Court of Appeals. In Maryland, the highest court is also the Court of Appeals. In all but a few sparsely populated states, an intermediate appellate court sits between the trial courts and the state supreme court.

Each state contains entities of local government: counties (parishes in Louisiana), cities, towns, and various types of authorities (e.g., fire districts). Local government entities (e.g., counties) pass laws called ordinances. For example, most counties have a curfew ordinance requiring teenagers to be home at night.

The Unique Role of the U.S. Supreme Court

The U.S. Supreme Court is one of the most important, revered, and, at times, reviled institutions in America. Decisions of the Supreme Court impact the lives of everyone. An example, just discussed, is the Court's monumental decision in *Brown v. Board of Education,* outlawing school segregation.

Another groundbreaking decision is *Loving v. Virginia* (1967), in which the Supreme Court struck down anti-miscegenation laws, or laws against interracial marriage. At the middle of the 20th century, 29 states prohibited interracial marriage.

The case involved Richard Loving and Mildred Jeter, who grew up in the tiny rural community of Central Point, Virginia. Richard was white. Mildred was part black and part Native American. When Richard was 24 and Mildred 18, they decided to marry, but marriage between races was a crime in Virginia. They drove to Washington, D.C., got married, and drove home to Virginia, where, a few weeks later, they were arrested in the middle of the night by the sheriff, who told them their marriage license was "no good here." The couple was charged with violating Virginia's Racial Integrity Act. A local judge convicted them and sentenced them to 1 year in jail, but said he would suspend the sentence if Richard and Mildred left Virginia for 25 years. The couple moved to Washington, D.C., but Mildred didn't like city life, and the Lovings and their children often snuck home to visit.

In 1963, Mildred wrote a letter to Robert Kennedy, Attorney General of the United States, asking if the Justice Department might help. Kennedy referred Mildred's letter to the American Civil Liberties Union. Two young ACLU lawyers, Bernard Cohen and Philip Hirschkop, both barely out of law school, took the case all the way to the U.S. Supreme Court. In the landmark *Loving* decision, the Supreme Court struck down Virginia's anti-miscegenation law as a violation of the Due Process Clause and the Equal Protection Clause of the Fourteenth Amendment. Writing for the Supreme Court, Chief Justice Earl Warren wrote:

> Marriage is one of the basic civil rights of man, fundamental to our very existence and survival. To deny this fundamental freedom on so unsupportable a basis as the racial classifications embodied in these statutes, classifications so directly subversive of the principle

> of equality at the heart of the Fourteenth Amendment, is surely to deprive all the State's citizens of liberty without due process of law. The Fourteenth Amendment requires that the freedom of choice to marry not be restricted by invidious racial discriminations. Under our Constitution, the freedom to marry or not marry, a person of another race resides with the individual and cannot be infringed by the State. (*Loving v. Virginia,* 1967, p. 12)

You may have noticed that in *Loving v. Virginia,* the U.S. Supreme Court, a *federal* court, struck down a *state* law. What gave a federal court the right to rule on a state law? The answer, which was mentioned earlier, is that the U.S. Constitution is the supreme law of the land, superior to state law. The U.S. Supreme Court is the final arbiter of the U.S. Constitution. Thus, the Supreme Court has authority to strike down state statutes that violate the federal Constitution. Although *Loving v. Virginia* was originally brought in state court, the case ended up in the U.S. Supreme Court because the Virginia anti-miscegenation statute violated the U.S. Constitution.

Loving v. Virginia struck down barriers to interracial marriage. In 2015, in *Obergefell v. Hodges* (2015), the Supreme Court did the same to barriers to same-sex marriage. The Court ruled that prohibitions against same-sex marriage violate fundamental principles of fairness and equality. Justice Anthony Kennedy, who wrote the majority opinion in *Obergefell,* stated:

> The Constitution promises liberty to all within its reach, a liberty that includes certain specific rights that allow persons, within a lawful realm, to define and express their identity. The petitioners in these cases seek to find that liberty by marrying someone of the same sex and having their marriages deemed lawful. . . . (p. 2593)
>
> The centrality of marriage to the human condition makes it unsurprising that the institution has existed for millennia and across civilizations. Since the dawn of history, marriage has transformed strangers into relatives, binding families and societies together. . . . There are untold references to the beauty of marriage in religious and philosophical texts spanning time, cultures, and faiths, as well as in art and literature in all their forms. . . . (p. 2594)
>
> That history is the beginning of these cases. The [opponents of same-sex marriage] say it should be the end as well. To them, it would demean a timeless institution if the concept and lawful status of marriage were extended to two person of the same sex. Marriage, in

> their view, is by its nature a gender-differentiated union of man and woman. This view long has been held—and continues to be held—in good faith by reasonable and sincere people here and throughout the world. (p. 2594)
>
> The petitioners acknowledge this history, but contend that these cases cannot end there. Were their intent to demean the revered idea and reality of marriage, the petitioners' claims would be of a different order. But that is neither their purpose nor their submission. To the contrary, it is the enduring importance of marriage that underlies the petitioners' contentions. This, they say, is their whole point. Far from seeking to devalue marriage, the petitioners seek it for themselves because of their respect—and need—for its privileges and responsibilities. (p. 2594)

This is inspiring prose from the Supreme Court, and one of its most important justices.

In any discussion of the U.S. Supreme Court, you may encounter the Latin term "writ of certiorari." A writ is a court order. A writ of certiorari is a writ issued by a superior court, ordering a lower court to send the record of the lower court to the superior court for review. Every year, the U.S. Supreme Court receives approximately 10,000 applications for writ of certiorari, asking the Supreme Court to review lower-court decisions. The Court grants only 75–80 writs a year. In the *Loving* and *Obergefell* cases, attorneys filed applications for the writ of certiorari in the Supreme Court. Fortunately, the Court issued writs and decided these landmark cases.

THE UNITED STATES IS A COMMON-LAW COUNTRY

Legislatures make law; they do so by passing statutes. Appellate courts also make law, but, of course, appellate courts do not pass statutes. Appellate courts make law through written opinions in individual cases. Judge-made law is called "common law."

For centuries in England, judges had the authority to create common law, and nations, or former colonies, that inherited the English legal system adopted the principle of judge-made common law. A California statute that is similar to statutes in other states acknowledges common law: "The common law of England, so far as it is not repugnant to or inconsistent with [federal and California law] is the rule of decision in all the courts of this state" (Cal. Civil Code § 22.2).

THE ADVERSARY SYSTEM OF JUSTICE

Disputes between individuals, and disputes between individuals and the government, are resolved many ways. The vast majority of disagreements are disposed of informally through negotiation and compromise. Abraham Lincoln (1850/1953), who practiced law in Illinois for 25 years before becoming president, urged his fellow lawyers to help people settle disagreements without going to court. He wrote, "Discourage litigation. Persuade your neighbors to compromise whenever you can. Point out to them how the nominal winner is often the real loser—in fees, expenses, and waste of time. As a peacemaker the lawyer has a superior opportunity of being a good man. There will still be business enough." When compromise and mediation are not possible, litigation in court "is society's last line of defense in the indispensable effort to secure the peaceful settlement of social conflicts" (Hart & McNaughton, 1958, p. 52).

In the United States, litigation is based on the adversary system developed long ago in England. The adversary system is premised on the belief that the most effective way to arrive at just results in court is for each side of a controversy to present the evidence that is most favorable to its position and to let a neutral judge or jury sift through the conflicting evidence and decide where the truth lies. In other words, the truth emerges from the clash of opposing evidence.

Professionals who are not trained in law sometimes shake their heads at the adversary process, and find themselves thinking, "These lawyers are a strange lot. How do they expect to find the truth when they seem to spend half their time hiding it from each other, and the other half obfuscating the facts with squabbles over inconsequential details?" There is an old lawyer joke: The kindly judge said to the witness, "You seem to be in some distress; is anything the matter?" The witness replied, "Well, your honor, I swore to tell the truth, the whole truth, and nothing but the truth, but every time I try, some lawyer objects!" Despite its shortcomings, the adversary system has stood the test of time. Perhaps a better system will emerge, but most likely not in your professional lifetime. When you head to court, the adversary system awaits you.

It is important to add that litigation is not always adversarial. Some court proceedings are designed to minimize confrontation. A good example is juvenile court protective proceedings intended to safeguard children and help parents. Hearings in juvenile court are typically informal and nonadversarial, although some juvenile court cases are highly contested. In family court litigation regarding divorce, child custody, and child support is often adversarial, although efforts are made to tamp down conflict. Many cities have specialized courts, such as drug courts and veterans' courts, where the emphasis is on treatment and positive reinforcement for constructive behavior.

Regardless of the type of case, lawyers are regarded as officers of the court and are expected to act civilly toward the judge, witnesses, and each other. In a California case in which the attorneys' aggressive behavior went over the top, the Court of Appeal reminded lawyers of the importance of civility, writing, "We close this discussion with a reminder to counsel—all counsel, regardless of practice, regardless of age—that zealous advocacy does not equate with 'attack dog' or 'scorched earth'; nor does it mean lack of civility. Zeal and vigor in the representation of clients are commendable. So are civility, courtesy, and cooperation. They are not mutually exclusive" (*Marriage of Davenport,* 2011, p. 1537).

In your dealings with lawyers in and out of court, you will find that most are honest and reasonable. Good heavens, some apparently intelligent people actually have been known to marry lawyers! Of course, there are some lawyers who are pugnacious, aggressive, and generally unpleasant. Such members of the bar are relatively uncommon, although they poison the well for the rest of the profession. One of my favorite lawyer jokes is: Ninety-eight percent of lawyers ruin things for the other 2 percent.

Lawyers are required by their code of ethics to be zealous advocates for their clients. In court, a lawyer's job is to win the case, and if winning necessitates being aggressive with witnesses, including expert witnesses, a lawyer will be aggressive. Non-attorneys sometimes shake their heads when they observe lawyers battling it out in court, only to see the same lawyers engaged in friendly conversation outside of court. In some respects, a lawyer is like a professional fighter, trying to knock out the opponent. When the fight is over, it is common for fighters to embrace. Fighters don't hate each other; they have a job to do. So do lawyers.

THE RIGHT TO JURY TRIAL

Federal and state constitutions guarantee the right to trial by jury in most criminal cases and in many civil matters. By long tradition, in most states, juries are not used in juvenile court and family court, for example, in divorce or child custody cases). When there is no jury, the judge fulfills the role performed by a jury: to determine the facts and reach a verdict. Trials without a jury are called bench trials or trials to the court. Lawyers often refer to the jury as the trier of fact. When there is no jury, the judge is the trier of fact.

AMBIVALENCE ABOUT LAWYERS

Americans love to hate lawyers. Yet, Americans understand that lawyers are indispensable to law and justice. Some of our greatest role models are lawyers. Think of Atticus Finch, the small-town lawyer in Harper Lee's classic *To Kill a Mockingbird*. Atticus epitomizes the best of the legal profession: honesty, integrity, self-sacrifice, patience, courage, and a fierce loyalty to justice. Think, too, of Thurgood Marshall, the African American lawyer for the NAACP, who, during the civil rights movement, repeatedly risked his life traveling in the Deep South to strike legal blows against segregation. Marshall became the first African American justice appointed to the U.S. Supreme Court. As mentioned earlier, Abraham Lincoln was a lawyer, and a darn good one. It seems fitting to let Mark Twain have the last word about lawyers. He captures Americans' ambivalence about the legal profession: "Lawyers are like other people—fools on the average; but it is easier for an ass to succeed in that trade than any other."

A useful way to understand the chasm that sometimes separates attorneys from mental health, medical, and social work professionals is to consider two hypothetical college graduates, Jill and Sara. Both have bachelor's degrees in psychology, and both have similar interests, temperament, and background. Jill goes to law school, and Sara seeks a master's in social work. From the first day of graduate school, the neophyte lawyer and social worker are embarked on different journeys.

Sara's first social work class is Introduction to Social Theory. The first 20 minutes consist of introductions to allow the students and the teacher to get to know each other. The remainder of the hour is a lecture.

Across campus at the law school, Jill's first class is Contract Law. Class is held in a theaterlike room with 150 seats, all focused on the podium in the well. Students sit nervously, awaiting the professor. The professor enters, places her book on the podium, and consults the list of students. The first words out of the professor's mouth are, "Good morning. This is Contracts. I am Professor Carter. Now, Ms. Jill Newman, what are the facts in the case of *Hawkins v. McGee*?" (146 A. 641 [N.H. 1929]). For the next 30 minutes, Professor Carter grills the terrified Jill with questions she cannot understand and points out the errors in her answers. When the professor asks the class, "Are there any questions?" Dead silence. There is no lecture—just dialogue between the professor and Jill. After class, Jill is surrounded by sympathizers who say, "You did great." To themselves, they think, "Thank heaven Jill was the target, not me."

Sara's experience in the school of social work is very different from Jill's in law school. Jill and her classmates got their first taste of the adversary system. They learned that their professors will force them to think critically under pressure, to analyze, question, argue, challenge, debate, and respond to criticism—in short, to think and act like a lawyer. As a social worker, Sara has the same need for critical thinking and rigorous analysis, but she learns these skills from a different perspective. The emphasis in social work is on cooperation rather than on competition, on building bridges rather than confrontation. From the first days of their professional lives, the social worker and the lawyer march to different drummers. Is it any wonder that at graduation, Jill and Sara seem to speak different languages?

Jill and Sara love children, and decide to devote themselves to helping victims of child abuse and neglect. Sara, the social worker, takes the plunge into child protective services (CPS), while Jill, the attorney, joins the child abuse unit at the district attorney's office. Not only must these young professionals struggle to learn the intricacies of their new callings, they must learn to communicate and cooperate with each other. Communication, cooperation, and, eventually, trust are essential because neither profession can achieve the goal of child protection alone.

CONCLUSION

Preventing and responding to interpersonal violence takes a team effort, and the role of clinicians is second to none. Deepening your understanding of law, and the roles of legal professionals, strengthens the team working on behalf of victims.

Now that we have described the basics of the legal system, Parts II through V discuss the system in more depth. Part II describes the criminal justice system. Part III focuses on the civil justice system, including family court, child protection and juvenile court, civil commitment, and related civil law issues. Part IV discusses clinicians' involvement in the legal system, including testifying, cross-examination, and client confidentiality. Part V focuses on the complex issues of how interpersonal violence is proved in court.

Part II

The Criminal Justice System

Part II provides an overview of the American criminal justice system. Chapter 2 is an introduction to crimes and defenses. Chapter 3 discusses criminal procedure. Chapter 4 analyzes hearsay evidence. You may be tempted to skip the hearsay chapter, thinking to yourself, "Hearsay is for lawyers to worry about. I don't have to be concerned about it." In truth, it is vital for clinicians who work with victims to understand hearsay evidence, so please think twice before skipping Chapter 4.

2

Crimes and Defenses

Every state has a criminal code that defines crimes, defenses to crime, and punishments. Criminal codes are lengthy and complex. California's Penal Code, for example, is more than 1,700 pages! The federal government has its own, lengthy criminal code. The law of crimes and defenses is called substantive criminal law.

The Model Penal Code (MPC) is a model law published by the American Law Institute. Although the MPC is not the actual law in any state, a number of states have adopted portions of the MPC (e.g., New York, Utah). Because the MPC is influential, it is mentioned a number of times in this chapter.

CASE STUDIES

To set the stage, consider three real cases. The facts of these cases are disturbing, but that, unfortunately, is the reality of criminal law. At the end of the chapter, we will return to these cases for further analysis.

SELF-DEFENSE?

A deputy sheriff was dispatched to the residence of John and Judy Norman. In a bedroom, the deputy found John lying in bed, dead. He had been shot three times in the back of the head as he slept. On the fatal day, Judy went to her mother's home, got a pistol, loaded it, and returned to shoot her sleeping husband.

Judy and John had been married 25 years. There was a long history of verbal and physical abuse of Judy. John was addicted to alcohol. He began drinking and beating Judy 5 years after they married. The couple had five children. When Judy was pregnant with her youngest child, John beat her and kicked her down a flight of steps, causing the baby to be born prematurely.

John never worked. He forced Judy to prostitute herself to support him. When she begged not to, he hit her. John required Judy to make a minimum of $100 a day; if she failed, he beat her.

John routinely called Judy dog, bitch, whore, and other names. When he was drunk, which was often, John beat Judy. He beat her with his fists, a flyswatter, a baseball bat, his shoe, a bottle—whatever was handy. He put out cigarettes on Judy's skin. He threw food in her face and refused to let her eat for days at a time. He threw ashtrays and beer bottles at her. He smashed a glass in her face. John made Judy bark like a dog. If she refused, he beat her. He often forced her to sleep on the floor. On several occasions, he forced her to eat dog food out of the dog bowl. Many times, John threatened to kill Judy.

On the fatal night, John slapped Judy and threw beer bottles at her. He ordered her to make him a sandwich. When she brought the sandwich to him, he threw it on the floor and told her to make him another. Judy made a second sandwich and brought it to him. Again, he threw it on the floor, telling Judy to wear gloves because he did not want her to touch the bread. Judy made a third sandwich, using a paper towel so her hands did not touch the bread. John smeared the sandwich in her face. John said, "I'll cut off your breast and shove it up your ass."

Judy was depressed and felt her situation was hopeless. When John went to lie down, Judy tried to lie down on a smaller bed, but John said, "No bitch. Dogs don't sleep on beds, they sleep on the floor." That's when Judy got the gun and shot him (*State v. Norman,* 1988).

Did Judy commit a crime? Is she a murderer? Should she be charged? If she is charged, does she have a defense? Could she claim self-defense? How could she say she acted in self-defense when John was asleep?

WHO COULD DO SUCH A THING?

Eight-year-old Ronnie Midgett Jr. lived with his father, Ronnie Sr., and his siblings. Ronnie Jr.'s mother did not live with them. Ronnie Sr. was 6 feet 2 inches tall and weighed 300 pounds. Ronnie Jr. weighed 40 pounds. Ronnie Jr. had been brutally beaten over many months by his father.

School personnel and a school counselor noticed bruises on Ronnie Jr. A child protective services (CPS) social worker visited the home. Ronnie Jr. would not tell the social worker how he got bruised or why he was so lethargic at school. The other children in the family were not abused.

Ronnie Jr. died on a Wednesday. On the Saturday before his death, Ronnie Sr. was drinking and beating his son. Ronnie Sr. made a fist and hit Ronnie Jr. twice in the stomach and twice on the back. He choked the boy.

On the day Ronnie Jr. died, Ronnie Sr. carried his body into the hospital emergency room and said, "There is something wrong." An autopsy showed Ronnie Jr. was malnourished. He had bruises on his lips, face, head, chest, forehead, back, stomach, and buttocks. He had healed rib fractures. Ronnie Jr. died of abdominal bleeding that resulted from his father's hitting him in the stomach (*Midgett v. State*, 1987).

What should happen to Ronnie Sr.? Why do you suppose the CPS social worker left Ronnie Jr. in the home? What should the CPS worker have done? How could a father do such horrible things to his child?

STEALING FROM AN OLD LADY

Eighty-six-year-old Erika lived in her home more than 50 years. She and her late husband owned the home. David was a neighbor. David and Erika's late husband didn't get along. After Erika's husband died, David inquired about buying Erika's home, but she refused to sell.

Erika broke her hip and went to live in a nursing home. Erika had cognitive deficits that got worse over time. One day, David arrived at Erika's bedside, handed her a document, and had her sign it. The document was a deed, conveying Erika's home to David.

Although David said he paid $50,000 for the house, there was no evidence that David paid a dime. Who owns the home? In a civil lawsuit, it should be possible to set aside the deed to the home, based on David's fraud, and Erika's dementia. Should David be criminally prosecuted?

These three cases, one involving severe, chronic domestic violence, and the victim's desperate response, one involving fatal child abuse, and one involving the financial exploitation of an incapacitated elder, represent a tiny glimpse into the vast universe of crime.

THE "REASONABLE PERSON" STANDARD IN LAW

Throughout criminal and civil law, as well as in professional ethics, you encounter the words "reasonable," "reasonable person," and "reasonably." For example, in the law of negligence, a person's conduct is judged by a reasonable person standard—what would a reasonably cautious person have done under the circumstances? If a person's behavior sank below that of a reasonably cautious person, causing injury, the person could be sued for negligence.

Reasonableness plays a key role in the crime of involuntary manslaughter. A person commits this crime when he or she kills *un*intentionally, but the death resulted from criminal negligence. Criminal negligence, like its civil counterpart, is judged by the reasonable person standard.

In standards of professional ethics, reasonableness is ubiquitous. For example, the American Psychological Association's (2010a) *Ethical Principles and Code of Conduct* discusses multiple relationships by stating, "A psychologist refrains from entering into a multiple relationship if the multiple relationship could reasonably be expected to impair the psychologist's objectivity, competence, or effectiveness . . ." (Ethical Standard 3.05[a], p. 6).

Reasonableness in ethics and in criminal and civil law is an *objective* standard, measured by what a reasonable person would do or know under the circumstances, *not* by what the person actually knew or was subjectively aware of. When reasonableness is the applicable legal standard, important legal consequences—civil and criminal—can attach to people who have *no intent to do anything wrong*; no intent to violate the law or ethical standards. For example, a person can be liable for negligently causing an auto accident even if the person was trying to drive carefully. A mental health professional might be negligent for prematurely releasing a suicidal patient from a hospital, even though the professional took what he or she thought were appropriate precautions. The reasonable person standard does not ask, "Was the driver or the mental health professional intending to act responsibly?" It asks, "How would a reasonable person have acted under those circumstances?" If the person's conduct fails to measure up to the reasonable person, the person is negligent.

CRIMES

Victims of interpersonal violence, as well as suspects, are often involved in the criminal justice system as witnesses or defendants. It is important for clinicians who work with victims or perpetrators to have a working knowledge of criminal law and procedure. Such knowledge enables clinicians to interact effectively with lawyers, judges, and the police because they can speak the same language. Knowledge of criminal law affords insight into what clients are going through, legally and emotionally.

The legislature defines crimes and also prescribes punishments. Although the details of criminal law vary from state to state, similarities across the states outnumber the differences.

Components of Crime: *Actus Reus* and *Mens Rea*

Crimes have two components: *actus reus* and *mens rea*. The *actus reus* is the physical part of crime; the act. For the crime of theft, for example, the *actus reus* is wrongfully taking someone else's property. For the crime of murder, the *actus reus* is killing a human being. For the crime of rape, the *actus reus* is use of force to penetrate the victim against his or her will. Every crime has an *actus reus*.

Mens rea is the mental part of crime, typically called criminal intent. The U.S. Supreme Court used colorful language to describe the twin components of crime. The Court wrote that crime requires an "evil-meaning mind and an evil-doing hand" (*Dixon v. United States*, 2006, p. 5).

The subject of criminal intent is complicated. Part of the complexity lies in the fact that the same word—"malice," for example—can be the *mens rea* for more than one crime and can have different meanings in each offense. For example, arson is defined as the *malicious* burning of a dwelling. Murder is the killing of a human being with *malice* aforethought. The meaning of *malice* is not the same in the two crimes. Other *mens rea* terms are reckless, intentional, willful, wanton, knowing, and negligent.

A person acts "recklessly" when she *is* aware that her conduct is highly dangerous, but she consciously disregards the danger and proceeds. Thus, Uma is reckless if she intentionally drives her Porsche at 100 miles an hour through a residential district where children are playing.

A person acts "negligently" when she is *not* aware that her conduct is dangerous, but a reasonable person in her position would be aware of the danger. Referring to Uma and her Porsche, suppose Uma is going the speed limit, but she is looking not at the road, but at her cell phone, while she texts. Uma in this situation is negligent.

The difference between negligence and recklessness lies in conscious awareness of danger. Recklessness is a more culpable mental state than negligence because the reckless person is consciously aware of the danger she creates and plows ahead anyway. The negligent person *should* be aware of the risk, but is blissfully ignorant.

In criminal law, "intentional" has several meanings. In one respect, a person acts intentionally when it is the person's conscious objective to act in a specified way or to achieve a specified result. Thus, if Uma wants to kill her rival, Bill, and Uma purposely drives her Porsche into Bill at 100 miles an hour, *in order to kill him*, Uma kills Bill intentionally—it is her conscious objective to kill Bill.

A person acts "knowingly" or "with knowledge" when the person is consciously aware that her conduct is almost certain to cause a particular result, even if the person does not want that result. For example, consider Dell, who wants to kill Paula. Dell plants a bomb on the passenger airplane on which Paula will fly. The bomb is set to explode when the plane reaches 30,000 feet. Dell does not want to kill anyone on the plane except Paula. Indeed, Dell hopes everyone but Paula will survive. The bomb goes off, and everyone dies. Who did Dell *intend* to kill? Only Paula, right? It was Dell's conscious objective to kill Paula, so Dell killed her intentionally. What about the crew and the other passengers? Dell didn't want them to die. Clearly, however, Dell acted knowingly regarding the passengers and crew. He knew that his act of planting the bomb was almost certain to bring about their death.

In fact, by long tradition, in situations like planting a bomb on a plane, where death is virtually certain to occur, many states take the position that Dell intended to kill everyone on board.

The term "willful" can mean simply that a person intends to act in a certain way. Or, the term can carry a connotation of bad motive or ill will.

The term "wanton" is defined in *Black's Law Dictionary* as "reckless, heedless, malicious; characterized by extreme recklessness or foolhardiness." That definition is about as clear as mud, reinforcing the point made earlier: The mental element of crime—*mens rea*—is complex, with some terms having the chameleon-like ability to assume different meanings in different crimes.

Selected Crimes

There are hundreds of federal, state, and local crimes spelled out in criminal codes across the country. This section outlines some of the more common offenses, beginning with murder and manslaughter.

Murder

People are repulsed and fascinated by murder, as evidenced by the number of TV shows that focus on the subject.

Homicide is the killing of a human being by another human being. Not all homicide is criminal. For example, a police officer commits homicide when the officer lawfully shoots a bank robber who threatens to execute a hostage. The officer's homicide is not criminal. It is justifiable homicide. A soldier in battle commits homicide when the soldier kills an enemy, but the killing is justified. Homicide is criminal when it is *not* justified or excused in the eyes of the law.

Criminal homicide was divided centuries ago into murder and manslaughter. Murder is the killing of a human being with malice aforethought. The word "aforethought" no longer has any meaning. "Malice," on the other hand, has great significance. In the crime of murder, "malice" has four meanings. A person kills with malice when (1) the person intends to kill the victim, that is, it is the killer's conscious object to kill (intent to kill murder); (2) the person does not intend to kill, but does intend to seriously injure the victim, and the victim dies from the wound (intent to cause serious bodily injury murder); (3) the person does not intend to kill, but does intend to engage in extremely reckless behavior that is likely to result in death (depraved heart murder); and (4) the person does not intend to kill, but does intend to commit a felony (e.g., robbery), and someone dies during the felony (felony murder).

All states recognize intent to kill murder and some version of depraved heart murder. Not all states recognize intent to cause serious bodily injury murder or felony murder. The MPC rejects felony murder.

Note that only one of the four meanings of malice requires intent to kill. A person can be a murderer without intending to harm anyone. In one case, for example, a person entered a store to rob it. He didn't want to hurt anyone; he just wanted money. Unfortunately, an employee in the store was so frightened that he had a heart attack and died. The robber was convicted of felony murder.

The crime of murder is divided into degrees. Most states have two degrees of murder; some states have three. Intent to kill murder is first-degree murder when the killing is premeditated; that is, the killer thought about killing and decided to go ahead. How long does it take to premeditate? Not long. Premeditation can occur in the few seconds it takes to consider the decision to kill and to proceed.

Intent to cause serious bodily injury murder and depraved heart murder are typically second-degree murder. So is intent to kill murder *without* premeditation, that is, an intentional killing that is an instant reaction to some provocation, without time to premeditate the decision to kill. Felony murder can be first- or second-degree murder, depending on the state and the facts of the case.

Manslaughter

As we've discussed, murder is the killing of a human being *with* malice aforethought. Manslaughter is the killing of a human being *without* malice aforethought. That's right, the definitional difference between murder and manslaughter is one word, "malice." The law of manslaughter is complicated. In California, for example, there are four kinds of voluntary manslaughter and seven kinds of involuntary manslaughter! The crime of manslaughter varies somewhat from state to state.

There are two basic types of manslaughter: voluntary and involuntary. Voluntary manslaughter is an intentional killing in response to a provocation that is so serious that a reasonable person—there's that reasonable person standard again—faced with such a provocation might lose control, lash out, and kill. A killing in response to such provocation, although still a serious crime, is, in some sense, understandable in light of the frailties of human nature. The provoked killer—one who strikes out in a heat of passion—deserves punishment, but not punishment as severe as a cold-blooded killer. Compare a professional hit man who calmly pulls the trigger for money, with a father who is strolling down the sidewalk with his 5-year-old child when a drunk driver careens onto the sidewalk and runs over the child right in front of him. In a rage, the father dashes to the drunk driver's car and strangles him. The hit man and the father killed on purpose, but who deserves harsher punishment? The hit man committed murder. The shocked, grieving father committed voluntary manslaughter.

Involuntary manslaughter is an accidental killing in which the offender acts with criminal negligence. Remember Uma and her Porsche? Suppose that while Uma is driving at the speed limit and texting, she accidently hits and kills a pedestrian. What crime should Uma be charged with? Recall the four meanings of malice required for murder. Is Uma guilty of intent to kill murder? Of course not. How about intent to cause serious bodily injury murder? No. Uma didn't want to hurt the pedestrian. Is driving while texting a good fit for depraved heart murder, which requires recklessness? Did Uma understand that her texting was highly dangerous, and did she consciously disregard the risk? Although I agree that driving 100 miles an hour through a residential district where children are playing is reckless, for me, driving while texting is a better fit for negligence than recklessness. You may disagree, but I rule out depraved heart murder. How about felony murder? Is texting while driving a felony? No. That means it isn't felony murder. Switching from murder to manslaughter, should Uma be charged with voluntary manslaughter? No, because, in voluntary manslaughter, the provoked offender *intends* to kill. That leaves involuntary manslaughter based on criminal negligence. A driver who causes a tragic death while texting fits the requirements for involuntary manslaughter.

Because so many people are killed on roadways due to careless driving, many states have specialized vehicular manslaughter statutes.

APPLY WHAT YOU HAVE LEARNED

"Don't scream or I'll slit your throat."

Twelve-year-old Polly had a slumber party with two friends from school. The girls played in Polly's room. Around 10:00 P.M., Polly's mom told the girls not to stay up too late. Mom went to sleep in her room. The girls decided to set up their sleeping bags. When Polly opened her bedroom door to retrieve her sleeping bag, Richard Davis, a stranger, was standing in the doorway holding a knife. Davis said, "Don't scream or I'll slit your throats." Davis promised not to hurt the girls, so long as they did as he ordered. He told them to lie face down, and not to look at him. He tied their hands behind their backs. Davis took Polly with him, and left the house. The other girls freed themselves and told Polly's mother, who called the police. A little while later, and a few miles away, Davis got his car stuck on a dark, private dirt road. The property owner called the sheriff. Two sheriff's deputies drove to the scene. Unfortunately, the sheriff and the local police did not use the same radio frequency, and the deputies were not aware that Polly had been abducted. Before the deputies arrived, Davis placed Polly on an embankment. The deputies had no reason to think she was there. The deputies helped Davis free his car. Thirty minutes later, Davis returned to the spot and retrieved Polly. Later that night, Davis decided to kill Polly because he didn't want to go back to prison. He strangled her and hid her body under a piece of wood. Months went by, but eventually, tenacious police work led to Davis, and he confessed and led police to Polly's decomposed body.

What crime should Davis be charged with? Murder? What type of murder? Manslaughter? California has the death penalty. If you were the prosecutor, would you seek the death penalty? If you were a member of Davis's jury, would you vote for death? In death penalty cases, the jury considers aggravating and mitigating evidence. Davis had a long criminal record of brutal attacks on women, as well as property crimes. As for mitigation, Davis's parents went through a bitter divorce, and Davis's mother did not treat him well. A psychiatrist diagnosed Davis as having avoidant personality disorder, antisocial personality disorder, and schizoid personality disorder. Does this information help with your decision to vote for or against the death penalty?—*People v. Davis,* 208 P.3d 78 (Cal. 2009)

Analysis: Davis was convicted of first-degree murder and sentenced to death. He remains on California's death row. If you Google Polly Klass, you will see pictures of Polly, and you can read more about her tragic death.

Rape and Other Sex Offenses

For much of the 20th century, rape was defined as sexual intercourse by a man with a woman, who was not his wife, without her consent, effectuated by force or threat of force. Under this definition, a married man could not "rape" his wife. Today, states have done away with the "marital exception" to rape. As well, laws are changing to make rape gender neutral.

Force is an element of the crime of rape. Force can be actual or threatened. The degree of force is evolving. Bennett Capers (2010) writes, "Since the 1980s, the trend has been to de-emphasize the presence of force and to instead emphasize the absence of consent" (p. 1354). Lack of consent is an element of rape. Consent is an act of free will. A victim who "consents" out of fear that the offender will hurt her does not consent freely.

Rape requires penetration. The slightest penetration is sufficient. The penis need not reach or enter the vagina. Penetration of the outer genitalia is sufficient. Although penetration is required, ejaculation is not necessary.

At an earlier time, the law required the victim to resist the attacker. If the victim failed to resist, there could be no prosecution. Today, the "resistance requirement" is all but gone.

In many rape cases, the accused admits to having sex, but claims the victim consented. Prior to the 1970s, the courts allowed defense attorneys to attempt to prove consent by offering evidence that the victim consented to sex with *other* men. The idea was that an "unchaste" woman was more likely to have consented to sex with the accused than a "virtuous" or "pure" woman. Evidence of unchaste character took three forms. First, if the victim testified, the defense attorney could cross-examine her about the details of previous sexual relationships with other men. Second, the defense attorney could offer a character witness to testify that the victim had a reputation in the community as unchaste. Third, the defense could call the victim's past lovers as witnesses and have them describe their sexual activities with the victim.

In the 1970s, as part of the feminist movement, advocates sought reform of the rape law. Among other things, advocates sought to restrict the use of evidence of a victim's sexual relations with other men. Advocates argued that the fact that a woman had consensual sex with others is not relevant to whether she consented to sex with the accused. This argument carried the day, and states enacted rape shield statutes that limit evidence of the victim's sexual conduct with others.

The crime of statutory rape is intended to protect underage girls and boys from sex with adults. In this offense, a minor consents to sex. Indeed, the minor may initiate sex. The adult is guilty, regardless.

The law criminalizes many sex offenses in addition to rape and statutory rape. Thus, it is a crime to entice a minor into prostitution. Pimping and pandering are against the law. Incest is punished. Sexual abuse of children is criminal.

Stalking

Stalking laws vary from state to state. Stalking is a crime, as well as a basis for a restraining order.

Statutes require the stalker's conduct to be intentional and use terms such as "purposeful," "intentional," "knowing," "malicious," and "willful." Proving intent in stalking cases is similar to proving intent with other crimes. Often, the defendant's own words are the best evidence. Obscene language and death threats are common. In many cases, the stalker's conduct is so outrageous it screams intent. Consider the case of *State v. Higginbotham* (2001). Higginbotham dated the victim's daughter. While dating the victim's daughter, he lived in the victim's home. The trouble started when Higginbotham became violent, and the victim called the police. After Higginbotham moved out, he started calling the victim several times a day, at all hours, cursing her when she picked up the phone. During one call, Higginbotham said, "I'm going to fuck you in the rectum till you die." In another call, he threatened to kill the victim. On several occasions, Higginbotham appeared near the victim's home, stared at her, shook his fist at her, and gave her "the finger." When the victim obtained a restraining order, Higginbotham said it wouldn't do any good. Higginbotham was prosecuted for criminal stalking. The Louisiana Court of Appeals ruled that these facts demonstrated that Higginbotham harassed the victim with intent to inflict emotional distress.

Then there was David Adams who, in *one* day, called his victim 270 times and sent her 100 obscene texts! Intent to harass? Could there be any doubt (*Adams v. State*, 2014)?

Stalking statutes prohibit a variety of acts that annoy, threaten, and frighten victims. Physical contact with the victim is not required for stalking. A threat may be expressed to a third person, who conveys the threat to the victim. Some stalkers harass the victim with phone calls, e-mails, texts, or letters. Stalking can occur without words. Following the victim is a common mode of stalking, including keeping the victim under surveillance. In *People v. Sullivan* (2002), the victim commenced divorce proceedings against her husband. When the victim refused to dismiss the divorce, as her husband requested, he burned her clothes in the backyard. The victim obtained a restraining order, but Sullivan continued contacting her. Sullivan had a global positioning device (GPS) installed on the victim's car so he could track her. Sullivan was convicted of stalking by surveillance.

Stalking statutes often require two elements. First, the stalker must intentionally and repeatedly follow or harass the victim. Second, the stalker must make a "credible threat." A threat does not have to be verbal. In *People v. Cross* (2001), the victim worked at a kiosk in a shopping center. For nearly 2 months, Cross went to the shopping center almost daily, when the victim was working. He would spend several hours sitting on benches near the victim's kiosk, staring at her. Occasionally he would circle the kiosk. Once, he approached the kiosk, tapped on it, smiled at the victim, and returned to the bench, where he watched her for 2½ hours until she got off work. One day, the victim went to church, only to see Cross watching her. Cross's behavior frightened the victim. The court found that Cross's behavior violated the stalking statute.

McNally v. Bredemann (2015) was a disturbing case in which a psychologist was stalked by a former client. The client, Bredemann, sent repeated emails to McNally, blaming her for his unhappiness. McNally told him to stop contacting her, but Bredemann persisted with his email campaign, employing various false names to contact her. Somehow, Bredemann learned McNally's home address, and showed up unannounced on her doorstep. McNally obtained a protective order.

Kivisto, Berman, Watson, Gruber, and Paul (2015) conducted research on the experience of psychologists who were stalked. They observe, "Along with public figures, mental health professionals appear to be among the occupations at highest risk of being stalked, threatened, or harassed in their line of work" (p. 278).

There are innumerable ways to threaten victims. In the case of *Moses v. State* (2001), for example, Moses repeatedly called his estranged wife. Eventually, the victim refused to talk to him. Over the phone, Moses said, "Call me before it's too late." This threat, in conjunction with the defendant's other conduct, supported a stalking conviction.

Some stalking statutes require proof that the victim suffered emotional distress. In *People v. Cross*—the shopping center case—the Colorado Court of Appeals found sufficient evidence of distress. "The victim testified that defendant's behavior caused her to change her work schedule, take days off from work, and feel unsafe; she was nervous and had trouble sleeping; and she felt she was constantly being watched by defendant. The statute is clear that serious emotional distress need not be such as would compel professional treatment or a breakdown."

As mentioned previously, a stalker's words are often powerful evidence against the stalker. Threatening text messages, emails, Facebook postings, telephone messages, and other communications, should be carefully preserved in case they are needed in court. However, professionals must be careful about advising victims to record telephone calls. In some states (e.g., California) it is a crime to record a telephone call without the consent of both persons on the call. It is not against the law for an answering machine to record calls, but recording live calls without consent is against the law in California. In other states, the law allows recording without consent (Myers, 2014a). Don't advise recording live calls unless you know the law in your state.

Intimate Partner Violence

Intimate partner violence is prosecuted two ways: first, under general crimes such as murder, assault, battery, sexual assault, and rape, and second, under specialized domestic violence laws. In California, for example, it is a felony to willfully inflict corporal injury upon a fiancé, cohabitant, or spouse (Cal. Penal Code § 273.5). In South Carolina, it is a crime to "cause physical harm or injury to a person's own household member" (S.C. Code §16-25-20(A)(1)).

In the immediate aftermath of domestic violence, it is common for victims to disclose the abuse to the police, doctors, nurses, friends, mental health professionals, or others. Later, some victims change the story and deny that anything happened. The victim may offer the old standbys, "I fell" or "I ran into a door." Victims of intimate partner violence have many reasons to recant. Some are threatened by the abuser. Others love the batterer and don't want him to go to jail. Still others are desperate because the offender is the breadwinner.

Victim recantation poses serious impediments to prosecution of intimate partner violence. Often, the victim is the only eyewitness, and when the victim changes her story, the prosecution's star witness evaporates. Quite a few prosecutions founder when the victim recants. Even in these circumstances, however, many prosecutions proceed, especially when there is medical evidence of assault, or when other people witnessed the violence, and describe it in court.

If the victim testifies *for* the abuser, the prosecutor is allowed to confront her with her earlier statements to the police, doctors, and others, describing the abuse. This use of a recanting victim's earlier statements is called impeachment with prior inconsistent statements and is discussed in Chapter 8 on testifying in court.

Whether the victim testifies for the abuser, for the prosecution, or not at all, the prosecutor may offer her statements to the police and clinicians as evidence of abuse. In countless cases, victim statements are the most powerful evidence of trauma. Yet, offering a victim's earlier statements to prove abuse implicates hearsay. As you recall, in the introduction to Part II, I argued that it is vitally important for clinicians to understand hearsay. You can see why. For victims of domestic violence, child abuse, rape, stalking, elder abuse, and other crimes, the police, clinicians, and social workers are in the best position to document what victims say shortly following traumatic events. As well, who is in the best position to document the circumstances and timing of victim statements? The answer is the same. In case after case, documenting what victims say, and how they say it, makes the difference between protecting victims and leaving them at risk. If you interact with victims, *you need* a working understanding of hearsay to properly document statements that can be used to protect the innocent and punish the guilty. Your involvement with hearsay really is that important.

Elder Abuse

Elder abuse can take the form of physical abuse, sexual abuse, financial exploitation, or neglect. Like intimate partner violence, elder abuse is prosecuted under general crimes and under specialized elder abuse statutes (Kohn, 2012). In addition to criminal prosecution, systems such as adult protective services are in place to protect elders from abuse and exploitation.

The most common form of elder abuse is financial exploitation. Financial exploitation includes outright theft, all manner of scams, fraud, exertion of undue influence over competent or marginally competent elders, and taking improper advantage of incompetent elders. In *Campbell v. Thomas* (2010), a New York appellate court ruled that a person who married an obviously incompetent elder in order to take unfair advantage of his condition for her own financial gain could not make a claim against his estate as a surviving widow.

Older people execute wills, deeds, trusts, contracts, checks, powers of attorney, and other legal documents that often lie at the heart of alleged financial exploitation. In some cases, they give their property away. Of course, competent adults have the right to do what they like with their property. Thomas Hafemeister (2003) writes, "It is difficult, even for experienced professionals, to distinguish an unwise but legitimate financial transaction from an exploitative transaction resulting from undue influence, duress, fraud, or a lack of informed consent" (p. 387).

In financial exploitation cases, the elder's mental capacity takes center stage. Did the person have the mental capacity to consent to a transaction? If the elder was capable of consent, was her free will overborne by undue influence? To lawfully consent to a transfer of property, a person must have sufficient mental capacity to make an intelligent choice and must act voluntarily, based on accurate knowledge of pertinent facts. Mere passivity does not constitute consent. Consent requires an act of free will.

In the law of wills and trusts, the term "undue influence" is generally used for situations in which the victim *was* mentally capable of executing a document, but signed it only because the victim's free will was overborne by improper influence from others. Undue influence takes many forms, including threats, physical or psychological coercion, and false protestations of love or flattery. Of course, requests, pleas, advice, or encouragement that does not usurp the free will of a competent elder do not sink to the level of undue influence.

Financial abuse is often difficult to prove. The perpetrator has every incentive to hide wrongdoing. Evidence of financial exploitation includes missing or suspicious documentation of financial transactions; implausible explanations from the elder or the suspect; the elder's lack of awareness of recent transactions; a new caretaker who moves in with the elder or takes over the elder's finances; marked departures from long-established banking or financial practices (e.g., an elder, who has always been frugal, suddenly starts writing large checks to cash or to a caretaker), the elder switches banks or lawyers after using the same bank or attorney for years; suspicious changes to a will, trust, title, or other documents; suspicious gifts; and an unemployed, dependent family member who abuses substances or who feels "entitled" to the elder's money.

A caretaker who is financially exploiting an older person typically isolates the elder from those who might discover the wrongdoing. The perpetrator may convince the elder that the elder's friends or family cannot be trusted and are "out to steal your money." The perpetrator sends the message, "I'm the only one you can trust." The older person may stop attending church or discontinue favorite social activities. The perpetrator may discourage contact between the elder and his or her friends, neighbors, and family members.

In many financial abuse cases, wrongful intent is established by tracing the flow of the elder's money away from the elder and into the pockets of the perpetrator. The party seeking to prove fraud or theft creates a timeline in which withdrawals from the elder's bank accounts coincide with deposits in the perpetrator's account or with major purchases by the perpetrator. *Sepulveda v. Aviles* (2003) is a civil case that nicely illustrates the situation in which an impaired elder is taken advantage of. In *Sepulveda,* the beneficiaries under the will of a woman who died at 83, with advanced Alzheimer's, sued the defendant, claiming the defendant fraudulently induced the deceased to convey title to an apartment building to him for an inadequate price. The beneficiaries alleged that the defendant falsely promised the elder she could live in the building rent-free, and that he would care for her for the rest of her life. The beneficiaries also alleged that the defendant misappropriated over $39,000 of the decedent's property.

The older woman met the 35-year-old defendant at a local bank. Two social workers who worked with the woman testified that she told them she'd met a "nice man" who promised to take care of her in exchange for title to the apartment building. The woman and the defendant had accounts at the same bank, and testimony from a bank employee established that mortgage payments allegedly made by the defendant to the woman were not in fact made. "By comparing the routing numbers and endorsements on 10 checks drawn on [the defendant's] account with various bank accounts and deposit slips, the bank employee determined that these checks, purportedly mortgage payments payable to [the elder], were redeposited back into [defendant's] own account." Eventually, the defendant stopped making the sham "mortgage payments." There was evidence that three checks in the amount of $15,000, drawn on the woman's account, were deposited in the defendant's account. The defendant used the woman's credit cards to the tune of some $30,000.

In addition to the financial evidence just summarized, the beneficiaries provided testimony from the social workers who worked with the woman. Finally, the beneficiaries provided expert testimony on her mental condition. The expert testimony established that, at all relevant times, the she was suffering from advanced dementia that impaired her decision-making capacity.

In concluding that the evidence of fraud was overwhelming, the New York court wrote:

> Clear and convincing evidence adduced by [the beneficiaries] reveal a series of transactions permeated by undue influence. [The defendant's]

> unfettered use of [the elder's] funds and credit cards, which [the defendant] admitted at trial, provides convincing evidence that he was exploiting [the elder's] impaired condition for his own financial gain. Finally, his brazen conduct in writing out mortgage checks to [the elder], having her endorse them, and then depositing them back into his own account raises the strongest inference that the mortgage agreement was a sham, and his intent was to obtain [the elder's] building through improper means. (p. 365)

Although *Sepulveda v. Aviles* was a civil case, the facts of the case would support criminal prosecution for fraud or theft.

Perpetrators of financial exploitation select vulnerable victims. In some cases, the most effective way to establish the defendant's intent is to put the elderly victim on the witness stand, so that the jury can see for itself the victim's impairment. The victim's confusion, faltering testimony, or outright inability to testify due to dementia or disability speaks volumes about the defendant's intent.

DEFENSES TO CRIME

There are five categories of defenses against criminal charges, and attorneys representing individuals accused of crime base their cases on one or more of these categories:

1. "I didn't do it! You charged the wrong guy."
2. "I did the *actus reus* of the crime, but I'm not guilty because I didn't have the *mens rea* for the crime—I didn't have criminal intent."
3. "I did the *actus reus,* and I had the *mens rea,* but I'm not guilty because what I did was the right thing to do under the circumstances—my conduct was justified."
4. "I did the *actus reus,* and I had the *mens rea,* but I'm not guilty because there is something wrong with me that makes me blameless—my conduct is excused."
5. "I did it, and I intended to do it. I'm guilty as heck, but you can't punish me because the statute of limitations has expired."

You may ask, "I am a clinician. Why should I read about defenses against criminal charges?" There are three reasons to do so. First, if you help victims of crime, your clients may be confused or angered when the attorney for the person who hurt your client raises a defense in an effort to escape responsibility. Knowledge of the defenses allows you to help clients come to grips with what is happening in the legal system. Second, mental health professionals, serving as expert witnesses, play important roles in some defenses. Third, knowledge of criminal law is incomplete without a basic understanding of defenses.

Mistaken Identity: "I didn't do it! You charged the wrong guy."

Sometimes, the wrong person is charged, and the job of the defense attorney is to persuade the prosecutor to drop the charges. If that doesn't work, and the case goes to trial, the defense attorney attacks the prosecution's evidence that pins blame on the defendant.

In some cases, the defendant offers an alibi: "I was in Abu Dhabi, delivering cookies, which I baked myself, to my aged grandmother, when the bank in Oklahoma City was robbed. I didn't do it."

If the prosecutor offers eyewitnesses who identify the defendant as the perpetrator, the defense may offer expert testimony describing the weaknesses of eyewitness memory. There is abundant psychological research on the foibles of eyewitness memory. Carla Jones (2015) summarizes the literature:

> Eyewitness identifications are among the most common and compelling evidence brought against criminal defendants. Ironically, eyewitness misidentification is also recognized as the leading cause of wrongful convictions nationwide, playing a role in nearly 73% of convictions overturned through DNA evidence. . . . Over two decades of scientific research shows that an array of variables can affect and dilute memory and lead to misidentifications. Generally, fallible eyewitness testimony is believed to result from memory and recognition issues and suggestive identification procedures. Recollection of a stranger can be distorted easily by circumstances, such as distance or lighting conditions. In addition, a considerable amount of research reveals that certain methods of conducting identifications are likely to promote false identifications by eyewitnesses. (p. 511)

"I did the *actus reus* of the crime, but I'm not guilty because I didn't have the *mens rea* for the crime—I didn't have criminal intent."

A person who commits the *actus reus* of a crime may not have the necessary *mens rea* to be guilty. Consider Dell, who lives on Row House Road, and who broke into his neighbor's house, thinking he was entering his (Dell's) own home? Dell committed the *actus reus* of burglary, but he lacked *mens rea,* the specific intent to commit a felony.

Judges and lawyers call Dell's situation "mistake of fact." Dell made a mistake that negated bad intent. As another example of mistake of fact, consider Sue, who went to dinner with friends. When Sue arrived at the restaurant, she checked her black wool coat at the cloak room and enjoyed a lovely meal. Afterward, she gave the cloak room attendant her ticket and was handed a black wool coat. Sue donned the coat and left. Unbeknownst to Sue, the coat was not hers. The attendant gave her the wrong coat. If Sue is charged with theft, is she guilty? Your gut tells you no, and you are right. Theft is the wrongful taking and carrying away of the personal property of another, *with the intent to steal.* Sue did the *actus reus* of theft—she trespassorily took and carried away someone else's coat—but she didn't intend to steal the coat. The mistake of putting on the wrong coat, *thinking it was hers,* negates the *mens rea* of theft.

Sometimes, mental illness robs a person of the intent necessary for a crime. The MPC provides, "Evidence that the defendant suffered from a mental disease or defect is admissible whenever it is relevant to prove that the defendant did or did not have a state of mind that is an element of the offense" (MPC § 4.02(1)). Paul Robinson (1984) writes, "The variety of mental disorders that have been admitted to negate [*mens rea*] seems to be as broad as they are for the insanity defense" (vol. 1, § 64, p. 272, footnote 1). In most states, judges allow evidence of mental illness to disprove *mens rea*. However, it is important to understand that mental illness that is offered to disprove *mens rea* is *not* the same as an insanity defense. The insanity defense is discussed later.

In states that recognize the distinction between general intent and specific intent crimes, mental illness that is offered to disprove *mens rea* is generally effective only against specific intent crimes. California recognizes the general intent-specific intent distinction. In the Golden State, burglary is a specific intent offense. In *People v. Wetmore* (1978), the defendant had a long history of mental illness. The defendant broke into the victim's apartment while the victim was away, and proceeded to live there, wearing the victim's clothes and cooking the victim's food. At his burglary trial, the defendant sought to introduce evidence that because of his mental illness, he thought the apartment was his. If he thought the apartment was his, then he lacked the specific intent to commit a felony in the apartment, and he was not guilty of burglary. The California Supreme Court ruled that the defendant's evidence of mental illness was admissible.

Could a state prohibit evidence of mental illness that is offered to prove lack of *mens rea*? The U.S. Supreme Court discussed this issue in

Clark v. Arizona (2006). Clark suffered from schizophrenia. He shot and killed a police officer. The trial judge ruled that Clark could not rely on evidence of mental illness to prove he lacked the *mens rea* for murder. When the case reached the U.S. Supreme Court, the Court ruled that Arizona law allowed at least some evidence of Clark's mental illness.

In some cases, defendants argue that they were so drunk or high when they committed an act that they lacked the *mens rea* for the crime. At an earlier time, voluntary intoxication was not a defense. In fact, intoxication was an aggravating factor, deserving harsher punishment. During the 19th century, intoxication was reformulated into a defense, and today, most states allow evidence of voluntary intoxication for two purposes: first, to prove that a defendant charged with first-degree, premediated murder, was too intoxicated to premediate, lowering the crime to second-degree murder, and second, voluntary intoxication may deprive a defendant of the capacity to form specific intent. Voluntary intoxication is generally not a defense to a general intent crime.

In Arizona and Montana, voluntary intoxication is not a defense at all. The Arizona statute (Ariz. Rev. Stat. § 13-503) provides: "Temporary intoxication resulting from the voluntary ingestion, consumption, inhalation or injection of alcohol, an illegal substance . . . or other psychoactive substances or the abuse of prescribed medications does not constitute insanity and is not a defense for any criminal act or requisite state of mind." The Montana law (Mont. Code Ann. § 45-2-203) states: "A person who is in an intoxicated condition is criminally responsible for the person's conduct, and an intoxicated condition is not a defense to any offense and may not be taken into consideration in determining the existence of a mental state that is an element of the offense unless the defendant proves that the defendant did not know that it was an intoxicating substance when the defendant consumed, smoked, sniffed, injected, or otherwise ingested the substance causing the condition." The U.S. Supreme Court ruled that Montana's statute does not offend the Constitution (*Montana v. Egelhoff,* 1996).

In *State v. Anderson* (2014), the Wisconsin Supreme Court ruled that "one who mixes prescription medication with alcohol is responsible for any resulting mental state" (p. 761).

Although acute voluntary intoxication is often not a defense, chronic abuse of drugs or alcohol can lead to a permanent "mental disease" called fixed or settled insanity. Settled insanity is an aspect of the insanity defense.

In sum, in most states, voluntary intoxication is a defense in *limited* circumstances. What about *in*voluntary intoxication? Involuntary intoxication is a defense in *all* circumstances. There are four kinds of involuntary intoxication: (1) coerced intoxication, (2) innocent or mistaken intoxication (e.g., spiked punch at senior prom), (3) an unanticipated reaction to a drug taken on medical advice, and (4) pathological intoxication (e.g., the defendant knew she was taking a drug, but the reaction was highly excessive). The MPC describes pathological intoxication as "intoxication grossly excessive in degree, given the amount of the intoxicant, to which the actor does not know he is susceptible" (MPC § 2.08(5)(c)).

In some states, involuntary intoxication is considered a form of the insanity defense (e.g., Illinois). In other states, insanity and involuntary intoxication are separate defenses.

Involuntary intoxication cases are uncommon. An interesting example is *United States v. MacDonald* (2014). The case involved a 19-year-old soldier with a completely clean record—he was an Eagle Scout before enlisting—who wanted to quit smoking. An Army doctor prescribed Chantix, a medication intended for this purpose. Not long after starting Chantix, the soldier started having strange thoughts, including thoughts of killing someone. Without provocation, the soldier took a knife and stabbed another soldier some 50 times, killing him. The Court of Appeals for the Armed Forces held that the trial judge was mistaken to refuse to give jury instructions on involuntary intoxication.

"I did the *actus reus,* and I had the necessary *mens rea,* but I'm not guilty because what I did was the right thing to do under the circumstances—my conduct was justified."

Conduct that normally would be criminal is sometimes morally and legally justified. In such circumstances, the law gives the actor a defense called a justification defense. The most well-known justification defense is self-defense. To successfully claim self-defense, a person who is charged with murder or assault presents evidence of the following:

1. The defender honestly believed she was in imminent danger of being killed or seriously injured.
2. The defender honestly believed that the immediate use of force was necessary to defend against the imminent danger.
3. The defender's belief in the need for self-defense was reasonable under the circumstances.
4. The defender did not start the confrontation—that is, the defender was not the first aggressor.

A person who is attacked with deadly force (e.g., gun, knife, tire iron) can defend with deadly force. A person who is attacked with nondeadly force can defend with nondeadly force. In many states, a victim may use self-defense not only against physical assault, but also to ward off rape or robbery.

When the law allows a person to use self-defense, the person does not have to run away or retreat before defending herself. The defender can stand her ground and defend.

One night, Pam was walking home from work, when she was attacked by a stranger who jumped out of an alley, brandishing a knife and threatening to kill her. Believing she was about to die, Pam pulled a gun from her purse and shot the attacker as he thrust the knife at her, a few inches from her heart. If these facts are true, Pam will probably not be charged with a crime. Police and prosecutors will likely decide that she acted in self-defense. On the other hand, if police or a prosecutor does not believe Pam's account, she may be charged with murder or manslaughter. At trial, Pam can offer witnesses, including herself, to prove she acted in self-defense. It will be up to the jury to decide where the truth lies.

How about the following scenario? Ann was married to Art for 20 years when she shot him as he stood in their kitchen. Shortly after they married, Art started beating Ann, twice breaking her nose, and blackening her eyes more often than Ann could remember. Art often drank to excess, and became mean when he did so. When he was drinking, he verbally abused Ann, calling her vile names. Often, the verbal abuse escalated into physical violence. After years of abuse, Ann could tell when Art was headed toward violence; she knew his pattern. On the fatal night, Art had been drinking all day. Twice he said, "I should take care of you once and for all, you worthless cow." Ann was in the kitchen when Art walked in and said "Fix my dinner, bitch." She made him a sandwich, which he grabbed, and walked toward the living room. At the door, he turned to face Ann, and threw the sandwich at her. Ann grabbed a gun out of a drawer and said, "You ain't gonna hit me no more. Get out or I'll call 911." Art smiled and made a fist. At that moment, Ann pulled the trigger, killing Art with one shot.

The prosecutor charged Ann with first-degree, intent to kill murder. The defense argued that Ann killed in self-defense. But Ann has a problem. When Ann shot Art, he was not attacking her. He was standing across the room, smiling! It is hard to argue that a man who is standing on the other side of a room and smiling poses a danger that justifies shooting him! Making a fist is not a license to open fire. At trial, Ann will be allowed to recount the long history of domestic violence inflicted by Art, which would shed some light on what was going through Ann's mind at the critical moment.

In addition to Ann's testimony describing the history of abuse, the defense attorney is likely to offer testimony from an expert on domestic violence. The expert witness explains to the jury how chronic domestic violence can influence the thinking and perception of victims. Behavior of an abuser that seems innocuous to most of us—smiling and making a fist—can be perceived as an imminent threat of attack to a survivor of domestic violence. The survivor picks up on precursors of violence that non-survivors miss. Judges generally allow such expert testimony.

In addition to describing how a victim of violence gains a "sixth sense" of impending violence, an expert witness can help jurors understand why Ann stayed in a violent relationship so long. The average juror is bound to wonder, "Why didn't she leave?" Indeed, the prosecutor may tell the jury, "If there was serious domestic violence, she would have left." The expert helps jurors understand the cycle of violence and why many victims cannot extract themselves from the situation.

Recall Judy's horrible abuse, described at the beginning of the chapter. The facts of Ann's case differ in an important way from those in Judy's. Judy shot her husband as he slept. Ann shot her husband as he stood across the room from her. We shall see when we revisit Judy's case at the end of the chapter that this difference in facts makes a difference in the final outcome.

APPLY WHAT YOU HAVE LEARNED

"I had no choice."

Valerie and Jim had a 10-year relationship, throughout which Jim abused Valerie mentally and physically. Valerie often escaped Jim's attacks by taking her daughter to a domestic violence shelter, her pastor's home, or her aunt's home. On three occasions, Valerie filed an application for a protective order, but didn't follow through in obtaining the order.

Valerie finally decided to end the relationship. She purchased a mobile home and moved into it with her child. Before long, however, Jim moved into the mobile home too. Fearing Jim, Valerie left the mobile home, and she and the child entered a shelter. Valerie filed an application for another restraining order, and the sheriff tried unsuccessfully to serve the application on Jim. Although Jim was not officially served with the application, he knew about it. A few days later, Valerie and her daughter emerged from a doctor's office to find Jim waiting for them in the parking lot. Jim threatened them. They all returned to Valerie's mobile home, where Jim threatened to kill Valerie and the child. Jim picked the child up by the hair and rolled her across the floor like a bowling ball. Afraid of what might happen next, Valerie retrieved Jim's pistol from a kitchen cabinet and shot him one time, hitting him between the eyes, and killing him instantly. At the time of the shooting, Valerie was 17 feet away from Jim. Immediately after the shooting, Valerie panicked, and put a shotgun in Jim's lifeless hand, with the idea of telling police she killed Jim in self-defense. Valerie then called police and told them she shot Jim.

The prosecutor charged Valerie with first-degree murder. At trial, Valerie claims she acted in self-defense. If you are a member of the jury, will you convict Valerie of murder, or acquit her on the basis of self-defense? If you are Valerie's attorney, would it be a good idea to offer expert testimony on the impact of chronic battering on a victim's thinking? What information could the expert impart to the jury that would help it evaluate Valerie's claim of self-defense?—*State v. Whittaker,* 650 S.E.2d 216 (W. Va. 2007)

Analysis: The jury acquitted Valerie of murder, but convicted her of voluntary manslaughter. She was sentenced to 10 years. The defense did not offer expert testimony on the effects of battering. Was that a mistake? The West Virginia Supreme Court affirmed Valerie's conviction and sentence. Justice Joseph Albright of the West Virginia Supreme Court disagreed strongly with the decision to affirm Valerie's conviction. Justice Albright wrote a passionate dissent, accusing the majority of the West Virginia Supreme Court of ignoring the realities faced by victims of domestic violence. Justice Albright wrote, "Despite the widespread recognition of domestic abuse and the legal system's efforts to protect the abused, the discomforting reality is that victims of abuse continue to find themselves in that proverbial setting of being between a rock and a hard spot. Until both the court and society fully appreciate the realities of domestic abuse and all its consequences, it seems unlikely that in the context of criminal prosecutions, our laws will adequately and fairly address the ramifications of such abuse" (p. 236).

"I did the *actus reus,* and I had the necessary *mens rea,* but I'm not guilty because there is something wrong with me, something that makes me blameless; therefore my conduct is excused."

Some people who commit horrible acts are morally blameless and do not deserve punishment. Not long ago, a young mother was killed by her 2-year-old son. Mom and her kids were at Walmart. The 2-year-old was seated in the shopping cart, next to Mom's purse. The purse contained Mom's loaded, legal pistol. The child went into the purse, found the gun, and accidentally shot his mom in the head. The 2-year-old committed homicide, but no one thinks him blameworthy.

Sometimes, adults and teenagers who commit terrible acts are as morally blameless as the 2-year-old. This usually happens when the adult is seriously mentally ill, and the illness deprives the individual of the cognitive ability to understand what he is doing, or, if he understands what he is doing, robs him of the ability to control his behavior. In this scenario, the person may defend against criminal charges with the insanity defense.

Contrary to popular belief, the insanity defense is rarely deployed, and when it is, it usually fails. Henry Fradella (2007) writes, "The insanity defense is used quite rarely. It is only raised in approximately 1% of all felony cases and, when invoked, the insanity defense is successful less than 25% of the time" (p. 15).

A high-profile example of a failed insanity defense involved the 2015 conviction by a Colorado jury of James Holmes for multiple counts of murder in the Aurora, Colorado, movie theater shooting. In 2012, Holmes killed 12 people and injured 70 others when he opened fire in a crowded theater with a shotgun, a semiautomatic rifle, and a pistol. Holmes had recently broken up with a girlfriend and flunked out of graduate school. He planned the crime meticulously. Defense attorneys raised the insanity defense, but the jury did not buy it.

The law has long recognized the impropriety of punishing someone whose mental illness deprives the person of culpability. As early as the 1700s in England, a "mad man" who did not know what he was doing any "more than a brute or a wild beast" was immune from punishment.

The American Psychiatric Association (2014) notes: "The insanity defense has always been grounded in the belief that there are defendants whose mental conditions are so impaired at the time of the crime that it would be unfair to punish them for their acts."

There are four variations of the insanity defense, each tracing its origins to the famous murder trial of Daniel M'Naghten in London in 1843. M'Naghten came to believe that the government was following and persecuting him. Armed with two pistols, M'Naghten went to the home of Prime Minister Robert Peel in London, intent on killing him. He followed a man he believed was Peel, pulled a pistol, and shot the man in the back. A police officer apprehended M'Naghten before he could shoot again. The victim was not the Prime Minister, but his private secretary, Edward Drummond, who succumbed to his wound. The jury acquitted M'Naghten, based on insanity. The acquittal caused an uproar that led to a revised test for legal insanity, the *M'Naghten* test.

The *M'Naghten* test, according to its original, 19th-century legalistic language, states: "To establish a defense on the ground of insanity it must be clearly proved that, at the time of committing the act, the party accused was laboring under such a defect of reason, from disease of the mind, as not to know the nature and quality of the act he was doing, or, if he did know it, that he did not know that what he was doing was wrong."

The *M'Naghten* test's "disease of the mind" refers to mental illness or intellectual disability. This is not to say that mental illness itself is a defense. Most seriously mentally ill defendants, including those with schizophrenia, do not meet the *M'Naghten* standard.

Psychopathy is a personality disorder listed in the *Diagnostic and Statistical Manual of Mental Disorders* (DSM-5; American Psychiatric Association, 2013), where it is called antisocial personality disorder (p. 659). Could a psychopathic person use the disorder as a basis for an insanity plea? No. Courts and legislatures agree that psychopathy is not "insanity" for purposes of the insanity defense. The MPC provides, "The terms 'mental disease or defect' do not include an abnormality manifested only by repeated criminal or otherwise antisocial conduct" (MPC § 4.01(2)).

The *M'Naghten* test focuses on the defendant's cognitive ability to understand one of the following: (1) the nature and quality of her act, that is, what she was doing or (2) if she understood what she was doing, she did not understand that what she was doing was wrong. Suppose an individual with psychosis strangles the governor, thinking the governor is a zombie trying to eat her brain. The defendant's psychosis deprived her of an understanding of what she did—she thought she was strangling a zombie, not a human being. Alternatively, suppose the defendant knew she was strangling the governor, but she did it because auditory hallucinations told her the governor was about kill everyone in the state. In this scenario, defendant knew what she was doing, but she didn't know it was wrong.

The meaning of "wrong" in *M'Naghten* has caused confusion. Does "wrong" mean against the law? Or does it mean morally wrong? Must the defendant be *subjectively* aware that her conduct is against the law and/or morally wrong? In *United States v. Ewing* (2007), the Federal Court of Appeals explained, "We conclude that wrongfulness for purposes of the federal insanity defense statute is defined by reference to objective societal or public standards of moral wrongness, not the defendant's subjective personal standards of moral wrongfulness" (p. 621). In *State v. Singleton* (2010), the New Jersey Supreme Court wrote, "A majority of states following the *M'Naghten* test have interpreted 'wrong' as encompassing legal as well as moral wrong" (pp. 295–296).

Approximately half the states and the federal government retain the *M'Naghten* test for insanity. The federal insanity defense states: "It is an affirmative defense to a prosecution under any Federal statute that, at the time of the commission of the acts constituting the offense, the defendant, as a result of a severe mental disease or defect, was unable to appreciate the nature and quality or the wrongfulness of his acts. Mental disease or defect does not otherwise constitute a defense" (18 U.S.C. § 17(a)).

M'Naghten focuses entirely on the defendant's cognitive capacity to know what she was doing, or to distinguish right from wrong. *M'Naghten* disregards the impact that mental illness can have on a person's ability to control her behavior, or volitional control. A few states that use *M'Naghten* combine it with the so-called "irresistible impulse test." This test allows a defendant who knew what she was doing, and knew it was wrong, to argue that her mental illness deprived her of self-control.

Both *M'Naghten* and the irresistible impulse tests are difficult for defendants to satisfy. In most cases, mental illness, even serious mental illness, does not completely destroy a person's cognitive capacity to know what she is doing, or to understand that it is wrong. Yet, destruction of cognitive capacity is required by *M'Naghten*. Paul Robinson and his colleagues (Robinson, Kussmaul, Stoddard, Rudyak, & Kuersten, 2015) write that *M'Naghten* "requires absolute inability to tell that one's conduct is wrong" (p. 78). Similarly, according to the irresistible impulse test, in most cases, mental illness does not completely eliminate volitional control.

More than a dozen states have broadened the *M'Naghten*/irresistible impulse test by adopting the MPC test for insanity, which provides: "A person is not responsible for criminal conduct if at the time of such conduct, as a result of mental disease or defect, he lacks *substantial* capacity either to appreciate the criminality [wrongfulness] of his conduct or to conform his conduct to the requirements of the law" (MPC § 4.01(1)).

Use of the word "substantial" in the MPC introduces shades of gray into the insanity defense. The Explanatory Note to § 4.01 states, "The standard does not require a total lack of capacity, only that capacity be insubstantial" (MPC § 4.01, Explanatory Note, p. 174). A delusional defendant who has *some* idea of what she is doing, or that it is wrong, is not insane under *M'Naghten,* but might lack *substantial* capacity under the MPC. Even under the MPC's more flexible test, however, few mentally ill defendants qualify for the insanity defense.

When a defendant is found not guilty by reason of insanity, the defendant does not walk out of court a free person. If the acquitted defendant poses a danger to her- or himself or others, the person is committed to an institution.

Four states have abolished the insanity defense: Idaho, Kansas, Montana, and Utah (see Idaho Code § 18-207(1); Kan. Stat. Ann. § 22-3220; Mont. Code Ann. § 46-14-104; Utah Code Ann. § 76-2-305). Abolition of the insanity defense does not mean that evidence of mental illness or intellectual disability is irrelevant. Evidence of mental illness or intellectual disability can be used as proof that the defendant lacked the *mens rea* for the crime.

To complete our discussion of the insanity defense, it is important to mention the so-called product rule. The product rule originated in New Hampshire in 1871, and it remains the law in the Granite State. In 1954, the United States Court of Appeals for the District of Columbia adopted the product rule in *Durham v. United States* (1954). In *Durham,* the court ruled that a defendant "is not criminally responsible if his unlawful act was the product of a mental disease or defect" (pp. 874–875). The product rule sounded simple, but proved unworkable in practice, and the D.C. Circuit abandoned the rule in 1972, in favor of the MPC approach (*United States v. Brawner,* 1972). Today, the product rule is used in New Hampshire and the Virgin Islands (see *Petric v. People,* 2014).

States differ in the procedures used for the insanity defense. Generally, a defendant who intends to rely on this defense must give advance notice to the prosecution and the judge. The judge appoints one or more psychiatrists or psychologists to evaluate the defendant and testify at trial. As well, the defendant can hire additional expert witnesses.

A number of states bifurcate the trial when the insanity defense is raised. In the first phase of trial, the defendant is presumed to be sane, and the jury decides guilt or innocence. If the defendant is convicted at phase one, the case moves to phase two, and the jury hears evidence on the insanity defense (see *People v. Mills,* 2012 [California]; *Jackson v. United States,* 2013 [District of Columbia]; *State v. Anderson,* 2014 [Wisconsin]).

If a defendant wants to raise the insanity defense, the defendant must start the ball rolling by offering evidence of insanity. This requirement is called the burden of producing evidence, or the burden of going forward with evidence. If the defendant fails to meet this burden, then the insanity defense is not "in the case" and is not an option for the jury to consider.

Assuming the defendant meets the burden of producing evidence of insanity, the next question is: Which side has the burden of proving or disproving insanity? In many states, the defendant has the burden of proving insanity. In about a dozen states, once the defense meets its burden of producing evidence of insanity, the prosecution has the burden of *dis*proving insanity.

Expert testimony from mental health professionals plays a vital role in the insanity defense. As mentioned previously, when a defendant raises this defense, the judge appoints psychiatrists or psychologists to evaluate the defendant and testify at trial. Additional experts may testify.

There is no psychological test that determines whether someone meets the insanity defense. The fact that a defendant has a DSM-5 diagnosis is not enough. Gary Melton and his colleagues (2007) write, "A diagnosis, standing alone, is virtually useless to the legal system" (p. 243).

A psychological evaluation regarding insanity should be comprehensive. In addition to interviewing the defendant, the mental health professional reads records and contacts collateral sources to shed light on the defendant's mental condition at the time of the offense.

With the insanity defense, the issue is the defendant's mental state *at the time of the offense*. There is no gainsaying the difficulty of reconstructing a person's mental state months or years earlier. Mental health professionals cannot be certain about what was going through a defendant's mind—what the defendant thought, believed, intended—when the defendant acted. According to Gary Melton and his colleagues (1998), "Clinical testimony can be useful here, but only to the extent the clinician sticks to providing informed speculation about the defendant's judgment, concentration, focus of attention, interpersonal functioning, and other aspects of experience at this particular point in time" (p. 243). The Rhode Island Supreme Court grappled with this issue in *State v. Gardner* (1992), wherein the Court wrote:

> The trial [judge] expressed concern over the difficulty and potential unreliability of a retroactive diagnosis. We agree with the trial [judge] that the process of diagnosing a defendant after a crime and relating that diagnosis back to the time of the offense is an elusive undertaking. In a meta-physical sense it may be impossible to know the mental state of the defendant at the time of the criminal conduct. Absolute scientific certainty, however, it not the standard for the admissibility

> of expert testimony. Whatever judicial skepticism may exist regarding psychiatric science is best resolved through the factfinder's determining the credibility and weight to be given the expert's testimony instead of resolving the uncertainty by a total exclusion. The trial [judge] in this case could have and, indeed, should have addressed the problems posed by [the expert's] testimony by permitting the state to question his testimony on cross-examination. (p. 1129)

Expert testimony from a psychologist or psychiatrist stating that a defendant meets the requirements of the insanity defense can go a long way with jurors, especially if the expert couches the opinion in the language of the insanity defense. Thus, the expert might testify, "The defendant's mental illness is a disease of the mind. Due to his mental illness, at the time of the act, the defendant did not know the nature and quality of the act he did, and he did not know that it was wrong."

Concerned that expert testimony that uses the legalistic language of the insanity defense carries too much weight with jurors, Congress amended Federal Rule of Evidence (FRE) Rule 704(b) to provide, "In a criminal case, an expert witness must not state an opinion about whether the defendant did or did not have a mental state or condition that constitutes an element of the crime charged or of a defense. Those matters are for the trier of fact" (Fed. R. Evid. 704(b)). The judges and lawyers who wrote Rule 704(b) explained:

> The purpose of [Rule 704(b)] is to eliminate the confusing spectacle of competing expert witnesses testifying to directly contradictory conclusions as to the ultimate legal issue to be found by the trier of fact [e.g., insanity]. Under [Rule 704(b)], expert psychiatric testimony would be limited to presenting and explaining their diagnoses, such as whether a defendant had a severe mental disease or defect and what the characteristics of such a disease or defect, if any, many have been. The basis for this limitation on expert testimony in insanity cases is ably stated by the American Psychiatric Association (2013):
>
>> It is clear that psychiatrists are experts in medicine, not the law. As such, it is clear that the psychiatrist's first obligation and expertise in the courtroom is to "do psychiatry," i.e., to present medical information and opinion about the defendant's mental state and motivation and to explain in detail the reason for his medical-psychiatric conclusions. When, however, "ultimate issue" questions are formulated by the law and put to the expert witness who must then say "yea" or "nay," then the expert witness is required to make a leap in logic. He no longer addresses himself to medical concepts but instead must

> infer or intuit what is in fact unspeakable, namely, the probable relationship between medical concepts and legal or moral constructs such as free will. These impermissible leaps in logic made by expert witnesses confuse the jury. Juries thus find themselves listening to conclusory and seemingly contradictory psychiatric testimony that defendants are either "sane" or "insane" or that they do or do not meet the relevant legal test for insanity. This state of affairs does considerable injustice to psychiatry and, we believe, possibly criminal defendants. In fact, in many criminal trials both prosecution and defense psychiatrists do agree about the nature and even the extent of mental disorder exhibited by the defendant at the time of the act.
>
> Psychiatrists, of course, must be permitted to testify fully about the defendant's diagnosis, mental state, and motivation (in clinical and commonsense terms) at the time of the alleged act so as to permit the jury or the judge to reach the ultimate conclusion about which they and only they are expert. Determining whether a criminal defendant was legally insane is a matter for legal fact finders, not for experts.
>
> Moreover, the rationale for precluding ultimate opinion psychiatric testimony extends beyond the insanity defense to any ultimate mental state of the defendant that is relevant to the legal conclusion sought to be proven. The committee has fashioned its Rule 704 provision to reach all such "ultimate" issues, for example, premeditation in a homicide case or lack of predisposition in entrapment. (Advisory Committee's Note to Rule 704(b))

Christopher Mueller and Laird Kirkpatrick (2012) explain how Rule 704(b) is designed to work: "Under FRE 704(b) a psychiatrist or other expert should not couch her testimony in terms of the legal elements in the insanity defense. Instead she should stay one step back, explaining the basis for her diagnosis, describing the defendant's condition by giving the diagnosis itself and the characteristics of the affliction, and saying how such a condition would or might affect the ability of an ordinary person to appreciate the nature and quality or wrongfulness of his acts or conform his conduct to the law, although these last points get so close to the ultimate issue that courts sometimes balk. What FRE 704(b) aims to prevent is expert testimony that goes directly to the legal conclusion. An expert should not testify, for example, that the defendant could not appreciate the wrongfulness of his acts or conform his conduct to the requirements of law" (§ 7.13, pp. 678–679).

Despite Rule 704(b), the Advisory Committee Note, and the opinions of the American Psychiatric Association (2013), and professors

Mueller and Kirkpatrick, experts in insanity cases routinely violate the spirit and letter of Rule 704(b) by opining on what was going through a defendant's mind at the time of a crime, and whether the defendant knew the nature and quality of the act, or whether it was wrong. Unless the judge prohibits such testimony, it is up to the cross-examining attorney to critique the expert's testimony.

You may find the events that led Congress to amendment Rule 704(b) and expert testimony on insanity interesting. In 1981, John Hinckley shot and nearly killed President Ronald Reagan. Hinckley was trying to impress actress Jodie Foster, and Hinckley thought killing the President would do the trick. At his trial, Hinckley relied on the insanity defense. Numerous experts testified for and against Hinckley. The jury found Hinckley not guilty by reason of insanity. Congress, and many people in the nation, were outraged that Hinckley "got away with it." In response, Rule 704(b) was amended, as just explained, to limit expert testimony.

Although expert testimony plays a central role in insanity defense trials, the jury is not obligated to accept expert testimony. The Wisconsin Supreme Court observed in *State v. Kucharski* (2015), "A [jury] is not required to accept the opinion of an expert, even if uncontradicted" (pp. 701–702). The Indiana Supreme Court's decision in *Satterfield v. State* (2015) makes the same point. The defendant killed his mother and burned down her home. At trial, he raised the defense of insanity. There was expert and lay testimony. The jury found the defendant guilty, rejecting his mental illness defense. The Indiana Supreme Court wrote:

> There was conflicting evidence on whether Satterfield was insane. . . . The jury's right to determine the facts allows jurors to disbelieve expert testimony of a defendant's insanity . . . and rely instead on other sufficient probative evidence from which a conflicting inference of sanity or mental illness can reasonably be drawn. Demeanor evidence, lay opinion testimony, and the circumstances of the crimes are just a few examples of the additional evidence that juries may consider and use to either accept or reject expert testimony—even when the expert testimony is unanimous. (pp. 348–349)

Related to the insanity defense, some states recognize a partial defense called temporary insanity. In Texas, for example, voluntary intoxication is not a defense, but evidence of intoxication may be admissible as evidence of "temporary insanity" to mitigate punishment (see *Johnson v. State,* 2014).

A number of states have a defense called diminished capacity. The details of the defense vary from state to state. Generally, diminished capacity is not a complete defense. In some states, mental illness that falls short of the insanity defense can lower the seriousness of an offense. A defendant charged with first-degree, premeditated murder, for example, may persuade the jury that his mental illness prevented him from premeditating, thus reducing the offense from first- to second-degree murder.

In 1975, Michigan became the first state to allow a verdict of guilty but mentally ill (Mich. Laws. Ann. § 768.36). Several states followed suit. This verdict is available when a defendant raises the insanity defense, but the jury rejects the defense. At that point, the jury can find the defendant not guilty, guilty, or guilty but mentally ill. A defendant who is found guilty but mentally ill is sentenced, but receives treatment instead of prison time.

Voluntary intoxication as a defense was briefly discussed earlier. Voluntary intoxication is not considered insanity for purposes of the insanity defense. The MPC states, "Intoxication does not, in itself, constitute mental disease within the meaning of" the insanity defense (MPC § 2.08(3)). In *Commonwealth v. DiPadova* (2011), the Massachusetts Supreme Judicial Court explained: "Voluntary consumption of alcohol or drugs, intoxication and even alcoholism or drug addiction do not qualify as mental diseases or defects in the [insanity defense]; as a result, a defendant whose lack of substantial capacity is due solely to one of these conditions, and not to any mental disease or defect, is criminally responsible."

"I did it, and I intended to do it. I'm guilty as heck, but you can't punish me because the statute of limitations has expired."

A statute of limitations is a law that places a time limit (measured in years) on how long a person can be prosecuted for a crime. Statutes of limitations are based on fairness. If many years have elapsed before a person is put on trial, it may be difficult for the person to mount a defense. Witnesses may have died or moved away. Memory fades. Evidence disappears.

There is no statute of limitations for murder. Thus, you will see cold case prosecutions for murders that happened years—even decades—ago.

CASE STUDIES REVISITED

Now that we have spent some time studying crimes and defense, let's return to the case studies discussed at the beginning of the chapter.

SELF-DEFENSE?

Remember Judy, who shot her sleeping husband? Judy's horror story is real. Indeed, in this brief retelling, I omitted many horrible things John perpetrated on Judy. Did Judy commit murder? The prosecutor thought so, and charged her with first degree, premeditated murder. How could it be otherwise? Judy put three bullets in the brain of her sleeping husband. That is intent to kill. As well, she clearly premeditated the act. It looks like a clear-cut case of intent to kill murder.

At her murder trial, Judy's attorney asked the judge to give the jury an instruction on self-defense, but the judge refused. Thus, the jury was not allowed even to consider the possibility that Judy acted in self-defense. As you recall, a person kills in self-defense when the person is under attack or is in imminent danger of attack. Judy's husband was sleeping. He was not attacking her. He posed no imminent danger to Judy. With very rare exceptions, self-defense law does not allow preemptive strikes. If there is time to call the police or get help, a person cannot act in self-defense. Self-defense is lawful only when a threat of assault is *imminent*. A sleeping man, even one as evil as John, poses no imminent threat. Thus, the judge refused to give the jury the option to consider self-defense.

After listening to the evidence, including an expert witness on the effects of chronic domestic violence, the jury refused to convict Judy of murder, but did convict her of voluntary manslaughter. The judge sentenced Judy to 6years.

Judy appealed, and the North Carolina Court of Appeals ruled the trial judge was wrong to refuse Judy's request to instruct the jury on self-defense. The Court of Appeals ruled that even though John was asleep, he posed an imminent threat to Judy. He could kill her the moment he woke up (*State v. Norman,* 1988).

The prosecutor appealed the Court of Appeals' decision to the North Carolina Supreme Court, and the high court reversed the Court of Appeals (378 S.E.2d 8 (N.C. 1989)). The Supreme Court wrote, "We conclude that the evidence introduced in this case would not support a finding that [Judy] killed her husband due to a reasonable fear of imminent death or great bodily harm, as is required before a defendant is entitled to jury instructions concerning self-defense" (p. 9).

The North Carolina Supreme Court's decision is in line with decisions in other states. Courts generally rule that self-defense cannot be claimed when a victim of domestic violence shoots a sleeping batterer or stabs him in the back while he watches TV. Nor can a victim of domestic violence claim self-defense if she hires a "hit man" to kill the batterer.

WHO COULD DO SUCH A THING?

As related earlier, Ronnie Midgett Sr. beat his little boy to death. Midgett Sr. was convicted by a jury of first-degree murder, but the Arkansas

Supreme Court lowered the crime to second-degree murder because there was no evidence Midgett Sr. intended to kill his son (*Midgett v. State,* 1987). Rather, he intended to keep him alive in order to further abuse him.

Three justices of the Arkansas Supreme Court dissented, taking the position that the first-degree murder conviction should be upheld. In his dissent, Justice Hickman wrote, "I cannot fathom how this father could have done what he did; but it is not my place to sit in judgment of his mental state, nor allow my human feelings to color my judgment of his accountability to the law. The law has an objective standard of accountability for all who take human life. If one does certain acts and the result is murder, one must pay. The jury found Midgett guilty and, according to the law, there is substantial evidence to support that verdict. That should end the matter for us. He is guilty of first-degree murder in the eyes of the law. His moral crime as a father is another matter, and it is not for us to speculate why he did it" (p. 417).

In response to the decision in *Midgett,* the Arkansas legislature changed the definition of first-degree murder to state, "A person commits murder in the first degree if the person knowingly causes the death of a person fourteen years of age or younger" (Ark. Code Ann. § 5-10-102(a)(3)).

If you were the judge, what punishment would you impose on Midgett Sr.? Apart from the punishment imposed by law, are you like Justice Hickman, baffled at how someone could do that to a child? Where does such evil come from?

STEALING FROM AN OLD LADY

In this financial exploitation case, David was convicted of larceny from a person 60 years of age or older. Today, police departments and prosecutors in many cities have specialized units that investigate and prosecute financial exploitation of older adults.

CONCLUSION

Interpersonal violence is far too common. The criminal justice system exists to prevent violence when prevention is possible, and to hold accountable those who are not deterred. Mental health and medical professionals play key roles at nearly all levels of criminal law.

3

Criminal Investigation and Trial

Chapter 3 addresses the investigation and prosecution of crime. The chapter is divided into two parts: the first part describes the law governing the investigation of crime, and the second part focuses on how the trial of a criminal case is conducted.

INVESTIGATION OF CRIME

If you are among the millions who enjoy an occasional episode of *Law and Order, CSI,* or other crime procedural on TV, you have seen the police arrest the suspect, give him or her *Miranda* warnings, interrogate prisoners, conduct lineups, search buildings, and use some level of force. In the real world of criminal investigation, medical and mental health professionals are seldom involved. Nevertheless, if your work involves the criminal justice system, or if you are simply curious, it behooves you to know something about the legal rules governing the investigation of crime—called, generally, criminal procedure. If nothing else, you will be in a better position to critique whether TV shows get it right!

The starting place in understanding criminal procedure is the U.S. Constitution. The Fourth, Fifth, and Sixth Amendments to the Constitution guarantee citizens important rights in the criminal justice system. The Fourth Amendment provides: "The right of the people to be secure in their persons, houses, papers, and effects, against unreasonable searches and seizures, shall not be violated, and no Warrants shall issue, but upon probable cause, supported by Oath or affirmation, and particularly describing the place to be searched, and the persons or things to be seized." The Fifth Amendment guarantees the right against self-incrimination—the right to remain silent. The Sixth Amendment guarantees the right to a speedy and public trial, the right to confront the prosecution's witnesses, and the right to an attorney.

Every year, American judges decide thousands of cases interpreting these amendments. Here, we discuss key particulars of criminal procedure that are likely to be germane to your work.

Arrest

An arrest is a "seizure" under the Fourth Amendment. To arrest someone, a police officer must have probable cause to believe that the person committed a crime. One would expect there to be a simple definition of "probable cause," but one would be wrong. The meaning of probable cause is distilled from two competing values. First, as a society, we do not want police officers running roughshod over our liberty by arresting people willy-nilly. The police need a good reason to put someone through the trauma, embarrassment, and loss of liberty entailed by arrest. Second, and on the other hand, we don't want to make it so difficult for the police to arrest suspects that guilty people remain at large to commit new crimes. Probable cause accommodates these values by requiring police officers to have pretty strong evidence to arrest, but not so much evidence that crime prevention is stymied.

Whether probable cause exists depends on the facts of each case. The U.S. Supreme Court wrote in *Illinois v. Gates* (1983), "Probable cause is a fluid concept—turning on the assessment of probabilities in particular factual contexts—not readily, or even usefully, reduced to a neat set of legal rules" (p. 232). The arresting officer's experience is a factor. A veteran officer may see evidence of a crime that would elude you or me. In the final analysis, the question is whether a reasonably cautious police officer in that situation would believe a crime occurred and the suspect committed it (yet another example of reasonableness in the law).

As just noted, the Fourth Amendment says, "No Warrants shall issue, but upon probable cause." Sometimes, the police get an arrest warrant from a judge. Most arrests, however, occur without an arrest warrant. A police officer can make a warrantless arrest when the officer has probable cause to believe the suspect committed a felony. The officer does not have to see the felony being committed. For misdemeanors, an arrest warrant is required unless the misdemeanor occurs in the officer's presence.

A police officer may use reasonable force to make an arrest. State laws limit the use of deadly force in arrests. Generally, an officer may use deadly force only when he or she is attempting to arrest someone for a dangerous felony. When a police officer who is trying to make an arrest reasonably believes the suspect poses a threat of death or serious harm to the officer or others, the officer may use deadly force to prevent the suspect from escaping or harming the officer or others.

Stop and Frisk: *Terry* Stops

An arrest requires probable cause, and is a Fourth Amendment "seizure." Many interactions between citizens and the police have no Fourth Amendment implications. Thus, a police officer is free to approach you on the street and attempt to engage you in conversation. You are free to leave.

It often happens that a police officer suspects that a crime has or is about to occur—"crime is afoot"—but the officer lacks probable cause to arrest. In such circumstances, an officer may briefly detain a suspicious person and ask questions. If the officer reasonably believes the person might be armed, the officer can pat down the person's clothing to check for weapons. This type of encounter is called "stop and frisk," or a *Terry* stop, after the U.S. Supreme Court decision authorizing such stops in *Terry v. Ohio* (1968).

To conduct a *Terry* stop, a police officer must have a reasonable suspicion that a crime has or will soon occur. What is a reasonable suspicion? It is less than probable cause. The U.S. Supreme Court defined reasonable suspicion as "some minimal level of objective justification" (*INS v. Delgado,* 1984, p. 217). In the *Terry* case, a police officer with many years of experience observed three men repeatedly walk past a store window and look in, as if they were "casing" the store for a robbery. The officer approached the men and asked them to identify themselves. When the men mumbled an answer, the officer patted down their clothing to check for weapons and discovered pistols on two of them. The Supreme Court ruled that the officer had reasonable suspicion to stop and question the suspicious men. Because the officer feared for his safety, he was justified in frisking for weapons.

Miranda Warnings

Before a police officer questions a suspect who is under arrest, he or she gives the suspect the well-known *Miranda* warnings: "You have the right to remain silent. Anything you say can and will be used against you in a court of law. You have the right to an attorney. If you cannot afford an attorney, one will be appointed for you."

In 1963, Ernest Miranda was suspected of kidnapping and raping an 18-year-old girl in Phoenix, Arizona. Police arrested Miranda at his home, took him to police headquarters, and questioned him for 2 hours. Miranda was not informed he had a Fifth Amendment right to remain silent. Miranda confessed, and his confession was used against him at his trial in state court. Miranda was convicted, and his conviction was affirmed by the Arizona Supreme Court. The U.S. Supreme Court took the case, and used it to create the *Miranda* warnings.

Police do not have to *Mirandize* a person *prior* to formal arrest. Thus, because a stop and frisk is not an arrest, *Miranda* warnings are not required. Similarly, when a cop pulls you over for speeding, you are not under arrest, and the officer does not *Mirandize* you.

Contrary to popular belief, *Miranda* warnings are not required upon arrest, but only when police interrogate an arrested person. If the arrestee asks for a lawyer, all questioning must stop.

APPLY WHAT YOU HAVE LEARNED

Not the First Time

Sherronica and her husband, Rich, got into a heated argument at home. Sherronica told Rich, "Get your stuff and get out." Rich responded by calling Sherronica a bitch. Sherronica went to the kitchen and got a knife. She started slapping Rich with one hand, while holding the knife in the other. Rich punched Sherronica in the face with his fist, knocking her to the floor. Sherronica stood up and stabbed Rich in the chest. Rich died later that day.

Sherronica was taken to the police station. Two hours after the stabbing, a police officer informed Sherronica that Rich was dead. Sherronica became extremely upset. Half an hour after being told her husband was dead, a police officer gave Sherronica the *Miranda* warnings. Sherronica signed a document indicating that she understood her rights and was willing to answer questions. During the questioning, Sherronica made incriminating statements.

Sherronica is subsequently charged with murder. At her trial, her attorney argues that the incriminating things Sherronica said after waiving her *Miranda* rights should not be allowed as evidence against her. The attorney argues that Sherronica did not understand her rights because she had just been told that her husband was dead, and she was in shock. If you are the judge, how will you rule on the defense attorney's argument? Will you suppress Sherronica's post-*Miranda* statements, or will you allow them to be used against her? Would it change your mind if you learned—as was the case—that this was not the first time Sherronica stabbed Rich? Should Sherronica's attorney have her evaluated by a mental health professional, who could testify about her mental state when she was questioned by the police officer? In your opinion, is it possible for a clinician to know what was going through someone's mind months earlier?—*McKenzie v. State,* 670 S.E.2d 158 (Ga. Ct. App. 2008)

Analysis: Sherronica was convicted of manslaughter. The Georgia Court of Appeals ruled that Sherronica's statements to the police could be used against her since she understood her *Miranda* rights. The Court of Appeals also ruled that the jury should be told about the prior stabbing because it shed light on Sherronica's intent when she inflicted the moral wound.

Search and Seizure

The Fourth Amendment protects you from unreasonable government searches of your person (body and clothing), house (dwelling, business, motel room, etc.), papers, and effects (your car is an effect). Observe that the Fourth Amendment does not limit all searches, only searches that are unreasonable. When is a search reasonable? That is a question on which we could spend weeks of discussion. America's leading Fourth Amendment scholar, Wayne LaFave, and his colleagues wrote a book on the subject that is more than 3,800 pages (LaFave, Israel, King, & Kerr, 2015)!

Before describing search law, it is important to mention once again the Fourth Amendment's "warrant requirement": "No Warrants shall issue, but upon probable cause." The probable cause needed for a judge to issue a search warrant is very similar to the probable cause required for the police to arrest a suspect. The U.S. Supreme Court has stressed that the Constitution has a strong preference for police officers to obtain a warrant before conducting a search. This is especially so when officers intend to search a home. The warrant requirement is at its zenith in the home. Although the Constitution prefers search warrants, there are the following exceptions to the warrant requirement, now briefly summarized.

- ***Search incident to arrest.*** When a police officer arrests a suspect, the officer may conduct a full search of the person, and the person's clothes, incident to the arrest. The officer may also search the area near the arrestee into which the person might lunge for a weapon.

If the police can search you incident to arrest, can the police also search the contents of your cell phone? This question reached the U.S.

Supreme Court in 2014 in the case of *Riley v. California* (2014). A unanimous Supreme Court ruled that, except in emergencies (called exigent circumstances), police must get a warrant to search a cell phone.

Suppose a client sends a series of emails or text messages to your cell phone, and the police are investigating the client. May the officer get a warrant to search *your* cell phone? If there is probable cause to believe your phone could contain evidence of wrongdoing by the client, the answer is yes.

- ***Exigent circumstances.*** If there is no time to secure a warrant from a judge, police officers with probable cause can conduct a warrantless search.

- ***Car searches.*** Although police officers don't have carte blanche to search any car they like, the law gives them broad authority to search cars, especially when the car is mobile and could be driven away.

- ***Consent searches.*** The owner or occupant of a home, car, boat, or plane can consent to a search. With consent, there is no need for a warrant. Indeed, with consent, the officer doesn't need probable cause. Thus, if a police officer pulls you over for a broken taillight, and asks, "Do you mind if I search the car?" your "Go ahead" allows a warrantless search.

- ***Plain view.*** Police are not required to close their eyes when they see evidence of crime. As long as a police officer is in a place where she has a right to be, she may seize evidence in plain view.

The Exclusionary Rule

If the police violate the Fourth Amendment by conducting an unreasonable, that is, illegal, search, what is the remedy? The person whose constitutional rights were violated can sue the police. Much more common than lawsuits, however, are requests (called motions) asking a judge to exclude illegally seized evidence from a criminal trial. The so-called exclusionary rule provides that evidence gathered in violation of the Fourth Amendment cannot be used in court against the person whose Fourth Amendment rights were violated. The purpose of the exclusionary rule is to deter police from violating the Fourth Amendment.

Confessions/Interrogation

A staple of TV crime shows is interrogation, in which the skillful detective gets the suspect to "spill the beans." Often on TV, interrogation involves threatened or actual violence. The real world is less entertaining. It is true that police occasionally resort to threats or force, but such instances are rare—not to mention illegal. The best interrogators rely on psychology, not force.

A confession that is voluntary can be used against the suspect in court. By contrast, an involuntary confession cannot be used. At the extreme, confessions obtained by torture are inadmissible. Interrogation techniques falling short of torture can nevertheless render a confession involuntary. To determine whether a confession was voluntary, judges consider all relevant circumstances, including the suspect's age and intelligence, length of questioning, whether the suspect was given food, drink, or an opportunity to sleep, use of force or the threat of force, promises of leniency or reward for confessing, psychological coercion that overbore the suspect's free will, and anything else that sheds light on voluntariness.

TRIAL OF A CRIMINAL CASE

When a person is charged with a crime, an adjudication process begins. As a mental health, medical, or social services professional, you may be involved at various stages of this process. Here we describe the criminal trial process in general. Chapter 9 discusses a key element of trials, expert testimony, in detail.

Competence to Stand Trial

A person who is incompetent cannot be put on trial. A person is competent to stand trial if he or she is able to understand the charges and assist the defense attorney (*Dusky v. United States,* 1960). A child who is accused of juvenile delinquency, like an adult accused of crime, has a right not to be tried while incompetent (*In re R.V.,* 2015).

Doubts about competence to stand trial typically surface when a defense attorney visits a client in jail and sees that the client is seriously mentally ill. Sometimes, family members bring their doubts to the defense attorney's attention. In some cases, a judge, a mental health professional, or a prosecutor raises the issue.

When doubts arise about a defendant's competence to stand trial, the judge orders the defendant evaluated by mental health professionals. A court hearing may be necessary to determine whether the defendant is competent to stand trial. The evaluators testify. If the defendant is competent, the trial proceeds. If the defendant is not competent, the judge puts the prosecution on hold, and orders treatment for the defendant in jail or in a secure mental health facility. If treatment restores the defendant to competence, proceedings resume. If treatment is ineffective, states have procedures to release the incompetent defendant or, if the defendant is dangerous, to commit the defendant to a psychiatric facility.

An evaluation for competence to stand trial consists of interviews with the defendant. A number of screening tools are available. The Competency Screening Test, for example, is a 22-item sentence completion test that probes the subject's understanding of the legal process. The Competency to Stand Trial Assessment Instrument is a semi-structured interview protocol that yields a numeric score. Except for obviously incompetent defendants, there is no substitute for thorough clinical assessment by an experienced mental health professional.

In an effort to restore a defendant to competence to stand trial, may the government medicate the defendant against the defendant's wishes? In *Sell v. United States* (2003), the U.S. Supreme Court said yes, "but only if the treatment is medically appropriate, is substantially unlikely to have side effects that may undermine the fairness of the trial, and, taking account of less intrusive alternatives, is necessary significantly to further important governmental trial-related interests" (p. 179).

After a defendant is convicted, he or she must be competent to be sentenced. The Supreme Court's *Sell* standard is used when it is necessary to medicate a defendant so that he or she is competent to be sentenced.

In a 2014 case that presages an emerging issue with our aging population, the Indiana Supreme Court considered how to handle the case of a 67-year-old defendant who was charged with sexually abusing his granddaughter. The defendant was incompetent to stand trial because of dementia (*State v. Coats*, 3 N.E.3d 528 (Ind. 2014)). Experts agreed that the defendant would never be restored to competence, and the issue was whether he should be committed to an institution. Ultimately, the state supreme court concluded that state law required commitment to an institution.

Pretrial Discovery

Pretrial discovery is designed to allow each side of a civil or criminal lawsuit to find out about the other side's evidence. The rules on pretrial discovery differ in civil and criminal litigation. Generally, discovery is more limited in criminal cases. Every state has detailed statutes that govern pretrial discovery. In addition to statutes, the U.S. Constitution requires the prosecution in criminal cases to turn over to the defense evidence that is favorable to the defendant (exculpatory evidence), including evidence that could be used to undermine prosecution witnesses (*Brady v. Maryland,* 1963).

Plea Bargaining

Most criminal cases do not end in a trial. Most are resolved through plea bargaining. With a plea bargain, the accused agrees to plead guilty in exchange for the prosecutor's agreement to drop some of the charges or to recommend lenience at sentencing.

Jury Selection

For cases that are not resolved through plea bargaining, a trial is held. One of the first trial issues is whether there will be a jury. The defendant can waive a jury, in which case, the judge serves the role normally performed by a jury.

If there is a jury, the case begins with jury selection. The judge and/or attorneys question prospective jurors, a process called voir dire. Each attorney looks for jurors he or she believes will be sympathetic to the attorney's case.

Attorneys have two types of challenges to prospective jurors: challenges for cause and peremptory challenges. A prospective juror can be challenged for cause if the juror is not qualified to serve on the jury (e.g., not a U.S. citizen). A prospective juror may be challenged for cause if the juror is related to the defendant, is biased, or admits he or she has already formed an opinion about the defendant's guilt. Attorneys have an unlimited number of challenges for cause.

Attorneys have a limited number of peremptory challenges. The number depends on the seriousness of the crime. A peremptory challenge allows an attorney to dismiss a prospective juror for any reason except race, ethnicity, gender, religion, or, in some states, sexual orientation. For example, I was once called for jury duty, and was in the pool of prospective jurors being questioned to serve on the jury for a child molestation trial. When the defense attorney learned that I am a law professor who has written books on how to prosecute child abuse, the defense attorney told the judge, "Your honor, the defense would like to thank and excuse Mr. Myers." He dismissed me from the jury pool. The defense attorney did not say why he booted me—he was not required to give a reason for his peremptory challenge.

If an attorney suspects that the other attorney is using peremptory challenges to excuse potential jurors on the basis of race or another prohibited classification, the attorney can make an objection based on the U.S. Supreme Court's decision in *Batson v. Kentucky* (1986). The objecting attorney presents evidence of improper exclusion. The other attorney then has the opportunity to defend the exclusion, by explaining the nondiscriminatory reason the juror was rejected (see *Foster v. Chatman*, 2016).

Trial

Once members or the jury are selected and each takes the juror's oath, the case begins with opening statements from the prosecutor and the defense attorney. The purpose of the opening statement is to help jurors understand what the attorneys believe the evidence will show. Each attorney paints a picture for the jury of what the attorney will try to prove. It is common for an attorney giving an opening statement to say, "Ladies and gentlemen, the evidence will show ____________."

Following the opening statements, a trial proceeds in three phases: (1) prosecution case-in-chief, (2) defense case-in-chief, and (3) prosecution case-in-rebuttal.

During the prosecution case-in-chief, the prosecutor offers evidence to prove the *actus reus* and *mens rea* of the crime, and to establish that it was the defendant who committed the offense. Evidence consists of testimony by witnesses, documents, and other items, such as a weapon, DNA samples, or fingerprints. The defense attorney has the right to cross-examine prosecution witnesses. (Cross-examination is discussed in Chapters 8 and 9.) The prosecutor, though, is not allowed to call the defendant as a witness during the prosecution's case-in-chief. When the prosecution finishes offering evidence, the prosecution rests its case.

The defendant in a criminal case has no obligation of offer evidence; no obligation to put on a defense case-in-chief. The defendant is entitled to argue that defense evidence is not necessary because the prosecution failed to prove its case.

If the defense attorney decides to offer evidence, then witness testimony, documents, and other items are offered that point toward innocence. If the defendant testifies, the testimony occurs during the defense case-in-chief. The prosecutor has the right to cross-examine defense witnesses, including the defendant, if the defendant testifies. At the end of the defense case-in-chief, the defense rests.

After the defense rests, the prosecutor may offer evidence to rebut evidence offered during the defense case-in-chief. This is the prosecution's case-in-rebuttal.

When all the evidence is presented, and both sides have rested their case, the attorneys make closing arguments. The prosecutor goes first and summarizes the evidence pointing to guilt. Defense counsel argues the opposite.

After the closing arguments are completed, the judge instructs the jury on the law it is required to apply to the facts of the case. The jury retires to the jury room to deliberate and decide the defendant's fate: Guilty? Not guilty? Not guilty by reason of insanity? Guilty but mentally ill?

If the verdict is not guilty, the defendant is acquitted. The prosecution can*not* appeal a not-guilty verdict. Nor can the prosecution charge the defendant a second time for the same crime following an acquittal because doing so violates the Double Jeopardy Clause of the Fifth Amendment to the U.S. Constitution. If the jury finds the defendant guilty, the defendant *can* appeal to a higher court, in an effort to convince the appellate court that the trial judge made mistakes that warrant a new trial.

SENTENCING

"Let the punishment fit the crime."
"An eye for an eye."
"Don't do the crime, if you can't do the time."
"Lock 'em up and throw away the key."
"Crime doesn't pay." (usually)

These and similar sentiments concern punishment, a subject that has occupied philosophers, lawmakers, judges, and the public for centuries. *Black's Law Dictionary* defines punishment as "Any fine, penalty, or confinement inflicted upon a person by the authority of the law and the judgment and sentence of a court, for some crime or offense committed by him."

The literature on punishment is voluminous and contentious. Five principle justifications are offered for punishment: deterrence, retribution, incapacitation, rehabilitation, and revenge.

Deterrence is of two kinds, general and specific. General deterrence is aimed at the public at large: We obey the law not only because it is the right thing to do, but because we realize we will be punished if we get caught. Specific deterrence is restricted to the individual lawbreaker. The unpleasantness of punishment deters the criminal from doing it again.

Retribution was defined by philosopher H.L.A. Hart "as the application of the pains of punishment to an offender who is morally guilty" (1968, p. 9). Punishment is inflicted because it is deserved. How much punishment is deserved introduces the concept of proportionality and depends on the seriousness of the crime—let the punishment fit the crime.

The idea behind incapacitation is simple: While a criminal is serving time in prison, the community is safe from further depredations at his hands.

The goal of rehabilitation is to "fix," or rehabilitate, the criminal so he decides to no longer engage in crime. Clearly, mental health professionals play a major role in rehabilitation.

The desire for revenge seems part of human nature. You hurt my family; I will exact revenge upon you and yours. Scholars have long debated whether revenge should have a seat at the table when it comes to punishment. Some argue that revenge has no place in an advanced civilization. Indeed, a primary purpose of the law is to replace private vengeance with punishments that are dispassionately administered by the state. Others disagree and argue that revenge is in our DNA. While it is true that private vengeance is unacceptable, society itself has the right, for itself, and on behalf of victims, to "hate" the criminal and to administer punishment as revenge.

The justifications for punishment, alone, and in combination, have been debated since time immemorial. Plato (427–347 B.C.E.) argued in his Dialogue *Gorgias* that an unjust man is "miserable," and is more miserable still "if he be not punished and does not meet with retribution." The miscreant is "less miserable if he be punished and meets with retribution at the hand of gods and men." The great religious texts grapple with the severity of punishment. The *Qur'an* states: "Cut off the hands of thieves, whether they are man or woman, as punishment for what they have done—a deterrent from God" (5.38). The idea of proportionality is at the heart of "an eye for an eye," found in various forms in the *Qur'an,* the *Talmud,* and the *Bible.* Thomas Hobbes (1588–1679), author of *Leviathan,* observed that punishment must be sufficient to deter would-be criminals: "For the punishment foreknown, if not great enough to deter men from the action, is an invitement to it: because when men compare the benefit of their injustice with the harm of the punishment, by necessity of nature they choose that which appeareth best for themselves" (Part II, Chapter 27). John Locke (1632–1704) argued in his second essay on government that people in "the State of Nature" are equal, and when one person in this state harms another, the measure of justice "is so much as may serve for reparation and restraint. For these two are the only reasons why one man may lawfully do harm to another, which is what we call punishment." Cesare Beccaria (1738–1794), who published *On Crimes and Punishments* in 1764, wrote: "The purpose of punishment is nothing other than to dissuade the criminal from doing fresh harm to his compatriots and to keep other people from doing the same. Therefore, punishments and the method of inflicting them should be chosen that, mindful of the proportion between crime and punishment, will make the most effective and lasting impression on men's minds and inflict the least torment on the body of the criminal" (p. 23). Two heavyweights in the debate over punishment are Jeremy Bentham (1748–1832) and Immanuel Kant (1724–1804). Bentham championed utilitarianism, and he justified punishment largely on its ability to deter crime. Kant rejected utilitarianism and argued that retribution is the justification for punishment—the criminal is punished because she deserves it. The debate goes on, probably never to be resolved, because each justification for punishment has merit.

Legislators decide what punishment is appropriate for particular crimes. A legislator can read the philosophical literature on punishment all day, but eventually the lawmaker must come to the difficult decision of prescribing particular punishments for particular crimes. There is no magic formula. In the final analysis, it is often little more than a gut feeling.

The best way to get a feel for the challenge of picking the right punishment is to try it yourself. As a thought experiment, prescribe the punishment for the following crimes: burglary, trespassing, theft, robbery, assault, rape, attempted rape, intent to kill murder, attempted intent to kill murder, and involuntary manslaughter based on negligence. Not easy, is it?

The Legislature sets punishments but often gives judges a range of possible punishments to choose from. The solemn responsibility of selecting and imposing punishment falls to the judge. The details of sentencing law vary considerably from state to state.

CONCLUSION

Police investigations and criminal trials are the stuff of TV programs, novels, films, and, for professionals working with victims of interpersonal violence, the real world. The criminal justice system has many failings, and innocent people are sometimes convicted. The guilty sometimes go free. Yet, despite its faults, in the run of cases, the system finds its way to truth, thanks to the dedicated efforts of police officers, prosecutors, defense attorneys, judges, and victim advocates. The legal system, and the legal professionals within it, are ably assisted in the search for truth by clinical professionals.

4

Hearsay

Hearsay evidence plays an important role in many interpersonal violence court cases. It is no exaggeration to say that the ability to keep victims safe often turns on the ability to use hearsay in court. It is equally no exaggeration to say that the ability to use hearsay often depends on whether clinicians know what to watch for and document. Therefore, as you read this chapter, it's important to understand that your knowledge of hearsay evidence may someday be of value to an attorney who can use such evidence to keep a child or an adult secure.

Hearsay is an out-of-court statement (an assertion of fact) that is repeated in court to prove the truth of the statement (the truth of the matter asserted). The law in all states, and in federal court, is that hearsay is inadmissible in evidence unless an exception to the rule against hearsay applies.

To better understand hearsay evidence, it is useful to divide the definition of hearsay into its three components. A person's words are hearsay when:

1. The person's words were intended by the person to describe something that happened (e.g., describing abuse).
2. The person spoke prior to the court hearing where the person's words are repeated (the person's assertion was "out-of-court").
3. The person's out-of-court statement (assertion) is repeated in court to prove that what the person said actually happened (the *out*-of-court assertion is repeated *in* court to prove the truth of the matter asserted).

The person who makes a hearsay statement is a "declarant." The person who comes to court to repeat a hearsay statement is not a declarant. For example, an elderly victim of abuse is taken by ambulance to the hospital. In the emergency department, the victim tells a nurse how she was injured and who hurt her. Later, at the trial of the abuser, the prosecutor calls the nurse as a witness and asks the nurse to repeat the victim's statements. In this scenario, the victim is the declarant. The nurse who repeats the victim's out-of-court statement is not a declarant.

To complicate matters, in some cases, the declarant comes to court and repeats her *own* hearsay statement. Consider, for example, 13-year-old Marcie, who was sexually abused by her stepfather. Marcie disclosed the abuse to her mother, a child protective services (CPS) social worker, a police officer, a forensic interviewer, and her counselor. At the stepfather's trial, Marcie testifies for the prosecution, and the prosecutor asks Marcie, "What did you tell your mom had happened to you?" The defense attorney makes a hearsay objection. The fact that Marcie—the declarant—is present in court does not eliminate the hearsay issue. Don't believe me? If you apply the three-part definition of hearsay, you will agree.

In addition to testimony from Marcie, the prosecutor may ask Marcie's mom, the social worker, the police officer, the forensic interviewer, and Marcie's counselor to repeat Marcie's out-of-court statement. With each witness, repeating what Marcie said involves hearsay.

However, since Marcie is in court, you may question why she should repeat her own out-of-court statements. Why not just ask her to describe what happened? In that way, hearsay is not involved because Marcie is not repeating what she said out-of-court. Like other eyewitnesses, she is simply describing what happened from memory. In some cases, that is how testimony unfolds, and hearsay issues are avoided. In other cases, however, the declarant's earlier hearsay statements are powerful evidence, and the attorney wants the jury to hear *both* the hearsay *and* the declarant's non-hearsay testimony. It all depends on the case, and what the declarant said out-of-court.

The best way to become adept at spotting hearsay is to practice applying the three-part definition. Give it a try. In many domestic violence cases, during the immediate aftermath of violence, the victim describes the abuse to police officers, family members, medical and mental health professionals, or others. Months later, however, when the trial of the abuser is under way, the victim is reluctant to testify. (This common scenario was described in Chapter 2.) Perhaps the victim has reconciled with the abuser. Perhaps the abuser has threatened her into silence. On the witness stand, the victim denies the abuse, or says, "I can't remember," or places the blame on herself. In such cases, the victim's initial statements to the police officer and others are powerful evidence of abuse. If the prosecutor calls the police officer, the family member, and the medical or mental health professional to repeat the victim's statements describing the abuse, however, the defense attorney will certainly make a hearsay objection.

Should the judge sustain the defense attorney's hearsay objection? First, the victim (declarant) described something that happened, in this case, domestic abuse. Second, her statements were out-of-court. Third, there is no doubt that the prosecutor is offering the victim's out-of-court statements to prove the truth of the matters asserted, that is, to prove the domestic violence. Thus, the victim's statements *are* hearsay.

In child abuse cases, the child's out-of-court statements are often the most powerful evidence in the case. Consider 4-year-old Beth. Beth is being examined by a physician because she told a friend that her father gave her "bad touches." In response to a question from the doctor, Beth points to her genital area and says, "Daddy put his pee-pee in me, down there. Then he took it out and shook it up and down and white stuff popped out and got all over me. It got in my mouth, and tasted yucky." Beth's words are powerful evidence of abuse. Criminal charges are filed against Beth's father, and the case goes to trial. The prosecutor calls the doctor as a witness and asks the doctor to repeat Beth's words, and to describe her pointing gesture. Before the doctor can speak, however, the defense attorney objects that Beth's words *and* gesture are hearsay.

Put Beth's words and gesture to the test. Are they hearsay? First, Beth intended to describe something that happened. Second, Beth made her statement prior to the court proceeding where the prosecutor asks the doctor to repeat Beth's words. Finally, the prosecutor offers Beth's words to prove that what Beth said actually happened—the truth of the matter asserted. Beth's out-of-court statement is hearsay.

But that's not all. Beth's gesture pointing to her genital area is also hearsay. The gesture was nonverbal communication intended by Beth to describe what happened. Nonverbal conduct that is intended as an assertion of fact can be hearsay.

In both the domestic violence and child abuse trials, the judge will sustain defense objections, unless the prosecutor persuades the judge that the hearsay meets the requirements of an exception to the rule against hearsay.

In both types of abuse cases, and in countless others, the prosecutor's ability to convince the judge that hearsay statements meet the requirements of exceptions to the hearsay rule depends *at least as much* on the documentation of the professionals to whom the declarant spoke as it does on the legal acumen of the prosecutor. If police officers, doctors, nurses, mental health professionals, social workers, and others know what to watch for and document when victims speak, and they take careful, verbatim notes of what the victim said about the abuse and how it was described, prosecutors are in a strong position to persuade judges to overrule hearsay objections and admit victims' hearsay statements in court. The next section describes what professionals need to watch for and document.

EXCEPTIONS TO THE HEARSAY RULE

There are more than 30 exceptions to the rule against hearsay, but only a handful of the exceptions play a day-to-day role in interpersonal violence litigation. Five frequently used hearsay exceptions are discussed here. Before delving into the exceptions, permit me once again to beat the drum I've been beating: It is important for frontline professionals to understand hearsay. It is you who are in the best position to document *exactly* what victims say out-of-court, *as well as* the facts that trigger hearsay exceptions, thus allowing victims' hearsay statements to be repeated in court for their protection. It is mistaken to think, "Hearsay exceptions are for lawyers, not me." Because you are in direct contact with victims, *you* are the one in the ideal position to document the information needed to open the courthouse doors to hearsay. It is no exaggeration to say that your knowledge of hearsay, and exceptions to the rule against hearsay, can make the difference between victims being safe or in danger.

Excited Utterance Exception

An excited utterance is a hearsay statement that describes a startling event. The statement must be made while the declarant is under the emotional stress caused by the startling event. The theory behind the excited utterance exception is that statements made under significant stress are likely to be true. All states have the excited utterance exception. Judges consider the following factors in deciding whether a hearsay statement is an excited utterance.

- ***Nature of the event.*** Some events are more startling than others, and the judge considers the likely impact a particular event would have on a person of a similar age and experience.

- ***Amount of time between the startling event and the statement relating to the event.*** The more time that passes between a startling event and a declarant's statement describing the event, the less likely a judge is to conclude that the statement is an excited utterance. Although passage of time is important, elapsed time is not the only factor judges consider. Judges have approved delays ranging from a few minutes to many hours. It's important, therefore, to document as precisely as possible how much time passed between the startling event and the declarant's statement.

- ***Was the declarant upset?*** Indications that the declarant was distraught when she or he described the event are important. Was the declarant crying, frightened, or otherwise upset when the statement was made?

- ***Declarant's speech pattern.*** In some cases, the way a person speaks, for example, the use of pressured or hurried speech, indicates excitement.

- ***Was the statement spontaneous?*** Spontaneity is a key factor in the excited utterance exception. The more spontaneous a statement, the more likely it meets the requirements of the exception.

- ***Did questions elicit the statement?*** The fact that a declarant was asked questions does not necessarily destroy the spontaneity required for the excited utterance exception. However, as questions become suggestive, spontaneity may dissipate, undermining the exception.

- ***First safe opportunity.*** In many abuse cases, the victim remains under the control of an abuser for hours after an abusive incident. When the victim is finally released to a safe person, the victim has the first safe opportunity to disclose what happened. A victim's statement at the first safe opportunity may qualify as an excited utterance even though considerable time has elapsed since the abuse occurred.

- ***Rekindled excitement.*** A startling event such as abuse may be followed by a period of calm, during which excitement abates. If the victim is later exposed to a stimulus that reminds the victim of the startling event, the victim's excitement may be rekindled. Rekindled excitement sometimes satisfies the excited utterance exception.

These foregoing factors and any additional information suggesting that a declarant was upset when describing traumatic events should be carefully documented.

Medical Diagnosis or Treatment Exception

All states have a medical diagnosis or treatment exception for certain hearsay statements to professionals who provide diagnostic or treatment services. The rationale for the diagnosis or treatment exception is that hearsay statements made to these professionals are reliable because the patient has an incentive to be truthful in these situations.

The person to whom a patient speaks may be a physician, psychiatrist, psychologist, nurse, social worker, paramedic, or an ambulance or medical technician. The medical diagnosis or treatment exception includes the patient's statements describing her medical history, as well as statements describing present symptoms, any pain, and other sensations. The exception includes the patient's description of the cause of the illness or injury.

Unlike the excited utterance exception, the patient does not have to be upset for the diagnosis or treatment exception to apply.

The diagnosis or treatment exception only applies to statements that are pertinent to the professional's ability to diagnose or treat. Thus, it is important to document why information disclosed by patients is pertinent to diagnosis or treatment. For example, after questioning a child, a professional might document that information provided by the child was relevant to deciding whether to test for a sexually transmitted infection (STI).

If the patient is a child, an adult may be the one who describes the child's history and symptoms. So long as the adult's motive is to obtain a diagnosis or treatment for the child, the adult's statements are admissible under the exception.

Professionals treating children can increase the likelihood that a child's statements satisfy the diagnosis or treatment exception by discussing with the child the clinical importance of providing accurate information and being forthcoming. A physician might say, "Hello, I'm Dr. Jones. I'm a doctor, and I'm going to give you a checkup to make sure everything is OK. While you are here today, I'll ask you some questions so I can help you. It's important for you to listen carefully to my questions. When you answer my questions, be sure to tell me everything you know. Tell me only things that really happened. Don't pretend or make things up. Your answers to my questions help me to do my job as a doctor, so it is important for you to tell me things that really happened."

If a patient identifies the perpetrator of abuse, document why knowing the identity of the perpetrator is pertinent to diagnosis or treatment.

For example, knowing the identity of the perpetrator is often important in deciding whether it is safe to send a child home. As well, the professional needs to know the perpetrator's identity if there is a possibility the child or adult victim was exposed to an STI. The decision to refer a victim for mental health services is influenced, in some cases, by the identity of the abuser, making the issue of identity pertinent.

The medical diagnosis or treatment exception has its clearest application with patients receiving traditional medical care in a hospital, clinic, or physician's office. Judges are less certain about the diagnosis or treatment exception for statements made to mental health professionals. Yet, judges generally conclude that the diagnosis or treatment exception extends to hearsay statements during mental health treatment.

Residual and Child Hearsay Exceptions

Most states have a hearsay exception known as a residual or catchall exception, which allows the use in court of reliable hearsay that does not meet the requirements of one of the traditional exceptions (e.g., excited utterance, medical diagnosis or treatment). In addition to a generic residual exception, which applies in all kinds of cases, most states have a residual hearsay exception for reliable statements by children in child abuse cases. Some states have a residual exception for domestic violence cases.

When a declarant's hearsay statement is offered under a residual or child hearsay exception, the most important issue to resolve is whether the statement is reliable. Professionals who interview, examine, or treat adult or child victims play a vital role in documenting the information judges consider to determine whether a victim's statements are sufficiently reliable to be admitted under a residual or child hearsay exceptions. The following indicators of reliability are important to document. The more spontaneous a victim's statement is, the more likely a judge is to find it reliable. Reliability may be influenced by the type of questions asked. When questions are suggestive, the possibility increases that the questioner influenced the victim's statement. It should be noted, however, that suggestive questions are sometimes necessary to elicit information from victims, particularly when the information is embarrassing. The smaller the number of suggestive questions, the more likely a judge is to conclude that a victim's statement is reliable. Reliability may be enhanced if a victim's description of abuse is consistent over time. When a victim's emotions are consistent with the victim's statement, the reliability of the statement may be enhanced. The play or gestures of a young child may strengthen confidence in the child's statement. For example, a child's use of dolls may support the reliability of the child's statement. A young child's developmentally unusual knowledge of sexual acts or anatomy supports the reliability of the child's statement. The presence in a child's statement of idiosyncratic details of sexual acts points to reliability. Children (like adults) hesitate to make statements they believe may get them in trouble. Therefore, if a child believed disclosing abuse could result in punishment, confidence in the child's statement may increase. Evidence that the child or an adult had or lacked a motive to fabricate affects reliability. The victim's statement may be corroborated by medical evidence. When a victim's behavior alters in a way that corroborates the victim's description of abuse, it may be appropriate to place increased confidence in the victim's statement. None of these factors, though, is a litmus test for reliability. Judges consider the totality of circumstances to evaluate reliability, and professionals can assist the legal system by documenting anything that indicates the victim was or was not telling the truth.

Prior Inconsistent Statements

Prior inconsistent statements were alluded to in the discussion of intimate partner violence in Chapter 2, and are noted again in Chapter 8. The law on prior inconsistent statements is complex, and there is no need here to delve into the details. Suffice to say, if a witness's prior inconsistent statement is offered to prove that the prior statement is true, then the statement is hearsay. State and federal courts have hearsay exceptions for some or all prior inconsistent statements.

Party Admissions

You have probably heard the expression, "Anything you say can be used against you." Well, in court, the expression is pretty much true. Any out-of-court statement that is relevant to a case, and that was made by a party to the case, can be used *against* the speaker by the opposing party. Such statements are called "party admissions."

THE IMPACT OF THE U.S. CONSTITUTION ON HEARSAY

There are two sources of law governing hearsay. First, there is the rule against hearsay, which is part of the law of evidence. Hearsay exceptions (e.g., excited utterance, medical diagnosis or treatment) are part of evidence law. Second, in addition to evidence law, with its hearsay rule and exceptions, the U.S. Constitution places limits on the use of hearsay in criminal cases. The Constitution's Sixth Amendment contains the so-called Confrontation Clause, which provides, "In all criminal prosecutions, the accused shall enjoy the right to be confronted with the witnesses against him." The U.S. Supreme Court interprets the Confrontation Clause to limit the types of hearsay evidence that can be used against defendants in criminal cases. To be admissible against the defendant in a criminal trial, hearsay must *both* satisfy the Confrontation Clause *and* fall within an exception to the rule against hearsay. In some situations, hearsay that fits a hearsay exception is inadmissible in court because it violates the Confrontation Clause.

The Sixth Amendment's Confrontation Clause does not apply when the defendant offers hearsay evidence against the prosecution. The Sixth Amendment protects the accused person, not the government. Of course, the hearsay rule applies regardless of which side offers hearsay evidence.

The U.S. Supreme Court's 2004 decision in *Crawford v. Washington* (2004), and decisions after *Crawford,* define the impact of the Confrontation Clause on the admission of hearsay in criminal cases. Before discussing *Crawford,* it is important to mention two rules. First, if the person who made a hearsay statement—the declarant—is able to testify in court and be cross-examined by the defense attorney about the hearsay statement, then the Confrontation Clause is satisfied, and the person's hearsay can be admitted without an affront to the Confrontation Clause. Of course, the hearsay still has to meet the requirements of an exception to the rule against hearsay. Second, the constitutional limits on hearsay apply only in criminal cases. Thus, the Confrontation Clause does not apply in civil proceedings, such as child protection proceedings in juvenile court or child custody litigation in family court.

In criminal prosecutions, the Confrontation Clause comes into play when a prosecutor offers hearsay against a defendant. As previously stated, if the declarant who made the hearsay statement can testify and be cross-examined about the hearsay, the Confrontation Clause is satisfied. However, when the declarant is unable or unwilling to testify, the constitutional question is whether the declarant's hearsay statement was "testimonial." If the court determines that a declarant's hearsay statement is testimonial, it cannot be admitted against the defendant. On the other hand, if the declarant's hearsay statement was nontestimonial, then the Confrontation Clause places no limit on use of the statement against the defendant.

Under the *Crawford* decision, the word "testimonial" is a term of art. A hearsay statement can be testimonial" even though it bears no resemblance to testimony in court. Hearsay is typically testimonial when the *primary purpose* of the declarant in speaking, or the primary purpose of the person questioning the declarant, is to create evidence for use in possible criminal proceedings. For example, a person's answers to questions during a formal interrogation at a police station are testimonial because the purpose of the questioning is to gather evidence for use in court.

Under the "primary purpose" test, statements made to parents, relatives, friends, foster parents, and babysitters are almost never testimonial. On the other hand, statements made to child protection workers conducting investigations are often testimonial. Children's statements made during formal forensic interviews at child advocacy centers are generally considered testimonial.

Hearsay statements made to physicians, nurses, and other medical professionals, and to mental health professionals, are nontestimonial when the professional's primary purpose for questioning is clinical. The fact that a professional is aware of the forensic implications of communicating with victims does not alter this conclusion. On the other hand, if a medical or mental health professional questions a person primarily for legal, evidence-gathering reasons, the person's statements are likely to be testimonial.

Although many statements made to police officers are testimonial, some are not. The answer depends on the circumstances in which the officer spoke to the person. Statements to the police are likely to be nontestimonial when the police question the victim in the context of an ongoing emergency. Thus, a victim's answer to a police officer's question "What happened?" shortly after the officer arrives in response to a 911 call, is often nontestimonial because the question is intended to assess the situation, to see whether medical help is necessary, and to determine whether the victim and the officer are safe. As the emergency abates, and the officer's questions shift from dealing with an emergency to gathering evidence, statements become testimonial.

In deciding whether statements made to police officers are testimonial, judges typically consider the following questions:

1. Was there an ongoing emergency?
2. Was the declarant safe or in danger?
3. Was medical assistance necessary?
4. Was the declarant alone or protected by others?

5. Was the declarant seeking help?
6. Was the declarant describing events that were happening? Or was the declarant describing past events?
7. How much time elapsed since the crime occurred?
8. What was the level of formality of the questioning?

To summarize, two independent, but overlapping, sources of law govern the admission of hearsay against the accused in criminal court. First, the hearsay rule and its exceptions. Second, the Confrontation Clause of the Sixth Amendment, which bars the admission of testimonial hearsay when the declarant does not testify. In many cases, the two sources of law reach the same conclusion: hearsay is or is not admissible in court. Sometimes, however, a hearsay statement that is admissible under hearsay law cannot be used in court because it runs afoul of the Confrontation Clause. Consider, for example, a case in which a prosecutor has a hearsay statement that meets the requirements of a hearsay exception. The statement is admissible under hearsay law. Be that as it may, if the statement is testimonial, and the declarant cannot testify, the statement is inadmissible in court because it offends the Confrontation Clause.

If you are analyzing the admissibility of hearsay against a defendant in a criminal case, it helps to keep the two sources of law separate. First, conduct a hearsay analysis to determine whether the out-of-court statement is hearsay and whether it meets the requirements of an exception. If no exception applies, the statement is inadmissible under hearsay law, and it is not necessary to consider the Confrontation Clause. However, if the statement is admissible under the hearsay law because it meets an exception, then analyze the Confrontation Clause. On that score, ask these two questions:

1. Is the declarant available to testify and be cross-examined? If so, the Confrontation Clause poses no barrier to admission of the hearsay, and this is true whether the hearsay is testimonial or nontestimonial.
2. If the declarant is not available to testify and be cross-examined, is the hearsay testimonial? If the hearsay is not testimonial, it is admissible. But if the hearsay is testimonial, then it is not admissible.

Finally, do not fall prey to a common mistake, the erroneous belief that testimonial hearsay is a hearsay exception. It is not. Testimonial hearsay is a concept under the Confrontation Clause, and is not a hearsay exception.

In 2015, the U. S. Supreme Court handed down an important decision on testimonial hearsay *Ohio v. Clark* (2015). In *Clark,* a 3-year-old child, L.P., was abused. The question was, who was the abuser? The mystery began in L.P.'s Cleveland, Ohio, preschool. Darius Clark dropped L.P. off at preschool. In the preschool lunchroom, a teacher noticed that L.P.'s left eye was bloodshot. The teacher asked, "What happened?" but L.P. said, "Nothing." A little later, L.P. said, "I fell." In the brighter light of a classroom, however, the teacher saw bruises on L.P.'s face, as though someone had whipped him. Alarmed, the teacher notified the head teacher, who asked L.P., "Who did this? What happened to you?" L.P. replied, "Dee Dee." The head teacher asked, "Is Dee big or little?" L.P. said, "Dee is big." The teachers took L.P. to the preschool supervisor, who lifted L.P.'s shirt to reveal more injuries. A report of suspected child abuse was filed, and a social worker with child protective services (CPS) was summoned to the preschool. Before long, Darius Clark arrived to take L.P. home. Darius, whose nickname is Dee, denied causing the injuries, and he quickly left with the child over the objections of the social worker.

The social worker searched for L.P., and located the child and his little sister at Darius's mother's house a day later. The children were taken to a hospital. A doctor examined L.P. and found a black eye, injuries from a belt on L.P.'s back and stomach, and bruises covering his body. L.P.'s little sister had similar injuries. The quick action of L.P.'s teachers, the CPS worker, and the hospital staff rescued the children.

Why were these children living with Darius Clark, who was not related to them? Where were the parents? The father was nowhere to be found. The mother was in Washington, D.C., working as a prostitute. Darius was her pimp. He sent her to Washington to work, while he "took care" of the kids.

A grand jury indicted Darius Clark for physically abusing both children, but Clark stated, "I didn't do it. You charged the wrong person. It was the mother who hurt the children. She already lost other children to CPS." Thus, the primary question was not whether L.P. was abused, but who committed the crime.

At Clark's trial, the prosecutor put the preschool teachers on the witness stand to describe what they saw and to repeat L.P.'s words: "Dee Dee" and "Dee is big." Clark's defense attorney made a two-part objection. First, he argued that repeating L.P.'s words would violate the rule against hearsay. Second, he argued that repeating L.P.'s words would violate the Confrontation Clause.

The judge overruled the defense counsel's objections. The judge ruled that L.P.'s words were admissible under Ohio's residual hearsay exception. As for the Confrontation Clause, the judge ruled that L.P.'s statements to the preschool teachers were nontestimonial. In court, the teachers repeated L.P.'s words, and Clark was convicted and sentenced to a long prison term.

Clark appealed his conviction to the Ohio Court of Appeals, where he prevailed. In the appellate court, Clark's attorney argued that L.P's answers to the preschool teachers' questions were testimonial because the teachers were mandated reporters under Ohio's child abuse reporting law. The defense argued that as a mandated reporter, a teacher's primary purpose in questioning a child is to gather evidence for use in court. The Court of Appeals agreed with this reasoning and ruled that admission of L.P.'s hearsay statements to his teachers were testimonial, and should not have been admitted. The prosecution appealed to the Ohio Supreme Court, but Ohio's highest court endorsed the position taken by the Court of Appeals: L.P.'s statements to his teachers were testimonial, and their repetition in court violated Clark's rights under the Confrontation Clause.

The U.S. Supreme Court granted a writ of certiorari, and, in *Ohio v. Clark,* it rejected the reasoning of the Ohio Supreme Court and ruled that L.P.'s statements to his preschool teachers were nontestimonial.

If it seems to you that there is a world of difference between a police officer investigating a crime and a preschool teacher trying to find out what happened to a 3-year-old child, you are on the same page as the U.S. Supreme Court. The Court ruled that the reporting law does not transform preschool teachers into investigators gathering evidence for the purpose of prosecution. L.P.'s statements to his teachers, therefore, were not testimonial. The Court wrote:

> There is no indication that the primary purpose of the conversation was to gather evidence for Clark's prosecution. On the contrary, it is clear that the first objective was to protect L.P. . . . [T]he conversation between L.P. and his teachers was informal and spontaneous. The teachers asked L.P. about his injuries immediately upon discovering them, in the informal setting of a preschool lunchroom and classroom, and they did so precisely as any concerned citizen would talk to a child who might be a victim of abuse. . . .
>
> L.P.'s age fortifies our conclusion that the statements in question were not testimonial. Statements by very young children will rarely, if

ever, implicate the Confrontation Clause. . . . [I]t is extremely unlikely that a 3-year-old child in L.P.'s position would intend his statements to be [used as evidence in court]. On the contrary, a young child in these circumstances would simply want the abuse to end, would want to protect other victims, or would have no discernible purpose at all. . . .

Statements made to someone who is not principally charged with uncovering and prosecuting criminal behavior are significantly less likely to be testimonial than statements given to law enforcement officers. (p. 2182)

APPLY WHAT YOU HAVE LEARNED

"Bang, bitch. You're dead."

Dawn and Bill lived together 17 years and had three children. Throughout the relationship, Bill physically and psychologically abused Dawn. Finally, Dawn separated from Bill, and got an apartment for herself and the children. Bill told Dawn he would not agree to give up custody of the children. In the months after the separation, Dawn told coworkers and friends that she was afraid Bill would kill her. Bill had obtained passports for himself and the children, and Dawn told friends she was afraid he would murder her and leave the country with them. Dawn was prescient. Bill asked his friend, Hoffman, to kill Dawn. Dawn and Bill had dinner. After dinner, Dawn told a friend that, at dinner, Bill asked Dawn to return home. When Dawn said no, Bill pointed his finger at her, like a gun, and said, "Bang, bitch. You're dead." The next day, Hoffman murdered Dawn.

Bill is charged with murder. At Bill's trial, the prosecutor wants to offer Dawn's statements to her coworkers and friends, in which she expressed her fears of Bill, as well as his after-dinner threat, "You're dead." Bill's attorney objects that the things Dawn said are hearsay and violate the Confrontation Clause. How should the judge rule? Should the jury be allowed to hear Dawn's statements to friends and coworkers?—*People v. Richter,* 977 N.E.2d 1257 (Ill. Ct. App. 2012)

Analysis: Dawn's statements to coworkers and friends are hearsay, as is Bill's statement to Dawn at dinner. It is difficult to see how Dawn's statements fit into any of the normal hearsay exceptions. For example, her statements are probably not excited utterances. However, Illinois has a special hearsay exception for hearsay statements by victims of domestic violence. The Illinois Court of Appeals ruled that Dawn's statements met the requirements of that exception, and could be used at Bill's trial. The court also ruled that Dawn's statements to coworkers and friends were not testimonial as that term is defined under the Confrontation Clause. Bill was convicted of first-degree murder and sentenced to 75 years in prison. The Court of Appeals affirmed his conviction.

You may ask, how could Bill be convicted of murder, when it was Hoffman who killed Dawn? The answer is twofold. First, Bill is an accomplice to murder, and an accomplice is as guilty as the one who pulled the trigger, even though the accomplice is nowhere near the scene of the crime. Second, Bill and Hoffman entered a conspiracy to kill Dawn, and, as a co-conspirator, Bill is guilty of the murder.

The three children are effectively orphans. Hopefully, family members will step up to give them a home, and clinical services will be provided to help them cope.

"It hurts to pee."

Three-year-old Susie was visiting her maternal grandparents' home, along with her sister, and her uncle, Maurice. The grandparents and sister were watching TV in the living room. Maurice was watching TV in a bedroom. During the day, Susie ran around the house, and was in and out of Maurice's room. At one point, Susie went into a bathroom and cried out in pain when she tried to urinate. Susie's grandmother went to see what was wrong, but Susie said nothing, and her grandmother noticed nothing out of the ordinary. Susie's mother picked Susie and her sister up and took them home. After a bath, Susie again tried to urinate and again cried out in pain. Her mother wrapped Susie in a towel and placed her on her bed. She looked at Susie's genitals and saw "dried blood on Susie's vaginal area." She asked, "Who made you hurt like this?" Initially, Susie said nothing and lowered her head. Her mother reassured her it was OK to talk, and Susie said Maurice hurt her with his finger. Her mother immediately took Susie to the hospital. Susie was referred to a clinic, where a nurse practitioner performed a physical examination and noticed "superficial breaks in the skin inside the labia majora, but outside the vagina." At the clinic, a psychologist talked to Susie, who told the psychologist that Maurice pulled down her pants and touched her with his finger.

Maurice is charged with sexually abusing Susie. Maurice denies touching the child inappropriately. At Maurice's trial, Susie testifies and describes how Maurice hurt her. In addition, the prosecutor offers Susie's statement to her mother shortly after Susie cried out in pain after trying to pee, and her statement to the psychologist at the clinic. Maurice's attorney makes hearsay and Confrontation Clause objections to Susie's statements to her mother and the psychologist. How should the judge rule on the objections?—*State v. Gordon,* 952 S.W.2d 817 (Tenn. 1997)

Analysis: The Tennessee Supreme Court ruled that Susie's statement to her mother was hearsay, but that it could be used in court as an excited utterance. For a hearsay statement to be an excited utterance, there must be a startling event, the hearsay statement must relate to the event, and the speaker must be sufficiently upset. The court ruled that the painful urination was sufficiently startling. Susie's statement related to why it hurt to pee, and it was clear that Susie was upset. The court ruled that Susie's hearsay statement to the psychologist could be admitted under the medical diagnosis or treatment exception to the hearsay rule. How about the Confrontation Clause? Statements to family members are almost never testimonial. The statement to the psychologist was not testimonial either.

The odds that Susie's hearsay can be used to protect her are increased when the mental health and medical professionals who talk to her know the rules about hearsay evidence, as outlined in this chapter.

A FINAL NOTE ABOUT DOCUMENTATION

Hearsay plays a vital role in protecting victims and punishing perpetrators. Mental health and social service professionals are in an excellent position to document hearsay statements. Without careful documentation of exactly what questions were asked and exactly what the victim said in response, the professional will not likely remember months or years later, when he or she is called as a witness and asked to repeat past statements. Documentation is needed not only to preserve the declarant's words, but also to preserve a record of the factors indicating whether the declarant's hearsay statements meet the requirements of an exception to the hearsay rule and whether the statements are testimonial.

Part III

The Civil Justice System

The civil justice system covers a vast range of legal issues—from laws related to contracts, torts, antitrust, and civil rights; to landlord–tenant disputes; to laws related to intellectual property, elections, employment, international relations, and professional malpractice; to family and adoption law; to the law of the sea and even to the law of outer space. Part III comprises three chapters that focus on key sectors of civil law that are likely to be germane to your work. Chapter 5 examines family law, especially laws regarding the custody of children. Chapter 6 describes child protective services and juvenile court. Chapter 7 addresses the legal aspects of voluntary and involuntary psychiatric hospitalization.

Another topic that falls under civil law is professional malpractice. Because the issues surrounding malpractice are crucially important to how you conduct yourself not only with clients in your office, but also when you interact with the legal system, we will discuss malpractice in Part IV (but if you can't wait to read about the subject, turn now to Chapter 11).

5

Family Law

This chapter examines family law. The definition of "family" has evolved and continues to do so. Fifty years ago, the typical American family was a married man and woman with an average of 2.5 children. According to Andrew Cherlin (2010), "The nuclear family of husband, wife, and children, which was predominant in the first half of the [twentieth] century, reached its zenith in the 1950s. . . . Since the 1960s, . . . the overall percentage of children not living with both parents rose sharply to more than 40%" (p. 404). Martha Minow (1992) adds, "Both the growing diversity in groups across the nation who claim to be families and diversity within the families themselves carry consequences for three basic issues in family law: (1) who is in 'the family,' (2) what benefits accompany family membership, and (3) what obligations accompany family role" (p. 275).

When you think of your own family, you probably think of your parents, brothers and sisters, grandparents, and relatives. Some of us include a stepparent, guardian, adoptive parent, or foster parent. An increasing number of children have "two mommies" or "two daddies." In 2013, California passed a law making it possible for a child to have more than two parents (Cal. Family Code § 7601(c)). In 2015, as noted in Chapter 1, the U.S. Supreme Court issued a landmark decision that a generation ago would have seemed unthinkable, when it ruled in favor of same-sex marriage (*Obergefell v. Hodges,* 2015).

Family law includes divorce, division of property, child and spousal support, and child custody. Many mental health professionals, judges, and attorneys lament the fact that family law proceedings too often exacerbate hard feelings and unhappiness, rather than give family members the tools they need to dissolve relationships peacefully and shape their future lives based on trust and cooperation. There is no escaping the fact that the legal system, including family law, is based on the adversarial model. Fortunately, there are practices, such as mediation, that exist to help couples resolve disputes and to help parents avoid fights over child custody. In fact, many states require or strongly encourage mediation of custody before a case can go to court.

Some divorcing couples choose "collaborative family law," in which they agree to avoid litigation. Collaborative law was described by the National Conference of Commissioners on Uniform State Laws (2010): "The distinctive feature of collaborative law . . . is that parties are represented by lawyers ('collaborative lawyers') during negotiations. Collaborative lawyers do not represent the party in court, but only for the purpose of negotiating agreements. The parties agree in advance that their lawyers are disqualified from further representing parties" if either party decides to fight in court.

DIVORCE

Divorce has existed since antiquity. In ancient Greece, an Athenian could petition a magistrate for a divorce. Divorce was also available in ancient Rome. As the Catholic Church gained power over the centuries, however, the law of marriage and divorce fell under ecclesiastical control. The church considered marriage a sacrament ordained by God, and, by the 10th century, the church put a stop to divorce.

Although complete divorce—in Latin, divorce *a vinculo matrimonii*—was not available under church law, the church allowed "legal separation"—divorce *a mensa et thoro,* or divorce from bed and board. Legal separation authorized a married couple to live apart, but the couple still remained married. Today, legal separation is available, although it is seldom used because absolute divorce is readily available, and most married couples who break up choose divorce.

In addition to permitting legal separation, the church authorized annulment of a marriage. Annulment is available today if certain conditions are met, although it is uncommon. To annul a marriage, there must have been a legal defect in the marriage *on the wedding day.* Because the vast majority of marriages are valid on the wedding day, annulment is usually not an option, and divorce is the only way to end the marriage.

Despite the fact that annulment is seldom an option, you may be curious about what the grounds for it are. Bigamous and incestuous marriages are void and can be annulled. The following marriages are voidable, that is, valid unless annulled:

1. One of the parties was too young to consent to marriage.
2. One of the parties was so mentally ill or intellectually disabled that the party lacked capacity to consent to marry.
3. The marriage was induced by fraud.
4. One party was forced to marry.

When the grounds for annulment exist, it is possible to get either an annulment or a divorce. It is a common misconception that if a marriage was not consummated, it can be annulled. Not so.

The United States inherited its divorce law from England. When divorce became available in England, in the 19th century, it was based on marital fault. Only a spouse who was innocent of fault could obtain a divorce. The spouse seeking a divorce commenced a divorce case in court and had to prove that their spouse was at fault. Grounds for fault-based divorce included adultery, physical or mental cruelty, desertion, fraud, impotence, conviction of a felony, habitual drunkenness, failure to support, and incurable insanity.

By the 1960s fault-based divorce became increasingly unpopular, and by 1985, all states had some form of no-fault divorce. In a no-fault divorce, neither spouse need prove marital misconduct; instead, a married person files a petition in court asserting that the marriage is "irretrievably broken" or that "irreconcilable differences" have caused the irreparable breakdown of the marriage. Basically, "irreconcilable differences" is whatever one spouse thinks is a good reason to end the marriage. Judges do not second-guess claims of irreconcilable differences.

Today, ending a marriage can be unilateral. That is, one spouse can get a divorce even if the other spouse wants to stay married. Some people think divorce is impossible unless both spouses "sign the divorce papers," but that is not true. A reluctant spouse can delay a divorce by refusing to cooperate, but cannot prevent the other spouse from terminating the marriage.

A family court has authority (called jurisdiction) to grant divorce if at least one spouse is domiciled in the state. A "domicile" is the place where a person lives with the intent to remain. All states have a residency requirement for divorce. California law, for example, provides, "A judgment of dissolution of marriage may not be entered unless one of the parties to the marriage has been a resident of this state for six months and of the county in which the proceeding is filed for three months next preceding the filing of the petition" (Cal. Family Code § 2320).

ESTABLISHING THE PARENT–CHILD RELATIONSHIP: PARENTAGE

In most situations, there is no doubt about parentage. Giving birth establishes the mother–child relationship. As for the father–child relationship, if a woman and man are married and living together at the time of birth, the law creates a strong presumption that the husband is the father. Of course, not every child born during marriage is the biological offspring of the husband, and the law grapples with that reality.

Issues of paternity arise most often when the mother is not married. To use the antiquated phrase, her child was born "out of wedlock." If the father steps forward and assumes parental responsibilities, issues of paternity seldom arise. Sometimes, however, the father is less than enthusiastic about assuming the mantle of parenthood, including child support. In some cases, more than one man could be the father. When an unwed mother receives public benefits to support her child, officials from child support services are keen to establish paternity and enforce the father's duty to support his child.

Historically, a child born out of wedlock was "illegitimate"—a "bastard." Early law treated "illegitimate" children harshly. For example, an "illegitimate" child could not inherit from his or her parents. A series of U.S. Supreme Court decisions in the 1970s struck down many restrictions on the rights of children born out of wedlock. Today, the term "illegitimate child" is falling into disuse, and states have largely abolished the concept of illegitimacy.

Despite the fact that with most children, there is no doubt about the mother–child relationship, and in many cases, the father–child relationship is equally clear, cases arise all the time in which paternity must be established. Statutes governing paternity vary by state and are complex. No two states have exactly the same laws, although results are generally consistent. States use some version of the Uniform Parentage Act (UPA). Under the UPA, genetic testing is typically employed to establish the parent–child relationship.

CHILD CUSTODY

Custody of children is the most emotionally charged aspect of family law. Fortunately, most parents who are divorcing, or who are ending a nonmarital relationship, agree on the custodial arrangement that is best for their family, and custody litigation is avoided. When parents agree on custody, a judge seldom disapproves. This is not to say that parental decisions regarding custody are binding on the court. In the final analysis, judges—not the parents—decide custody.

When parents cannot agree on custody, litigation may be necessary. Full-blown custody litigation breeds tremendous ill will and heartache. Custody fights are hard on parents and children. Even lawyers, who ostensibly are detached professionals, lose sleep over these cases. Indeed, some family law attorneys won't handle custody cases. Fortunately, as we pointed out earlier, many parents are able to avoid litigation with the help of a professional mediator.

The policy in child custody cases is to maximize the involvement of both parents in the child's life. Illinois law, for example, states, "Unless the court finds the occurrence of ongoing abuse . . . , the court shall presume that the maximum involvement and cooperation of both parents regarding the physical, mental, moral, and emotional well-being of their child is in the best interest of the child" (750 ILCS 5/602(c)). According to Michigan law, "If the parents agree on joint custody, the court shall award joint custody unless the court determines on the record based upon clear and convincing evidence that joint custody is not in the best interests of the child" (Mich. Comp. Laws § 722.26a(2)).

Evolution of Child Custody Law

For much of the 19th century, the courts ruled that fathers normally had the right to custody. Gradually, the presumption in favor of fathers was replaced with the "tender years" presumption, which held that young children should normally be with their mother. In the 1960s, critics of the tender years presumption argued that the presumption favoring mothers having custody constituted gender discrimination, and it was replaced with a gender-neutral preference for the "primary caretaker," that is, the parent who provides most of the day-to-day parenting. In child custody cases today, the overarching priority for judges is to make custody decisions that serve the best interests of the children.

The Impact of Divorce on Children

In research on the impact of divorce on children, most studies suggest that divorce is a risk factor for adjustment problems. According to Paul Amato (2010), who reviewed the literature, "Research during the last decade continued to show that children with divorced parents, compared with children with continuously married parents, score lower on a variety of emotional, behavioral, social, health, and academic outcomes, on average" (p. 653). Gary Melton and his colleagues (2007) found:

> [D]ivorce obviously has a negative effect. . . . [D]uring the first year after the divorce, conflict typically escalates as both parties deal with the depression and anger engendered by the divorce, as well as the practical problems resulting from separate households. The crisis for the children is exacerbated if there is very high conflict between the parents. In such cases, children are worse off when their parents remain in contact. . . .
>
> [L]ong-term effects may be very different from those during the first months or even years following the divorce. For example, preschoolers were the age group most traumatized by separation and divorce, but ten years later they were minimally affected by the experience. . . .
>
> [T]he available literature on the effects of divorce gives little basis for either policy or individual dispositions. . . . [The] literature gives little help in decision making about custody. Indeed, if anything, it suggests the pitfalls in making predictions from clinical assessments at the time of divorce. (pp. 550–551)

Another researcher, Hyun Kim (2011), states, "Children with divorced parents are disadvantaged regarding various life outcomes, including likelihood of dropping out of high school, cognitive skills, psychosocial well-being, and social relations" (p. 487). Yet, many children of divorce do well. Divorce is a risk factor, not a fate accompli. Indeed, a divorce that ends a bad, abusive marriage can be good for children. As Melton and his colleagues (2007) point out, "High conflict in *intact* families is even more deleterious for children than divorce" (p. 549).

Custody Terminology

State laws vary slightly in the terminology used to describe child custody. However, the critical distinction is between legal and physical custody. Legal custody is the right to make decisions for a child about medical care, about where the child goes to school, and about innumerable day-to-day issues. Physical custody is the right to have the child live with the custodial parent all or part of the time. Sole physical custody means the child lives full time with the custodial parent. Joint physical custody means the child lives part of the time with each parent. Parents can have joint legal and physical custody, or one parent can have sole physical custody while the parents share legal custody.

The Best Interests of the Child

In deciding child custody cases, judges employ the best interests of the child standard. The Vermont Supreme Court discussed best-interest analysis in *Miller-Jenkins v. Miller-Jenkins* (2010), "The family court's sole focus in a custody dispute must be the best interests of the child. Although the parents are the ones who appear before the court in a custody dispute, and it is therefore easy to become caught up in their rights and interests rather than the child's welfare, the family court must not take into consideration the competing, often antagonistic, desires of the parents without upsetting the delicate nature of custody proceedings and trivializing the welfare of the child" (p. 521).

The question is always: What custody arrangement is best for the child? In conducting a best-interest analysis, judges have broad discretion and consider all the evidence shedding light on a child's short- and long-term interests, or the totality of the circumstances.

Another question that arises in custody litigation is: Should children testify? Can you think of anything *less* appropriate than putting a child on the witness stand and asking the child to "pick a parent"? With older children, judges sometimes talk to the child alone, without the parents, in the judge's chambers.

I practice and teach family law. Most of my clients are victims of domestic violence or children. My child clients are involved in juvenile court or family court. I have personally observed judges interview children as young as 6, usually in the judge's office, not in the courtroom. The child's parents are not present. I have been impressed with the sensitivity and care judges take when they interview children.

Custody Evaluation

In contested custody cases, judges sometimes order custody evaluations from mental health professionals. In 2006, the Association of Family and Conciliation Courts adopted *Model Standards of Practice for Child Custody Evaluation* (AFCC *Model Standards*). The AFCC *Model Standards* define custody evaluation as: "The child custody evaluation process involves the compilation of information and the formulation of opinions pertaining to the custody or parenting of a child and the dissemination of that information and those opinions to the court, to the litigants, and to the litigants' attorneys." (For a discussion of the history of custody evaluation, see Stahl & Martin, 2013.)

A custody evaluator should be neutral, not a partisan for either parent. The AFCC *Model Standards* state, "Evaluators shall always function as impartial examiners" (Preamble ¶ 2). Many custody evaluators will only take cases when they are appointed by a court and when they are guaranteed access to both parents and the child.

There is no psychological test or battery of tests that determines a child's best interests. Melton and colleagues (2007) state:

> It is our contention that psychological tests assessing clinical constructs (e.g., intelligence, depression, personality, academic achievement) are frequently unnecessary and often used inappropriately. Tests of intellectual capacity, achievement, personality style, and psychopathology assess constructs that are linked only indirectly, at best, to the key issues concerning custody and visitation. . . . We recommend the use of traditional psychological tests only when specific problems or issues that these tests were designed to measure appear salient in the case. (pp. 559–560)

Evaluators do not have a magic wand that makes the custody decision an easy one. A good evaluation gives the judge insight into parenting style and psychological functioning. The evaluator provides information about the child's psychological needs. He or she offers suggestions regarding the "fit" between parenting attributes and the child's psychological needs. The American Psychological Association's (2010b) "Guidelines for Child Custody Evaluations in Family Law Proceedings" remark, "The most useful and influential evaluations focus upon skills, deficits, values, and tendencies relevant to parenting attributes and a child's psychological needs. Comparatively little weight is afforded to evaluations that offer a general personality assessment without attempting to place results in the appropriate context" (p. 864). Thus, an evaluation that says, "Mother is depressed" does little to help the judge. Plenty of depressed parents are wonderful with their children. The judge needs concrete information about the impact of parental strengths and weaknesses on day-to-day parenting (Patel & Choate, 2014).

As just mentioned, custody evaluators prefer to interview both parents. A mental health professional who has not personally evaluated a parent should not opine on the parent's psychological functioning. The American Psychological Association's (2010b) "Guidelines" provide:

> Psychologists provide an opinion of an individual's psychological characteristics only after they have conducted an examination of the individual adequate to support their statements and conclusions. The only exception to this occurs in those particular instances of record review, consultation, or supervision (as opposed, in each case, to

> evaluations) in which an individual examination is not warranted or necessary for the psychologist's opinion. The court typically expects the psychologist to examine both parents as well as the child. (p. 866)

Custody evaluators can provide valuable information. But should custody evaluators take the final step of offering specific recommendations regarding custody? Experts have differing opinions on this issue. The American Psychological Association's (2010b) "Guidelines" state, "The profession has not reached consensus about whether psychologists should make recommendations to the court about the final child custody determination (i.e., 'ultimate opinion' testimony)" (p. 866). According to Jelena Zumbach and Ute Koglin (2015), "[S]trong disagreements exist about whether experts should offer an ultimate opinion as to who should receive custody" (p. 227). Melton and colleagues (2007) argue that mental health professionals have little to offer regarding who should have custody:

> Thus the state of the literature does not promote confidence about the validity of opinions concerning dispositions judges might consider in custody cases. Indeed, there is probably no forensic question on which overreaching by mental health professionals has been so common and so egregious. Besides lacking scientific validity, such opinions have often been based on clinical data that are, on their face, irrelevant to the legal questions in dispute. (p. 540)

Determining a child's best interest can be difficult. Most experts agree that mental health professionals can assist courts, but custody evaluators do not have tools that are superior to those possessed by experienced, patient, and compassionate judges.

APPLY WHAT YOU HAVE LEARNED

The Doctor Who Forgot Basic Ethics

Vivian and Kirk were getting divorced. Kirk hired a psychiatrist to perform a psychiatric analysis of Vivian. Despite the fact that the psychiatrist never met Vivian, the doctor wrote a report in which he diagnosed Vivian with a personality disorder. The doctor submitted the report to the court.

Vivian sued the psychiatrist for malpractice. (Malpractice is discussed in Chapter 11.) According to Vivian's malpractice complaint, the doctor based his diagnosis entirely on what Kirk had told him, and prepared his report without meeting or examining Vivian.

The doctor filed a motion to dismiss the malpractice case. The doctor argued that he was entitled to absolute immunity from liability because he wrote the report in preparation for providing expert testimony in the divorce case. (Immunity is also discussed in Chapter 11.)—*Harrison v. Roitman,* 362 P.3d 1138 (Nev. 2015)

Analysis: Ethical principles place limits on diagnosing a person whom a professional has not met or examined. This is certainly so in divorce and child custody cases. The American Psychological Association's (2010b) "Guidelines" specify, "Psychologists provide an opinion of an individual's psychological characteristics only after they have conducted an examination of the individual adequate to support their statements and conclusions. . . . The court typically expects psychologists to examine both parents as well as the child" (p. 866).

It seems the good doctor ran afoul of basic ethics when he proffered a diagnosis of Vivian, whom he never met. Yet, he escaped liability because the Nevada Supreme Court ruled that mental health professionals providing reports for use in court cases have absolute immunity from liability for their reports and testimony. The court ruled that absolute immunity applies whether the professional is appointed by a judge to prepare a report or is retained by a party to the lawsuit, without court order. This case highlights the importance of practicing in accordance with ethical guidelines.

Gay and Lesbian Parents

In the not too distant past, gay and lesbian parents faced a steep uphill battle for custody of their children (Haney-Caron & Heilbrun, 2014). In *Bachman v. Bradley* (1952), the father in the case acknowledged bisexuality. The trial judge denied him custody, and the Pennsylvania appellate court affirmed, writing, "We think the cumulative weight of the evidence is to the effect that the children in the custody of [father] may be exposed to improper conditions and undesirable influences" (p. 382). In 1967, a California judge ruled that "the homosexuality of [mother] as a matter of law constitutes her not a fit or proper person to have the care custody and control of the minor child of the parties" (*Nadler v. Superior Court,* 1967, p. 524). The judge refused even to consider the facts of the case, ruling essentially that no gay or lesbian parent is fit for custody. In *Roe v. Roe* (1985), decided by the Virginia Supreme Court, the father lived with his same-sex partner. They slept in the same bed and were affectionate in front of the father's child, but did not "flaunt" their homosexuality. The Virginia court wrote, "The father's continuous exposure of the child to his immoral and illicit relationship renders him an unfit and improper custodian" (p. 694).

Times have changed. Courts today hold that sexual orientation itself has no bearing on custody. In *Miller-Jenkins v. Miller-Jenkins* (2010), the Vermont Supreme Court wrote, "The State of Vermont has determined that same-sex couples have the same rights and responsibilities as opposite-sex couples—thus, the sexual orientation of the parents is irrelevant in a custody determination" (p. 777).

What *can* be relevant to a child's best interests is sexual *behavior,* not sexual *orientation.* Exposing a child to inappropriate sexual behavior—gay or straight—between the parent and their partner or spouse is relevant to custody. The South Carolina Court of Appeals explained in *Reed v. Pieper* (2011), "A parent's morality, while a proper consideration in custody disputes, is limited in its force to what relevancy it has, either directly or indirectly, to the welfare of the child" (p. 434).

Race and Custody

Race and ethnicity are not relevant factors in custody decision making. The U.S. Supreme Court's 1984 decision in *Palmore v. Sidoti* (1984), addressed the constitutional dimension of race and child custody. Linda Sidoti Palmore and Anthony Sidoti, who are both white, divorced in 1980. Linda received custody of their 3-year-old daughter. A year later, Anthony sought to change custody because Linda was living with a black man, whom she later married. The trial judge concluded that the best interests of the child would be served by changing custody to Anthony. The judge wrote, "The father's evident resentment of the mother's choice of a black partner is not sufficient to wrest custody from the mother. . . . This Court feels that despite the strides that have been made in bettering relations between the races in this country, it is inevitable that Melanie will, if allowed to remain in her present situation and attains school age and thus more vulnerable to peer pressures, suffer from the social stigmatization that is sure to come" (p. 431). The U.S. Supreme Court disagreed, writing:

> A core purpose of the Fourteenth Amendment was to do away with all governmentally imposed discrimination based on race. Classifying persons according to their race is more likely to reflect racial prejudice than legitimate public concerns; the race, not the person, dictates the category. . . .
>
> It would ignore reality to suggest that racial and ethnic prejudices do not exist or that all manifestations of those prejudices have

> been eliminated. There is a risk that a child living with a stepparent of a different race may be subject to a variety of pressures and stresses not present if the child were living with parents of the same racial or ethnic origin.
>
> The question, however, is whether the reality of private biases and the possible injury they might inflict are permissible considerations for removal of an infant child from the custody of its natural mother. We have little difficulty concluding that they are not. The Constitution cannot control such prejudices but neither can it tolerate them. Private biases may be outside the reach of the law, but the law cannot, directly or indirectly, give them effect. Public officials sworn to uphold the Constitution may not avoid a constitutional duty by bowing to the hypothetical effects of private racial prejudice that they assume to be both widely and deeply held. . . . The effects of racial prejudice, however real, cannot justify a racial classification removing an infant child from the custody of its natural mother found to be an appropriate person to have such custody. (pp. 432–434)

Temporary Custody

At the outset of a divorce, one parent may seek an order for temporary custody. A temporary order remains in place until a court makes a final custody decision. A court may change temporary custody as the need arises.

Modification of Custody

A final custody decision is just that, final. In Latin legal parlance, it is *res judicata* (a thing decided). A parent who is dissatisfied with a judge's final custody decision cannot relitigate the same facts. However, the court retains jurisdiction over custody until the children reach adulthood. Following a custody decision, a parent may return to court and ask the court to modify custody. Before a judge will revisit a final custody order, however, the parent seeking modification must prove a substantial change in circumstances that warrants a fresh look at custody. The California Supreme Court described the changed circumstances rule in *Marriage of Brown and Yana* (2006):

> Once the trial court has entered a final or permanent custody order reflecting that a particular custodial arrangement is in the best interest of the child, the paramount need for continuity and stability in custody arrangements—and the harm that may result from disruption of established patterns of care and emotional bonds with the

> primary caretaker—weigh heavily in favor of maintaining that custody arrangement. In recognition of this policy concern, we have articulated a variation on the best interest standard, known as the changed circumstance rule. . . . Under the changed circumstance rule, custody modification is appropriate only if the parent seeking modification demonstrates a significant change of circumstances indicating that a different custody arrangement would be in the child's best interest. (p. 956)

In a similar vein, the Arkansas Supreme Court wrote in *Alphin v. Alphin* (2005):

> A judicial award of custody should not be modified unless it is shown that there are changed conditions that demonstrate that a modification of the decree is in the best interest of the child. . . . Courts impose more stringent standards for modifications of custody than they do for initial determinations of custody. The reasons for requiring these more stringent standards for modifications . . . are to promote stability and continuity in the life of the child, and to discourage the repeated litigation of the same issues. (p. 165)

What constitutes substantially changed circumstances? The facts of each case are unique. Remarriage of either parent is seldom a change of circumstances warranting changed custody. If the custodial parent dies, the non-custodial parent automatically has the right to custody, and does not have to get a court order.

Sometimes, the parent with custody frustrates the non-custodial parent's ability to visit the child. Does such obstructionist behavior amount to substantially changed circumstances? Judges seldom change custody on this basis, although a protracted course of deliberate interference with visitation might persuade a judge to revisit custody.

APPLY WHAT YOU HAVE LEARNED

"Mommy is a fireman."

Two years ago, Lourdes and José divorced. By agreement, Lourdes got primary physical custody of the two children, ages 4 and 6. José has parenting time every other weekend, and 1 day during the week, and always uses his parenting time. The parents are devoted to the children and get along well. A month ago, Lourdes graduated from college, and was hired by the local fire department, where she will be working 24-hour shifts.

When José learns this, he tries to persuade Lourdes to switch primary custody to him because his work schedule is more flexible. Lourdes does not agree and says her parents will take care of the kids when she is at work. When the grandparents are not available, the children will stay with Lourdes's sister. José thinks it will be best for the kids to live with him and visit Lourdes when she has days off, which will be often. He files a motion in family court, asking a judge to switch primary custody to him, with liberal parenting time for Lourdes.—*Collier v. Harris,* 261 P.3d 397 (Alaska 2011)

Analysis: If you are the family court judge, how will you rule on José's request to change custody? To modify an existing custody order, the parent seeking modification has to persuade the judge that a substantial change in circumstances has occurred that justifies a fresh look at what is best for the child. Lourdes's new job is certainly a change, but is it sufficiently substantial to change custody? The Alaska Supreme Court thought not.

Move-Away Cases

Beth and Phil fell in love and married in medical school. They had a baby girl, Joy, during their senior year. Upon graduation and completion of their residency training, Phil got a job with the state health department. Beth went to work in a private medical practice, as a surgeon, and worked extremely long hours. They bought a home and settled in. Unfortunately, the marriage deteriorated, and they divorced. They agreed on joint legal custody. They also agreed that Phil would have primary physical custody. Joy lives with Phil because his work schedule for the state is more flexible than Beth's demanding work schedule at the hospital. Beth has visitation 3 days a week, mostly around weekends. Several years pass, with Beth and Phil working cooperatively to coparent. Then, Phil gets an offer to join the faculty at a medical school across the country. Phil proposes to take Joy with him. Beth says, "No way. If you move, and take her with you, how am I supposed to be a mother?" This scenario plays out daily in our mobile society, and as I'm sure you see, there are no easy answers.

A large body of law addresses move-away cases, and quite a few states have statutes on the topic. The Colorado statute, for example, applies when a parent with primary custody plans a move that will substantially change the non-custodial parent's ties to the child (Colo. Rev. Stat. § 14-10-129). The statute instructs judges to consider all the factors relevant to the child's best interests. Specifically, the judge considers the reasons for the proposed move, the objections of the nonmoving parent, the quality of each parent's relationship with the child, the educational opportunities for the child and the presence or absence of extended family in the new versus the current home, the advantages of the child remaining with the relocating custodial parent, and the likely impact of the move on the child.

The facts of each case govern whether a parent will be permitted to move and take the children. If the parent who plans to move has been the primary custodian, and the move portends well for the parent *and* the children, the judge is likely to approve the move.

Custody Litigation and Active-Duty Military

Members of the armed forces defend the nation at considerable, and sometimes the ultimate, sacrifice to themselves and their families. In 1940, Congress enacted the Soldiers and Sailors Civil Relief Act to protect service members from civil lawsuits while the service member is deployed and not in a position to defend the case. The Act requires judges to halt civil proceedings against service members until the member is in a position to respond. The court may grant "a stay of proceedings for a minimum period of 90 days" (50 U.S.C. § 521(d)). The service member may request an additional stay. The Act is now called the Service Members Civil Relief Act, and it applies to divorce actions, including child custody proceedings.

Service members who are parents endure long separations from their children. For married couples, the stay-at-home parent keeps the home fires burning and cares for the children. Divorced and never-married parents who are deployed overseas face more challenging situations. Often, the at-home parent assumes full custody during deployment. Problems arise when a parent is deployed, and the other parent starts proceedings to obtain custody or modify an existing custody order. The Service Members Civil Relief Act can halt such actions.

In custody cases involving service members, should the judge consider the impact on children of lengthy military deployments? A number of statutes provide that military deployment cannot be the "sole" factor in determining custody or visitation. Should military service be a factor *at all*? Would you favor a law requiring judges to ignore military service, and long periods of deployment, when considering children's best interests?

What State Should Decide Custody?

Authority, or jurisdiction, regarding child custody is governed by two complex statutes, the federal Parental Kidnapping Prevention Act

(PKPA) (28 U.S.C. § 1738A) and the Uniform Child Custody Jurisdiction and Enforcement Act (UCCJEA). These laws determine which state has authority to make an initial custody decision and to modify a custody decision. Basically, the two laws provide that child custody should be determined by courts in the state where the child lives, called the child's "home state." A state becomes a child's home state once the child resides there 6 months.

The PKPA and UCCJEA place strict limits on which state may modify a child custody determination. The purpose of these limits is to prevent parents who are dissatisfied with a judge's custody order from "kidnapping" the child, taking the child to a different state, and seeking a different custody order there.

THE HAGUE CONVENTION ON CIVIL ASPECTS OF INTERNATIONAL CHILD ABDUCTION

Imagine you are married with two children, ages 9 and 11. One day you arrive home to find the children gone and the following note from your spouse, "I can't handle this relationship. I'm going to Germany to stay with my parents, and I'm taking the children with me. We won't be back. I'll email you when we arrive. I'm sorry, but I have to do this."

Once you recover from the initial shock, you wonder to yourself, "What can I do about the kids? I want them here. This is their home. This is nuts."

The United States and more than 100 other nations are parties to the Hague Convention on Civil Aspects of International Child Abduction, which was created in 1980 to deal with this growing problem. Although the Convention is complex, the basic idea is simple. When a parent wrongfully takes a child to another country or refuses to return a child to the child's home country (called "habitual residence") after a visit, the aggrieved parent can ask a judge to order the child returned. The judge does not decide which parent should have custody. The only question is *which* country should decide custody.

If the Convention applies because a child was wrongfully removed from the country of habitual residence, then the child must be returned to the habitual residence unless one of five defenses to return applies. In *Trudrung v. Trudrung* (2010), a North Carolina federal judge described the defenses to return:

> Upon a showing of wrongful removal or retention, return of the child is required unless the [parent who acted wrongly] establishes one of

> several affirmative defenses. . . . (1) that return would expose the child to a "grave risk" of "physical or psychological harm or otherwise place the child in an intolerable situation; (2) that return of the child would not be permitted by "fundamental principles of the United States relating to the protection of human rights and fundamental freedoms"; (3) that the petition for return was not filed within one year of the removal and the child is now well-settled in another country; (4) that the petitioner was not actually exercising his custodial rights at the time of the removal or had consented to or acquiesced in the removal; and (5) the child objects to being returned and has attained an age and degree of maturity at which it is appropriate to take account of his or her views. (pp. 574–575)

Cases brought under the Hague Convention can be filed in either state or federal court.

VISITATION

A parent who is not awarded custody receives visitation. Reasonable visitation is automatic unless the non-custodial parent forfeits the right through serious misconduct. Today, the word "visitation" is being replaced with "parenting time."

What types of misconduct might convince a judge to deny parenting time to a non-custodial parent? Chronic drug or alcohol abuse, illegal behavior, domestic violence, and child abuse are behaviors that stand out. It is important to note, however, that parents who are less than perfect have the right to spend time with their kids.

Some parents refuse to pay court-ordered child support, but nevertheless insist on visits with their children. Is it right that a parent who refuses to support his kids should nonetheless have the right to visit them? In most states, child support and visitation are not linked. A deadbeat parent does not forfeit visitation (see Myers, 2014b). The policy behind the rule is that children need their parents, even deadbeat ones.

Visitation with Nonparents

Do individuals other than parents have a right to visit children? This question comes up most often with grandparents. The issue of grandparent visitation reached the U.S. Supreme Court in the case of *Troxel v. Granville* (2000). The Court affirmed the right of parents to make decisions regarding their children, including decisions about visitation. It ruled that the decision about whether to allow grandparents to visit "is for the parent in the first instance. And, if a fit parent's decision of the kind at issue here becomes subject to judicial review, the court must accord at least some special weight to the parent's own determination" (p. 70).

States have laws that allow nonparents to petition a judge to authorize visits with children over parental objections. So long as a judge accords the wishes of parents the deference mandated by the Supreme Court in *Troxel v. Granville,* a judge may order visitation that will serve a child's best interests.

CONCLUSION

Family law is a complex, emotionally charged, and evolving field. Mental health professionals play important roles in family law. The stress and sadness of divorce leads many couples to the therapist's office. Mental health professionals serve as mediators and custody evaluators. Psychological research deepens our understanding of many aspects of family and child functioning.

6

Child Protective Services and Juvenile Court

The principal agencies that handle child protection are child protective services (CPS), law enforcement, and juvenile courts. Important secondary roles are played by professionals in medicine, nursing, mental health, and education. This chapter focuses on CPS and juvenile court. To start the ball rolling, let's consider three cases.

A TRAGEDY ON MANY LEVELS

Tyler was 9 years old when he was mauled to death by his 24-year-old sister's three pit bull dogs. Tyler's short life was chaotic. His father had serious mental health issues and could not care for him. Tyler's mother was addicted to drugs, and lived on the street, where she died. After her death, Tyler lived in foster care. CPS social workers allowed Tyler to have overnight visits with his sister, who lived in a small travel trailer with her pit bulls. The long-term plan was for Tyler to live permanently with his sister, and he was excited about having a home of his own. One day, after Tyler's sister returned from work, she found her brother's lifeless, mangled body and her dogs covered in blood. Accusations flew. Why had CPS social workers allowed Tyler to spend time with his sister, who had problems of her own, in a travel trailer that didn't have a working bathroom, and in the company of pit bulls?

PERIPATETIC KILLERS

In a small mountain town a concerned citizen called authorities to report that a young girl was neglected. A deputy sheriff found the 9-year-old girl locked in a parked car. The child was severely malnourished and had obvious injuries. She was whisked to the hospital, where doctors found multiple broken bones, broken teeth, bruises, and infections.

The sheriff arrested the adults who were "caring" for the child, 39-year-old Tami and her 17-year-old boyfriend, Gonzalo. During his questioning, Gonzalo told the deputies to look in a storage locker 140 miles away. Inside the storage locker, the police made the grisly discovery of the bodies of two murdered children, ages 6 and 3. The children had been killed 300 miles from the storage facility, and the peripatetic killers had been moving around the state to stay ahead of the law and CPS.

Before the little ones were murdered and the 9-year-old girl was tortured, a CPS worker had been to the home *four* times. After each visit, the children were left in the home. Of course, we do not know what the CPS worker saw when she went to the home. If abuse or neglect had been obvious, the worker would, presumably, have acted. Yet, after the fact, relatives were quick to condemn CPS for the deaths, and the media was happy to publish the relatives' indictment of the system. Interestingly, there was little mention in the press that the 9-year-old was rescued by the quick work of a concerned citizen, the sheriff, and the CPS worker. All attention focused on the system's apparent failure.

BORN IN A SHACK

Jane, 25, grew up in a small town. She started using drugs at 13, and she's been addicted to methamphetamine since she was 18. She now uses methamphetamine, alcohol, and any other drug she can get her hands on. Her parents tried to help, but Jane wouldn't cooperate. Jane does not work. She supports herself, and her habit, with occasional prostitution and petty theft. Jane has been convicted of passing bad checks, possession of illegal drugs, driving on a suspended license, and burglary. She is in and out of jail. Jane has a 7-year-old son, but she does not see the child. He lives with his dad in another state.

A year ago, Jane hooked up with Duane, also a drug addict and petty criminal, and became pregnant. She used drugs and alcohol throughout her pregnancy. She had only one prenatal medical exam, which occurred during a time she was in jail. The baby, Nathan, was born 6 weeks premature in December. Jane gave birth in a shack where she and Duane were living. The shack had no heat, running water, plumbing, or electricity. The couple decided not to take the baby to the doctor for a few days because they feared the baby would test positive for methamphetamine. They realized, however, that they needed to get the baby to a warm place, so they went to the home of a relative. The relative looked at the tiny boy and told Jane to see a doctor immediately, but Jane refused. The relative called CPS, and, within an hour, a social worker and a deputy sheriff arrived and observed that the baby did not look well. The social worker was advised by an emergency room doctor at the rural hospital to bring the baby in. The deputy sheriff took the baby into emergency protective custody, and straight to the emergency room. Following a medical examination, the baby was airlifted to the neonatal intensive care unit of a regional hospital, where he stayed for the first month of his life.

These three cases—all real—may be more dramatic than average, but cases like these, along with more mundane fare, confront social workers and other professionals who deal with child protection issues every day. Society depends on all these professionals to respond and to keep children safe, and also to help struggling parents. It is a Herculean task.

CHILD PROTECTIVE SERVICES

America's child protection system is enormously complex, and this discussion simply serves as an introduction to the topic. The history of child protection is fascinating, and, if you are a history buff, you may wish to look at my books, *Child Protection in America: Past, Present, and Future* (2006), *A History of Child Protection in America* (2004), or *The History of Child Protection in America* (2010).

The function of CPS is to respond to reports of suspected child abuse and neglect. In many cases, CPS social workers are able to help struggling parents so that children can live safely at home. When necessary, the agency removes children from unsafe environments and commences protective proceedings in juvenile court. Deciding to remove a child from an unsafe home is one of the most difficult decisions CPS workers make. Often, the decision is made in the middle of the night, in chaotic circumstances, and with less than complete information.

The U.S. Constitution places limits on the authority of CPS to remove children. The Fourteenth Amendment to the Constitution guarantees citizens due process of law, and the U.S. Supreme Court has interpreted the Fourteenth Amendment as protecting parental rights. As the Federal Court of Appeals for the Ninth Circuit put it in *Wallis v. Spencer* (2000), "Parents and children have a well-established constitutional right to live together without governmental interference" (p. 1137).

In addition to the rights guaranteed by the Fourteenth Amendment, the Fourth Amendment protects citizens from unreasonable seizures by police *and* government social workers. Removing a child from the home is a "seizure" for Fourth Amendment purposes.

Under the Constitution, CPS may not remove a child from parents unless (1) parents consent to removal; (2) prior to the removal of the child, CPS obtained a court order or warrant authorizing removal; or (3) an emergency exists that necessitates immediate removal to protect the child from serious harm or death. The emergency exception to the requirement of a warrant is called the "exigent circumstances exception." (See Chapter 3 for additional information on warrants and exigent circumstances.)

In emergencies, CPS workers balance the need to protect the child against the right of parents to custody of their children. The Federal Court of Appeals for the Fifth Circuit discussed the balancing of interests involved in emergency removal in *Gates v. Texas Department of Protective and Regulatory Services* (2008):

> There is no doubt that child abuse is a heinous crime, and the government's interest in stopping abuse and removing children from abusive situations is paramount. . . . Deciding what is reasonable under the Fourth Amendment will require an assessment of the fact that the courts are dealing with a child who likely resides in the same house, and is under the control of, the alleged abuser. The analysis cannot be divorced from that fact, but that fact does not override all other Fourth Amendment considerations.
>
> Therefore, we hold that the government may not seize a child from his or her parents absent a court order, parental consent, or exigent circumstances. Exigent circumstances in this context means that, based on the totality of the circumstances, there is reasonable cause to believe that the child is in imminent danger of physical or sexual abuse if he remains in his home. This is a flexible inquiry that considers all of the facts and circumstances with no one factor being dispositive. . . . Whether there was time to obtain a court order is . . . one factor that informs the reasonableness analysis. . . . Other non-exclusive factors . . . are the nature of the abuse (its severity, duration, and frequency), the strength of the evidence supporting the allegations of abuse, the risk that the parent will flee with the child, the possibility of less extreme solutions to the problem, and any harm to the child that might result from the removal. (p. 429)

On rare occasions, parents whose child was removed sue the responsible CPS workers. In such lawsuits, parents claim the removal violated their parental rights as guaranteed by the Fourteenth and Fourth Amendments of the U.S. Constitution. Most of these lawsuits fail because social workers were judged to have acted responsibly. Moreover, in most circumstances, CPS social workers have immunity from liability. (See the discussion of immunity in Chapter 11.)

Federal Leadership in Child Protection

Today, the federal government plays an important leadership, policy, and funding role in child protection. This has not always been the case. Prior to the 1970s, the federal government's role was limited. The Children's Bureau was created in 1912, although the Bureau devoted little attention to maltreatment until the 1960s. The Social Security Act of 1935 created Aid to Dependent Children and authorized the Children's Bureau "to cooperate with State-welfare agencies in establishing, extending, and strengthening, especially in predominantly rural areas, [child welfare services] for the protection and care of homeless, dependent, and neglected children, and children in danger of becoming delinquent." Yet, as late as 1973, U.S. Senator Walter Mondale wrote, "Nowhere in the Federal Government could we find one official assigned full time to the prevention, identification and treatment of child abuse and neglect." It was not until January 1974 that the federal government assumed a leadership role when President Nixon signed into law the Child Abuse Prevention and Treatment Act (CAPTA). CAPTA authorized federal funds to improve the response to physical abuse, sexual abuse, and neglect. It provided money to train professionals and to support multidisciplinary centers on child abuse and neglect and demonstration projects. Congress and the president periodically renew CAPTA, and it remains in force today.

Child abuse reporting laws first appeared in 1963. Reporting laws led to enhanced awareness of abuse and increased intervention. (See Chapter 10 for a further discussion of the reporting requirement.) In the 1970s, the rising number of children in foster care set off alarm bells in Congress, resulting in the 1980 passage of the Adoption Assistance and Child Welfare Act. The Act required all states seeking federal foster care funds to make "reasonable efforts" to avoid removing children unnecessarily from maltreating parents. When removal from the home was necessary, reasonable efforts were required to reunite families. Every child in foster care had to have a "permanency plan" to return the child home or move toward termination of parental rights. For children who could not go home, Congress provided financial incentives for adoption. The Act also provided financial support for adoptive parents who adopted children with special needs.

The effort to preserve families was a key component of the Adoption Assistance and Child Welfare Act. "Family preservation" was the dominant paradigm of child welfare in the 1980s, and family preservation programs worked well for many families. In the 1990s, however, critics argued that overreliance on family preservation sometimes led to tragedy. One forceful critic of overreliance on family preservation was Richard Gelles, who challenged the effectiveness of family preservation in his 1996 book, *The Book of David: How Preserving Families Can Cost Children's Lives.* Gelles criticized research supporting family preservation programs, and he argued for a shift in policy toward what he called "a new child-centered policy." He argued:

> The essential first step in creating a safe world for children is to abandon the fantasy that child welfare agencies can balance the goals of protecting children and preserving families, adopting instead a child-centered policy of family services. This is not a new policy, but rather a return to the policy of the early 1960s that established child safety as the overriding goal of the child welfare system. . . . It is time to abandon the myth that "the best foster family is not as good as a marginal biological family." The ability to make a baby does not ensure that a couple has, or ever will have, the ability to be adequate parents. The policy of family reunification and family preservation fails because it assumes that *all* biological parents can become fit and acceptable parents if only appropriate and sufficient support is provided. (pp. 148–149)

An equally forceful critique was made by Elizabeth Bartholet, who stated in her 1999 book, *Nobody's Children: Abuse and Neglect, Foster Drift, and the Adoption Alternative,* "There is no evidence that the treatment and other parent-support services which may be offered in the most serious abuse and neglect cases are helpful in reforming parents and protecting children" (p. 109).

The 1980 Adoption Assistance and Child Welfare Act helped many children and parents. Yet, the number of children in foster care did not decline. Many children languished in out-of-home care. Moreover, Gelles, Bartholet, and others charged that the reasonable-efforts and family-preservation requirements caused social workers to leave children in dangerous homes. Congress responded with the Adoption and Safe Families Act of 1997 (ASFA). Although ASFA did not abandon family preservation, it made child safety the top priority. When children were placed in foster care, ASFA established strict timelines to return them to their parents or to terminate parental rights so children could be adopted. In cases of sexual abuse and chronic physical abuse, ASFA authorized states to dispense with efforts to reunify the family and to proceed directly to termination of parental rights.

In the early 21st century, the most noteworthy development in child protection has been the spread of what is commonly called differential response (DR), also known as alternative response, or dual track. The Child Welfare Information Gateway (2014) describes this approach:

> Differential response . . . is a way of structuring child protective services (CPS) that allows for more than one method of initial response to reports of child abuse and neglect. . . . DR responses typically fall into two major categories:
>
> [1] Investigative response (IR) (also called the traditional response or high-risk assessment). These responses involve gathering forensic evidence and making a formal determination of whether child maltreatment has occurred or the child is at risk of abuse or neglect.
>
> [2] Alternative response (AR) [is] usually applied in low- and moderate-risk cases (p. 2), [and involves offers of help which parents are free to accept or reject].

A primary goal of DR is to adopt a positive, cooperative, voluntary, and "family friendly" approach to parents and to avoid the involuntary, and sometimes adversarial, investigative approach of traditional CPS. In 2010, Congress gave a boost to DR by requiring states to adopt policies to triage low-risk cases out of traditional CPS investigation and into DR.

DR is not a new idea. Since the earliest days of formal child protection in the 1800s, professionals have sorted between high- and low-risk cases, reserving formal investigation and court involvement for the former. Thus, DR is little more than a refinement and expansion of an existing practice.

Critics of DR are concerned that the expansion of voluntary services is draining already scarce resources away from traditional CPS (Bartholet, 2015). They also believe that funneling large numbers of children into voluntary services, where there is no meaningful investigation, places children at risk. It is true that several evaluation studies suggest that DR does not compromise child safety (Child Welfare Information Gateway, 2014, p. 10). Ronald Hughes and his colleagues (2013), however, published a critique of DR research, in which they noted, "In our review, we identified significant problems in research methodology and implementation that presented threats to internal, external, and construct validity, thereby calling into question the reliability and accuracy of many of the claims and conclusions made in these studies" (p. 6). Hughes and colleagues claim that research does not support the conclusion that DR keeps children safe: "[W]e conclude that the many claims found in DR research studies and program literature related to children's safety are overreaching" (p. 12). Elizabeth Bartholet (2015) also reviewed the research supporting DR, and concluded, "DR represents a dangerous direction for children" (p. 642).

DR may prove to be a flash in the pan; the latest in a long line of alternating approaches in child welfare. In all likelihood, traditional, investigation-based CPS will remain society's primary tool for keeping children safe. Ideally, CPS will integrate the best features of DR into its practices.

The history of child protection is replete with pendulum swings in the debate over family privacy versus intervention. These swings are reflected in the federal legislation described earlier. CAPTA contained fairly broad definitions of maltreatment, encouraging greater intervention. By contrast, the Adoption Assistance and Child Welfare Act of 1980, with its emphasis on family preservation, pushed the pendulum away from intervention. ASFA placed top priority on child safety, once again shifting the emphasis toward intervention. Finally, the DR movement pushes the pendulum away from intervention. The intervention pendulum swings back and forth, never reaching the extremes, and never standing still.

JUVENILE COURT

Juvenile court has authority over three groups of children: abused and neglected children, juvenile delinquents, and status offenders. In several states (e.g., New York, Hawaii, and Nevada), juvenile court is called family court.

Juvenile Delinquency

Juvenile delinquency is conduct by a minor that would be considered a crime if committed by an adult. When a minor is suspected of delinquency, the police investigate, and may question and search the minor. If the investigation points to the minor as a suspect, an arrest may follow. Once arrested on a serious matter, the minor is typically taken to a juvenile detention center. At the detention center, an intake worker, who is often a probation officer, interviews the minor, considers the police report and decides whether the minor should be released or detained. Soon thereafter, the intake worker and/or a prosecutor decide whether to file formal delinquency charges against the minor. If charges are filed, and the minor is detained, the minor must be taken before a juvenile court judge as soon as possible so the judge can rule on the legality of the detention.

If a minor is charged with delinquency, he or she has the right to an attorney. Because most minors (and their parents) cannot afford to hire private defense attorneys, the judge assigns a public defender to represent the minor. The public defender meets with the minor, explains the charges, listens to the minor's side of the story, and helps the minor decide whether to admit or deny guilt.

Plea bargaining occurs in juvenile court delinquency proceedings, and most minors plead guilty. Only a small percentage of minors deny guilt and insist on a trial, or, as it is called in many states, an adjudicatory hearing. A juvenile court adjudicatory hearing regarding delinquency looks much like the trial of an adult. The minor is represented by counsel. A prosecutor represents the government. Formal rules of evidence and procedure apply. Witnesses are called and cross-examined. The minor has the right to testify, but cannot be compelled to do so.

Adults charged with serious crimes have a right under the U.S. Constitution to a trial by jury. In juvenile court, however, the U.S. Supreme Court ruled in *McKeiver v. Pennsylvania* (1971) that minors accused of delinquency do not have a constitutional right to jury trial. The Supreme Court reasoned that the constitutional right to a jury trial does not apply in juvenile court because the nature of delinquency proceedings is, technically, civil rather than criminal.

Since the Supreme Court's 1971 decision in *McKeiver,* holding that the Constitution does not require juries in delinquency cases, a movement has developed across the country to "get tough" on juvenile delinquents. As a result, defense attorneys have renewed the argument that minors accused of delinquency should have the right to trial by jury in juvenile court. In 2008, the Kansas Supreme Court agreed, ruling in *In re L.M.* (2008), that Kansas minors accused of delinquency have a constitutional right to a jury. In 2009, by contrast, the Louisiana Supreme Court rejected the argument that minors accused of delinquency have a constitutional right to a jury trial in juvenile court (*In re A.J.,* 2009).

If a minor pleads guilty, or is found guilty following an adjudicatory hearing, the judge decides the appropriate disposition. Unlike criminal prosecutions against adults, in which the sentencing judge imposes punishment in the form of incarceration, a fine, or probation, the juvenile court judge is concerned more about rehabilitation than punishment. The judge, aided by a report from the juvenile probation officer, and input from counsel, fashions a disposition that is intended to turn the young offender away from crime. Most youth are placed on probation, and they may be ordered to go to school, obey their parents, perform community service, and stay away from bad influences. If the youth has mental health or substance abuse issues, the disposition may include therapy. To the extent that punishment will teach a lesson, it is part of the disposition in juvenile court. The goal of disposition is individualized intervention to turn the youth away from the negative influences pulling him or her in the direction of crime.

Some teenagers commit serious, calculated, and callous crimes and may deserve to be punished like adult criminals. Moreover, some teens are already committed to a life of crime and are unlikely to benefit from the therapeutic approach of juvenile court. The law allows such "hardened" youth to be transferred from juvenile court to criminal court, where they are prosecuted as adults. In making the transfer decision, juvenile court judges consider the minor's age and IQ, the nature and seriousness of the crime, whether the youth is naive or sophisticated in the ways of crime, whether the minor has been in trouble before, and the likelihood the minor can be rehabilitated in juvenile court.

Consider the sad facts of *People v. Superior Court* (1998). Melvin and Marcus were 15-year-old cousins. They were average students in high school and participated in school and church activities. Neither youth had been in trouble before. They wanted to go to the high school prom, but since they did not have enough money, they decided to rob a convenience store to get it. Melvin borrowed a gun from a friend. The cousins consumed alcohol to work up the necessary courage, and then walked to a local store. Before entering the store, they checked the gun. A bullet was in the chamber, and the gun was cocked. They tried to remove the bullet so the gun would not go off accidentally, but they could not figure out how the gun worked. As they stood outside the store, they were recognized by people from the neighborhood. Before entering the store, they donned masks and one glove each. Melvin entered first and pointed the gun at the clerk. The gun went off accidentally, killing the clerk. Melvin and Marcus stole the money, which they dropped as they ran to Melvin's home. They were promptly arrested.

Should these remarkably stupid and incredibly unsophisticated teenage "criminals" be prosecuted for murder as adults in criminal court? Or should their cases be handled in juvenile court, where the goal is rehabilitation rather than punishment? The prosecutor agreed that both boys could be rehabilitated through juvenile court. Yet, because of the seriousness of the crime, the prosecutor charged them as adults, and the California Supreme Court agreed.

The overarching theory of the juvenile court system is that youth are malleable, and that with the right package of individualized services, many youth can be saved from the downward spiral that leads to crime as a career. Sadly, there are times when the theory of the juvenile court gets lost in crowded court dockets, overworked professionals, and underfunded programs. Today, juvenile courts are under considerable strain. Yet, few observers would argue that the juvenile court system should be abandoned as a failure. Every day, dedicated judges, probation officers, social workers, and attorneys pour their energies into turning young people away from crime. Failure is common, but success stories abound. Thousands of youth benefit from interaction with the juvenile court.

Status Offenses

As conceptualized at the beginning of the 20th century, the juvenile court was intended as a refuge for a broad range of children in difficulty. Thus, the court had authority over delinquent children, abused and neglected children, and children who were simply poor. In addition, the juvenile court had authority over so-called status offenders. A status offense is conduct by a minor that is not a crime, but that nevertheless justifies intervention by the juvenile court. The traditional status offenses include running away from home, truancy, and underage smoking and drinking. In addition, juvenile court had authority over so-called "ungovernable children"—that is, older children who refuse to obey the "reasonable" demands of their parents. A parent at wit's end with his or her teenager's disobedience could ask a juvenile court judge to assume control of the child and order the child to behave or face the possibility of commitment to reform school or some other institution.

In the closing decades of the 20th century, experts recommended narrowing or eliminating juvenile court authority over status offenses. In particular, experts called for an end to placing status offenders in institutions with delinquents. Congress responded in 1974 by passing the Juvenile Justice and Delinquency Prevention Act. This law required states receiving federal funds to stop institutionalizing status offenders in facilities with delinquents.

Today, juvenile courts in many states retain authority over status offenses. In many communities, however, juvenile courts are so overwhelmed with delinquency and maltreatment cases that little time and few resources are available to help status-offending youth.

ABUSE AND NEGLECT: DEPENDENCY PROCEEDINGS IN JUVENILE COURT

Juvenile court has the authority to intervene in the family to protect children from abuse and neglect. Definitions of abuse and neglect vary slightly from state to state. The following definitions are the most common.

• ***Physical abuse*** is nonaccidental physical injury inflicted on a child by an adult. Physical abuse takes many forms, such as hitting with hands, fists, or weapons; kicking; burning; poisoning; twisting arms or legs; squeezing; drowning; stabbing; and strangling. Devastating and often fatal brain injuries are inflicted when babies are shaken by frustrated caretakers, resulting in shaken baby syndrome. Much physical abuse results from "corporal punishment" that goes too far.

• ***Sexual abuse*** is sexual activity between a child and an adult. Sexual abuse also includes sexual activity between a child and an adolescent. Sexual activity includes inappropriate sexual touching, penetration, and use of children in pornography.

• ***Psychological abuse*** is a pattern of adult behavior that conveys to a child the idea that the child is worthless, unloved, unwanted, or all three. Sexual abuse is essentially psychological abuse. Many physically abused or neglected children are also psychologically abused.

• ***Neglect*** occurs when a caretaker deliberately or inadvertently fails to provide a child with essential food, clothing, shelter, medical care, or love. At its core, neglect happens when the "care" is missing from "caretaker."

The Decision to Involve Juvenile Court

Cases of possible child abuse and neglect come to official attention when reports of suspected maltreatment are received. Quite a few reports are screened out or referred to other agencies (e.g., child support or mental health services). If the agency employs differential response, reports are sorted accordingly. For cases that require a traditional CPS response, workers conduct an investigation. If no maltreatment is detected, the case is closed. On the other hand, if abuse or neglect is substantiated,

CPS workers make a series of decisions. How serious is the maltreatment? What is the risk the child will be hurt again? Is it safe to leave the child at home, or must the child be removed and placed with relatives or in a foster home? Can the case be handled safely and effectively without involving the juvenile court? In quite a few cases—particularly in neglect cases—CPS workers decide that juvenile court is not needed, and the agency offers various services to alleviate neglect.

Juvenile court is invoked when maltreatment is serious, when the abused or neglected child is at risk, when it is unsafe to leave the child at home, and when maltreating parents increase the risk to the child by refusing to cooperate.

When a child is removed from the home in an emergency, the law requires CPS to immediately file a petition in juvenile court. The petition contains a brief description of the facts of the case and an allegation that the child is abused or neglected and in need of the court's protection. A copy of the petition is given to the parents.

When a child is removed in an emergency, a hearing is held before a juvenile court judge. The purpose of the hearing is to determine whether the child should remain in out-of-home care or be returned to the parents. At the detention, or initial, hearing the judge informs the parents of the nature of the proceedings, including the allegations in the petition. At the detention hearing, CPS is represented by a government attorney. The judge assigns attorneys for the parents and, in many states, for the child as well. After listening to the attorneys, the CPS social worker, and the parents, the judge decides whether CPS made reasonable efforts to avoid removing the child from the home. Assuming reasonable efforts were made, the judge decides whether to "detain" the child in out-of-home care or return the child to the parents. The detention hearing is often quick—from a few minutes to an hour.

With the detention hearing out of the way, the attorneys turn to the task of resolving the case or preparing for a trial, often called an adjudicatory hearing. As is true with all types of litigation, few juvenile court cases go all the way to a contested adjudicatory hearing. Most cases are settled. The attorney for CPS—working with CPS professionals—negotiates with the attorneys for the parents and the child in an effort to reach a solution that is acceptable to all parties.

In cases that are settled, the parents acknowledge that they need help. The parents, the CPS worker, and the parents' and child's attorneys agree that the child meets one or more of the definitions of maltreatment. The agreement is presented to the judge, who typically approves the agreement and makes a ruling that the child is subject to the juvenile court's authority. The child is then called a "dependent of the court" or a "child in need of protection."

Once a judge rules that a child is a dependent of the court, the next step is the disposition—what is the goal for this child and family? The CPS worker typically prepares a report for the judge, outlining the agencies' goals for the family and the services that will be provided to help the parents achieve these goals. In most cases, the goal is reunification of the family.

Cases that are not settled go to a contested adjudicatory hearing before a juvenile court judge, referee, or commissioner. In most states, there is no jury in juvenile court. At the adjudicatory hearing, CPS is represented by its attorney. The parents have the right to hire an attorney of their choosing. Most parents, however, cannot afford to hire an attorney, and the judge appoints an attorney to represent the parents and, in many cases, for the child as well.

In addition to appointing an attorney for the child, juvenile courts in many states appoint a court-appointed special advocate (CASA) for children in dependency proceedings. CASAs are volunteers—usually, college students, retirees, and parents—who are interested in helping abused and neglected children. CASAs receive training about child maltreatment, the child protection system, and juvenile court. Typically, each CASA volunteer is assigned only one or two children. The CASA gets to know the child, and, in most communities, the CASA goes to court when their child's case comes up. Juvenile court judges often place great stock in the opinions of CASA volunteers because it is common for the CASA to know the child better than the professionals assigned to the case.

If the judge sustains the petition that CPS originally filed, and rules that the child was maltreated, the next step is disposition. Similar to cases that are settled without a trial, the judge receives recommendations from the CPS worker, considers the parents' wishes, consults the child if the child is old enough to have a useful opinion, and listens to the attorneys.

If the child can live safely at home, then home placement is the preferred disposition. The judge's dispositional order outlines the services the parents will receive to keep the child safe and reduce the likelihood of further maltreatment. The order may provide that the child and/or parents receive therapy or another intervention.

If the child cannot live safely at home, the dispositional order provides for the child's placement, and approves a plan to work toward family reunification (Smith, 2015). In some cases of severe maltreatment, there is no realistic hope of reunification, and the disposition is to move expeditiously to the termination of parental rights.

Postadjudication Placement and Review

Every year, some half a million children enter America's foster care system. A rural county may have a dozen children in out-of-home care, while an urban county has thousands. Keeping track of these children, and providing services to the children and their families, is one of the greatest challenges facing child welfare agencies.

Child welfare agencies have procedures to prevent children from falling through cracks in the foster care system. In tandem with efforts by child welfare social workers, the juvenile court holds periodic post-adjudication hearings to review progress. The timing of review hearings varies from state to state, but a common approach is to review what progress has been made every 6 months.

To prevent children from languishing in out-of-home care, the Federal Adoption and Safe Families Act (ASFA) requires states to consider the termination of parental rights for children who have been in foster care for 15 of the previous 22 months. ASFA's emphasis on termination is not required for children in the care of relatives and in cases where termination is not in a child's best interest.

Termination of Parental Rights

There is no relationship more revered than the relationship between parent and child. The parent–child relationship is protected by the U.S. Constitution from unwarranted government interference. Yet, some parents are so thoroughly incompetent, incapable, or abusive that, in order to save the child, society must sever the parent–child relationship. The solemn responsibility for determining when severance is necessary is entrusted to judges of the juvenile and family courts.

The states have detailed laws governing termination of parental rights. The party seeking termination, usually a child welfare agency in juvenile court, has the burden of proof, and must establish the grounds for the termination with clear and convincing evidence.

To terminate the parent–child relationship, a child welfare agency must establish serious parental fault, such as abandonment of the child, mental illness that is incompatible with minimally adequate parenting, or serious maltreatment that is likely to persist. If fault is established, the judge determines whether the termination of parental rights is in the child's best interest.

A judgment terminating parental rights permanently severs the legal parent–child relationship. The "parent" no longer has rights to custody, visitation, or even contact with the child. Severance of the parent–child relationship frees the child for adoption.

Guardianship for Foster Children

Guardianship is an option for some foster children who cannot return to their parents and for whom adoption is unlikely. Often, the guardian is a member of the child's family, such as a grandparent, aunt, or uncle. Guardianship is a legal relationship established by a judge.

A guardian receives legal custody of the child, including the decision-making authority normally exercised by parents. Once formal guardianship is established, the child leaves the child welfare system. Guardianship lasts until the child turns 18. The principal advantage of guardianship is that the child has a permanent family. An additional advantage in many cases is that the biological parents can remain part of the child's life because guardianship does not terminate parental rights.

Foster Care

Foster care is intended to be an interim stop, a way station on the journey to a permanent home. Most foster children eventually are reunified with their parents. When reunification is impossible, the journey takes a different turn, often in the direction of adoption.

The federal government defines foster care broadly as "24-hour substitute care for children outside their own homes" (45 C.F.R. § 57). Under the federal definition, foster care includes children living with relatives, nonrelative foster family homes, group homes, institutions, and preadoptive homes. State definitions of foster care vary.

The number of children in foster care has fluctuated over time. Throughout the 20th century, approximately 1% of American children were in foster care, with a higher percentage among poor children today, the foster care population hovers around 500,000.

Children of color are overrepresented in foster care. African Americans make up 15% of the U.S. population but 32% of the foster care population. Native Americans and Alaskan Natives represent 1% of the U.S. population but 2% of children in foster care. Whites are 60% of the population but 40% of the foster care population.

Every year, approximately 20,000 foster children reach age 18, and age out of the child welfare system. Unfortunately, many of these young people do not fare well. Children who age out of foster care have increased rates of homelessness, incarceration, and mental illness. Some sell drugs to earn money. Others sell their bodies. In 2005, Mark Courtney and his colleagues described a longitudinal study of former foster youth in Illinois, Iowa, and Wisconsin:

> In summary, youth making the transition from foster care are faring worse than their same-age peers, in many cases much worse, across a number of domains of functioning. They approach the age of majority with significant educational deficits and relatively few of them appear to be on a path that will provide them with the skills necessary to thrive in today's economy. They are less likely to be employed than their peers, and earnings from employment provide few of them with the means to make ends meet. This is reflected in the economic hardships many of them face and the need that many of them have for government assistance. A large number continue to struggle with health and mental health problems. Too many of them have children for whom they cannot provide a home. They are much more likely than their peers to find themselves involved with the criminal justice system. (p. 71)

It is important to keep in mind that foster care itself is not responsible for the difficulties children experience. Stephanie Berzin (2005) compared outcomes for foster youth and similarly situated youth who were not in care. From her comparison research, Berzin concluded:

> [Y]outh with foster care experience and matched youth do not differ to a statistically significant degree on any of the outcomes measured. This finding differs from the results of previous research, which suggests that many educational and employment outcomes are worse for youth with foster care experience than for other youth. This study does not find such differences. . . . The results challenge the notion that foster care placement is uniquely responsible for negative outcomes. . . . [V]ulnerabilities for foster youth seem to stem from characteristics that existed well before youth's placement in care. (p. 190)

In popular media and professional literature on foster care, children are seldom heard from. An early, historical exception was the 1885 Annual Report of the Massachusetts Society for the Prevention of Cruelty to Children. The report described a motherless girl who was rescued by the society from a brutal and drunken father. Following her placement in a rural foster home, she wrote to the society: "I had a lovely time last winter, sliding downhill. I went to private school last winter. I have been may-flowering and got some lovely ones. I sent you a box of them, which I hope you received all right. I think I am a happy girl, and would not exchange for anything of my own accord." Another little girl was removed from an "intemperate mother," who forced the child to sing in saloons. From her foster home in the country, the child wrote: "I like my place very much. I love Mr. and Mrs. C. and call them papa and mamma. I have been going to school. The teacher is Miss C. and she is very nice. We spelt for headmarks and I got the second prize. I can play 'Sweet By and By' and 'Yankee Doodle' on the organ, and mamma is learning me the notes. I had a splendid Christmas and New Year's. I have four pets; two pigs, a chicken, and a calf."

We would hardly expect the Massachusetts Society to publish children's letters expressing a longing for their parents or complaining about foster care. Some children weren't happy, and unfortunate placements occurred. Child welfare isn't perfect. Yet, these touching letters attest success.

How do today's foster children describe their circumstances? Adair Fox, Karie French, and Jill Berrick (2000), prepared a report on California's foster care system based on a series of questions foster children were asked, including, "In what ways has your social worker been helpful to you?" Among children's answers we find a 12-year-old saying, "Every Monday she takes me to the library, she takes me shopping, and she came to my graduation." A 7-year-old said, "She helped me because she came to my school and talked to my teacher." A 10-year-old remarked, "She takes me places. She makes sure I get to see my mom, [that] I have what I need, that I'm happy." An 8-year-old stated, "She helps my mommy learn to take care of us better." A 10-year-old said, "She takes care of things when I have a problem. She plays with me and always answers my questions."

Obviously being away from their parents is difficult for children. As part of the report, foster youth were asked, "Is there anything else that you think I should know about what it's like for children who live separate from their birth mother?" An 11-year-old spoke for many when she said, "It's sad. It's not fun. You cry sometimes. You miss them a lot. You want to be with them every day." A 10-year-old remarked, "It's scary, and you don't know what's gonna happen." One child said simply, "I miss my mom."

When asked what they liked about foster care, a 12-year-old said, "They are taking care of me. They treat us right. They do not beat us."

An 8-year-old replied, "I have friends. I love my sisters." A 9-year-old's answer was, "[They have] lots of toys and food, and my mom cooks good too." A 13-year-old said, "I like it good. We eat chicken every day. Good house. Clothes on my back." An 8-year-old stated, "My foster mom is the best. She treats me well. When she puts me in the corner I know why. And I like it here a lot." A 13-year-old said, "I feel how it is to have a family that loves you."

Every foster child has a story. Some are happy; some are sad. Research tells us that for many foster children, the passage into adulthood is stormy. Yet, as we read the statements from these and other foster children, we see many young people who are better off in foster homes than in their own homes. We see children who are cared for and, in many cases, loved by substitute mothers and fathers. We see children who have a future, thanks to foster care.

The foster care system has its faults: Too many children are in care too long, and too many children are shifted from home to home. Despite these problems, we are fortunate that hundreds of thousands of adults open their homes and hearts to abused and neglected children. The great majority of foster parents provide competent, stable homes. Caring for children who have been through so much is stressful, yet foster parents persist and give these children the tremendous gift of a home where a kid can be a kid. Although researchers, policymakers, and legislators must continue efforts to improve foster care, they should devote just as much effort to supporting the existing system. The foster parents, foster children, and professionals in the child welfare system deserve praise and support.

Foster care is not ideal for all children. No one doubts that children are better off with loving biological parents than with substitute caretakers. Yet, there are biological parents who parent in name only: parents who are so incompetent, stoned, drunk, perverted, mentally ill, or violent that they cannot or will not provide what children need. Children in such "families" are better off in foster care.

Some observers view foster care as a problem rather than a solution. They lament that a half a million children live in foster care. This is a legitimate concern, yet we should not lose sight of the fact that for many abused and neglected children, foster care is an improvement. Joseph Reid (1959) observed long ago: "For thousands of children foster care is preferable to their being in their own homes, for there simply is no own home and no possibility for one. . . . The need for foster care programs cannot be eliminated and communities should not blame themselves for this necessity" (pp. 388–389).

The Indian Child Welfare Act (ICWA)

Prior to 1978, 25–35% of Native American children were removed from their parents for alleged abuse or neglect. The majority of these children were placed in non-Indian foster homes, adoptive homes, and institutions. In 1974, Congress held hearings on the issue. Calvin Isaac, Chief of the Mississippi Band of Choctaw Indians, testified before Congress:

> One of the most serious failings of the present system is that Indian children are removed from the custody of their natural parents by non-tribal government authorities who have no basis for intelligently evaluating the cultural and social premises underlying Indian home life and childrearing. Many of the individuals who decide the fate of our children are at best ignorant of our cultural values, and at worst contemptuous of the Indian way and convinced that removal usually to a non-Indian household or institution can only benefit an Indian child. (quoted in *Mississippi Band of Choctaw Indians v. Holyfield,* 1989, pp. 34–35)

As a result of these hearings, Congress enacted the Indian Child Welfare Act in 1978. The law is intended to reduce the number of Native American children inappropriately removed from their homes. According to Congress, "The wholesale separation of Indian children from their families is perhaps the most tragic and destructive aspect of Indian life today" (*Adoptive Couple v. Baby Girl,* 2013, p. 2561).

In juvenile court, social workers and the judge inquire whether a child is Native American. If there is reason to believe the child is Native American, the child's tribe must be notified, and the tribe has a right to participate in the proceeding.

Interstate Compact on the Placement of Children

Juvenile courts sometimes place children in homes or institutions across state lines. When they do so, it is necessary to comply with the Interstate Compact on the Placement of Children (ICPC), which is in force in every state. The purpose of the ICPC is to enhance cooperation between the states with the result that children are placed in appropriate foster homes, institutions, or adoptive homes.

Social workers seeking to place a child in another state send a detailed form to social workers in the receiving state. The placement does not occur until social workers in the receiving state notify social workers in the sending state "that the proposed placement does not appear to be contrary to the interests of the child" (ICPC Article III(d)). Once a child is placed across state lines, the sending state retains authority over the child, as well as financial responsibility for the child.

The ICPC does not apply to cross-border placements with parents and other close relatives (ICPC Article VIII(a)). As the California Court of Appeal phrased it in *In re Z.K.* (2011), "The ICPC governs conditions for out-of-state placement in foster care or as a preliminary to a possible adoption. . . . The ICPC is applicable only to foster care and possible adoption—neither of which would involve natural parents. Accordingly, compliance with the ICPC is not required for placement with an out-of-state parent." The ICPC does not play a role in child custody litigation in family court.

CONCLUSION

This chapter began with three cases, two of which involved the death of children. The third case focused on Nathan, who was born in a shack. Of course, there is no shame in being born in a shack. Long ago, another baby was born in humble surroundings, in a manger if I recall, and he turned out ok. The problem with Nathan's parents, Jane and Duane, is not the fact that they are poor, but that their poverty stems from their criminal lifestyle and their chronic substance abuse, including Jane's abuse of drugs and alcohol during pregnancy. Is it in Nathan's best interest to have parental rights immediately terminated so he can be adopted while he is still a baby? On the other hand, don't Jane and Duane deserve an opportunity to get their lives together and parent their child? The law generally favors giving parents that chance. Should the juvenile court judge keep Nathan in foster care and order Jane and Duane into drug treatment for 6 months? Of course, while we wait to see if Jane and Duane can overcome their addictions, Nathan becomes attached to his foster parents, an attachment that will be broken if he is returned to Jane and Duane when they are "cured." Moreover, given the rate at which addicts relapse, there's a strong chance that reunification will fail, and Nathan will again be torn from the ones he loves. If parental rights are terminated now, Nathan will be adopted, and his life chances will be improved dramatically.

Nathan was my client in juvenile court. As part of my duty to investigate the case, I tracked down the shack where he was born so I could take a picture to show the judge. I visited Nathan at the neonatal intensive care unit that saved his life, where I saw his tiny body, snug and warm in a baby blanket, gently rocked by a machine designed to mimic the rocking a parent normally provides. When Nathan was finally released from the hospital, I visited him in the foster home that took him in with the hope of adoption. When Nathan's parents did nothing meaningful to accept responsibility, I joined with CPS in arguing that parental rights should be terminated as quickly as possible. The thoughtful and wise juvenile court judge agreed, and, today, Nathan has a chance at a better life, with his loving adoptive family.

7

Voluntary and Involuntary Mental Health Treatment

Readers of this book understand the importance of mental health treatment. Most treatment is outpatient and voluntary. Sometimes, however, involuntary treatment is needed, and this chapter discusses the laws governing civil commitment to treatment.

No freedom is more precious than freedom from confinement, and no act of the government strikes a deeper nerve than depriving people of their liberty. Citizens with mental illness share the passion for freedom, yet some people with serious mental illness cannot live safely in the community. Some are dangerous to themselves; some are dangerous to others. The law of civil commitment seeks the proper balance between liberty, on one hand, and the government's interest in helping mentally ill persons and protecting the community, on the other.

A SHORT HISTORY OF INVOLUNTARY COMMITMENT

In the 1800s, a person could be involuntarily committed to an insane asylum on the basis of an application by a family member that was approved by a physician. John Parry (2009) observes, "Typically, if a judge or the facility administrator, often without any prior medical exam, concurred with the petitioner—usually a husband, father, or guardian—that the proposed mental patient needed treatment, the confinement was almost certain to be authorized. Too often wives were committed for disobeying their husbands; children, for appearing to be different, being defiant, or simply being unwanted" (p. 10).

In the early 1900s, many states passed laws requiring judicial approval of involuntary civil commitment. When an application for commitment was filed, a physician examined the person and testified at a commitment hearing before a judge. During that time, many states also built large mental hospitals housing hundreds of patients. By the 1950s, more than half a million people lived in state mental hospitals. Conditions in some hospitals were deplorable, spurring both calls for reform and exposés, such as Ken Kesey's novel *One Flew Over the Cuckoo's Nest,* made into the 1975 Academy Award–winning film starring Jack Nicholson.

Deplorable conditions in mental hospitals were due partly to overcrowding and partly to a lack of medications that the staff could use to alleviate the suffering of patients. The antipsychotic drugs in use today were not discovered until the 1950s.

By the 1960s, large mental hospitals were regarded as a failure. In 1963, President John F. Kennedy signed into law the Community Mental Health Centers Act, with the goal of creating community-based outpatient mental health services across the nation, thereby reducing the need for institutional care. As a result, many large hospitals closed as part of the deinstitutionalization movement of the 1960s and 1970s.

Unfortunately, plans for outpatient treatment services in the community did not pan out. There was never enough money invested in community-based mental health to cope with the onslaught of seriously mentally ill patients leaving mental hospitals. Today, hundreds of thousands of mentally ill individuals are homeless in America, many without access to treatment. Jails and prisons are home to thousands of seriously mentally ill individuals.

SHORT-TERM EMERGENCY HOSPITALIZATION

The law allows for emergency, short-term (e.g., 72-hour) hospitalization of persons who appear to be seriously mentally ill, and who pose an immediate threat to themselves or others. Typically, the law allows a police officer to take the person to a hospital. Some states require the officer to consult a mental health professional before hospitalizing the patient. Other states allow an officer to act alone. In addition to the police, states allow physicians and mental health professionals to initiate emergency hospitalization. Usually, a judge is not involved at this stage.

Once the patient is at the hospital, he or she is evaluated by a mental health professional. Some patients are allowed to leave following an evaluation. Others check themselves into the hospital voluntarily. For patients who need hospitalization, but don't want it, a mental health professional starts the process to civilly commit the patient.

LEGAL STANDARDS FOR CIVIL COMMITMENT TO INPATIENT TREATMENT

The states have detailed laws governing civil commitment. The procedure starts with a family member or professional filing a petition or similar document in court. The individual has the right to a court hearing and an attorney. Generally, the individual has a right to a jury trial, in which the burden of proof is on the government to prove the need for commitment by clear and convincing evidence (*Addington v. Texas,* 1979).

The role of the patient's attorney in civil commitment proceedings raises difficult ethical issue for attorneys. Normally, an attorney is a zealous advocate for the client's wishes: It is the client, *not* the attorney, who makes the critical decisions in a case. But what is an attorney to do when the client is seriously mentally ill? For example, must an attorney zealously advocate for the wishes of a psychotic client who is opposed to hospitalization, and who thinks that the FBI is trying to kill him, and who intends to travel to Washington, D.C., at the first opportunity, to blow up FBI headquarters? What if the client is an 18-year-old who is deeply depressed and has tried recently to kill herself, but who says, "I don't want to go to the hospital. I want to be with my boyfriend. Can you help me?" There are no easy answers for the lawyers who do this work.

Although the exact wording of civil commitment laws varies from state to state, the legal standard is similar across the country. The government must prove (1) the person is mentally ill; (2) as a result of mental illness, the person poses an immediate threat of substantial harm to the person or others; and (3) there is no less restrictive alternative to hospitalization that can address the person's mental health issues.

The concept of dangerousness is at the heart of civil commitment. Yet, as Michael Perlin (2008) observes, "No question in the area of the involuntary commitment process has proven to be more vexing than the definition of the word 'dangerousness'" (vol. 1, p. 93). In some cases, dangerousness posed by the individual is obvious. In others, it is exceedingly difficult to tell whether the legal standard is satisfied.

Evidence of dangerousness is often a combination of lay and expert testimony. A lay witness might describe a recent assault by the person or threats to hurt someone. Expert testimony from mental health professionals is typically the most important evidence in civil commitment hearings. The expert describes the person's symptoms and diagnosis. Often, the expert offers an opinion on whether the individual is dangerous. In addition to evidence of dangerousness, a few states require proof that the person engaged in "either recent overt acts or recent expressed treats of violence" (see, e.g., Ga. Code Ann. § 37-3-1).

In addition to requiring civil commitment based on dangerousness to self or others, quite a few states allow the commitment of persons whose mental illness renders them gravely disabled. Alaska's definition of gravely disabled is similar to the law in other states, and it defines a person as gravely disabled when, due to mental illness, the individual "is in danger of physical harm arising from such complete neglect of basic needs for food, clothing, shelter, or personal safety as to render serious accident, illness, or death highly probable if care by another is not taken; or will, if not treated, suffer or continue to suffer severe and abnormal mental, emotional, or physical distress, and this distress is associated with significant impairment of judgment, reason, or behavior causing a substantial deterioration of the person's previous ability to function independently" (Alaska Stat. § 47.30.915(7)).

Iowa has an interesting law that allows commitment of a mentally ill person who "is likely to inflict serious emotional injury on members of the person's family or others who lack reasonable opportunity to avoid contact with the person with mental illness" (Iowa Code § 229.1(17)(b)).

RISK ASSESSMENT: PREDICTING DANGEROUSNESS

Predicting dangerousness is central to civil commitment, yet the subject is complex and controversial. Michael Perlin (2008) comments, "No question in involuntary civil commitment law is more controversial than the extent to which psychiatrists are accurate in their predictions of future dangerousness" (vol. 1, p. 104). The American Psychiatric Association (2012) states, "While psychiatrists can often identify circumstances associated with an increased likelihood of violent behavior, they cannot predict dangerousness with definitive accuracy. Over any given period some individuals assessed to be at low risk will act violently, while others assessed to be at high risk will not."

The traditional approach to risk assessment involves a mental health professional interviewing a subject and drawing on clinical experience to estimate dangerousness. Pure clinical assessment is often unreliable, however. Gary Melton and his colleagues (2007) point out,

"Clinicians' involvement in violence prediction is extremely controversial. . . . [M]yriad factors limit clinicians' abilities in this area; many have questioned whether mental health professionals' predictions of violent behavior are sufficiently accurate to meet acceptable scientific or legal standards" (p. 277). Guy, Douglas, and Hart (2015) add, "Unstructured clinical approaches have no association with violence" (vol. 1, p. 70).

Today, mental health professionals generally supplement clinical interviews with more statistically based actuarial risk-assessment tools. Guy and colleagues (2015) offer the following description of actuarial risk assessment.

> At the opposite end of the spectrum from the unstructured clinical approach [to violence assessment] is the actuarial approach. . . . [T]he actuarial approach is seen as "a formal method [that uses] an equation, a formula, a graph, or an actuarial table to arrive at a probability, or expected value, of some outcome." Risk factors are identified through various statistical procedures and are selected based on the strength of their association with violence. . . . Risk factors also may be assigned weights. . . . The hallmark, or defining feature, of the actuarial model of prediction is the derivation and use of reproducible unvarying rules for amalgamating predictive factors. (vol. 1, p. 42)

Guy and colleagues (2015) emphasize that although actuarial risk assessment is far from perfect, it is not worthless. They write, "Decades of research have shown that structured, validated approaches to assessing an individual's risk of violence have on average moderate levels of predictive accuracy" (vol. 1, p. 70).

LEGAL STANDARDS FOR OUTPATIENT COMMITMENT

In addition to civil commitment to inpatient treatment, most states authorize the courts to involuntarily commit mentally ill individuals to outpatient treatment. Outpatient commitment has proved to be controversial. In 2001, John Monahan and his colleagues (2001) noted, "In many states a take-no-prisoners battle is under way between advocates of outpatient commitment—who call this approach assisted outpatient treatment—and its opponents—who use the term 'leash laws'" (p. 1198).

Legal standards for outpatient commitment vary from state to state. Generally, outpatient commitment is allowed for mentally ill patients who require treatment, but who do not require hospitalization. With outpatient commitment, there is less focus on dangerousness, and a greater concentration on preventing individuals from decompensating to the point where they require inpatient care. Thus, Alabama law allows outpatient commitment for mentally ill individuals who will "continue to suffer mental distress and will continue to experience deterioration of the ability to function independently" (Ala. Code § 22-52-10.2). Georgia law considers whether outpatient treatment is needed to avoid the risk that the individual will imminently become an inpatient (Ga. Code Ann. § 37-3-1). Hawaiian law determines whether the individual "is now in need of treatment in order to prevent a relapse or deterioration which would predictably result in the person becoming imminently dangerous to self or others" (Haw. Rev. Stat. § 334-121(4)). Laws in both California and Florida require a clinical determination that the individual is unlikely to survive safety in the community without treatment (Cal. Welfare & Institutions Code § 5346(a)(3); Fla. Stat. § 394.4655(1)(c)). Some states require evidence that the individual has recently received inpatient treatment or has committed dangerous acts (e.g., Florida, Hawaii, and Louisiana).

THE RIGHT TO REFUSE TREATMENT

People have the right to refuse medical and mental health treatment. This right extends to people who are civilly committed for psychiatric care. Except in emergencies, a committed individual cannot be medicated against the person's will without a court order (*In re R.K.L.*, 2016). The Alaska Supreme Court wrote in *Myers v. Alaska Psychiatric Institute* (2006), "In keeping with most state courts that have addressed the issue, we hold that, in the absence of emergency, a court may not authorize the state to administer psychotropic drugs to a non-consenting mental patient unless the court determines that the medication is in the best interests of the patient and no less intrusive alternative treatment is available" (p. 238).

The right to refuse treatment extends to electroshock therapy (ECT). When an individual's mental illness renders the person incapable of consenting to ECT, a proceeding may be started in court, in which a judge is asked to approve the treatment (see *Conservatorship of Pamela J.*, 2005; *In the Matter of A.A.*, 2005).

PERIODIC REVIEW OF CIVIL COMMITMENT

Decades ago, during the era when large state hospitals housed hundreds of patients, it was common for civilly committed individuals to disappear into institutions and be forgotten. Today, civil commitments typically last a set number of days, and then must be reviewed on a regular basis. The patient has a right to seek release.

If mental health professionals determine that a civil commitment should be extended, legal procedures exist to do so. In Wisconsin, for example, "the extension of an involuntary mental health commitment . . . requires the circuit court to find by clear and convincing evidence that the individual is mentally ill and is a proper subject for treatment and that there is a substantial likelihood, based on the subject individual's treatment record, that the individual would be a proper subject for commitment if treatment were withdrawn" (*Mental Health Commitment of James H.*, 2015, p. 529).

CIVIL COMMITMENT OF PERSONS WITH INTELLECTUAL DISABILITY

States have laws creating procedures to place persons with intellectual disability in institutions when they cannot live independently. The law in Florida is typical. A petition is filed in the appropriate county court, stating, "The person lacks sufficient capacity to give express and informed consent to a voluntary application for services and lacks the basic survival and self-care skills to provide for the person's well-being or is likely to physically injure others if allowed to remain at liberty" (Florida Stat. § 393.11(2)(c)(4)). The court appoints experts to evaluate the person. The person has the right to an attorney. A hearing is held, and there must be clear and convincing evidence to commit the person to care.

CIVIL COMMITMENT OF CHILDREN

Parents have the right to consent to medical care for their children. But does this include the right to admit a child to a mental hospital? Skeptics of unfettered parental authority worry that some parents who are fed up with troublesome teenagers will "dump" their children in hospitals to get rid of "the problem." People who support parental authority respond that such abuses are rare, and, when they occur, it is important to remember that parents cannot unilaterally admit children to a mental hospital. A mental health professional must agree that the child needs hospitalization.

The U.S. Supreme Court waded into this minefield in *Parham v. J.R.* (1979), in which it determined that children have a right to be free from unnecessary restraint. The Court also acknowledged the importance of parental authority, writing, "Most children, even in adolescence, simply are not able to make sound judgments concerning many decisions, including their need for medical care or treatment. Parents can and must make those judgments" (p. 603). As for the government, it has an interest in conserving scarce mental health resources, and not wasting them where they are not needed.

The Court ruled that, although parents play the dominant role in deciding whether hospitalization is necessary, "parents cannot have absolute and unreviewable discretion to decide whether to have a child institutionalized" (p. 604). It also ruled that a judicial commitment hearing is not necessary for children. Indeed, the Court worried that court hearings would discourage parents from getting help for their children. According to the Court:

> The State in performing its voluntarily assumed mission also has a significant interest in not imposing unnecessary procedural obstacles that may discourage the mentally ill or their families from seeking needed psychiatric assistance. The *parens patriae* interests in helping parents care for the mental health of their children cannot be fulfilled if the parents are unwilling to take advantage of the opportunities because the admission process is too onerous, too embarrassing, or too contentious. It is surely not idle to speculate as to how many parents who believe they are acting in good faith would forgo state-provided hospital care if such care is contingent on participation in an adversary proceeding designed to probe their motives and other private family matters in seeking the voluntary admission. (p. 605)

The ruling held that the Constitution is satisfied so long as there is "some kind of inquiry by a neutral factfinder to determine that hospitalization is required. The factfinder can be a mental health professional, and need not a judge. No formal hearing is required. Due process is not violated by use of informal traditional medical investigative techniques" (p. 607).

CIVIL COMMITMENT OF SEX OFFENDERS

Sex offenders, some of whom are dangerous, can pose a risk to public safety when they are at-large. Yet, when their prison term expires, they are entitled to release. Most such offenders cannot be committed for traditional psychiatric treatment because they do not have the mental illness required for civil commitment.

In the middle of the last century, a number of states had laws that permitted involuntary commitment of dangerous sex offenders. In the 1970s and 1980s, those laws fell into disuse. In the 1990s, however, states resurrected laws allowing the involuntary civil commitment of sexually violent predators.

In 1997, the U.S. Supreme Court upheld the constitutionality of Kansas' sexual predator commitment law (*Kansas v. Hendricks,* 1997). In 2002, the Court revisited the Kansas law and ruled that in commitment proceedings, the Constitution requires the state to prove that the sexually dangerous individual has some degree of inability to control himself (*Kansas v. Crane,* 2002).

Mental health professionals who evaluate individuals in sex offender commitment proceedings use clinical judgment and actuarial instruments to assess the risk of reoffending. In *In re Detention of Thorell* (2003), the Washington Supreme Court observed, "There are two broad approaches to conducting risk assessments: clinical judgment or actuarial assessment. The clinical approach requires evaluators to consider a wide range of risk factors and then form an overall opinion concerning future dangerousness. The actuarial approach evaluates a limited set of predictors and then combines these variables using a predetermined, numerical weighting system to determine future risk of re-offense which may be adjusted (or not) by expert evaluators considering potentially important factors not included in the actuarial measure" (p. 724).

The tragic facts of *State Department of Hospitals v. Superior Court* (2015), illustrate the importance, and limitations, of risk assessment. Gilton Pitre was scheduled to be paroled from prison. Before his release, the state department of mental health evaluated Pitre to determine whether he should be civilly committed as a dangerous sexual predator. The department did not request Pitre's commitment. Four days after leaving prison, Pitre raped and murdered a 15-year-old girl.

APPLY WHAT YOU HAVE LEARNED

The Pedophile across the Street

Seven-year-old Megan lived with her parents in a quiet subdivision. Megan's parents were unaware that a convicted sex offender, named Jesse, lived across the street. Early one evening, while it was still light, Megan walked down the street to visit a friend. A few minutes later, Megan's mother looked for her daughter, but could not find her. The police were called, and an intensive search ensued, but it was too late. Megan was dead. Jesse had lured Megan into his house with the promise of showing her a puppy. Once inside, Jesse sexually assaulted Megan, and she screamed. Jesse strangled her with a belt and placed a plastic bag over her head. After she was dead, he put his fingers in her vagina. He drove her body to a park and dumped her in the weeds.—*State v. Timmendequas,* 737 A.2d 55 (N.J. 1999)

Analysis: The senseless murder of Megan Kanka led to the adoption, nationwide, of laws called Megan's laws. These laws, which vary from state to state, require various forms of notification of the whereabouts of sex offenders. We will never know what Megan's parents, and other parents, might have done had they known a convicted sex offender lived on their block. They never got the chance to know. Today, they could have that chance.

If Jesse had been civilly committed as a dangerous sexual predator, he would not have murdered Megan. Yet, sex offenders have rights too. Only the most dangerous offenders merit commitment. We will never know if Jesse could have been committed.

The appropriate societal response to individuals with a history of sexual offending is one of the most difficult and urgent challenges facing the field of interpersonal violence. We cannot eliminate all tragedies like Megan's, but we have to try. A unified effort is required from clinical, legal, and legislative professionals to tackle this problem in ways that are not alarmist or irrational, but that offer the hope of meaningfully reducing the rate of sexual offending.

VOLUNTARY HOSPITALIZATION

Most people in mental hospitals are *not* committed; they are in the hospital voluntarily. Many individuals with serious mental illness are competent to consent to hospitalization and treatment. Others, however, are so ill or out of touch with reality that they lack the capacity to consent to hospitalization. Who is then responsible for seeing that these individuals consent to hospital admission? It would be quite a Catch-22 to deny hospital care to a person who needs it, but whose illness deprives that person of the ability to consent to care.

Some people who lack capacity to consent to care can enter the hospital through civil commitment. Yet, the civil commitment process is time-consuming, expensive, and adversarial. As well, many people who need inpatient treatment do not meet the criteria for involuntary civil commitment.

It does not make sense medically, legally, or humanely for civil commitment to be the only way into the hospital for some patients who are too ill to consent to care. States have developed alternatives to civil commitment. In some states, family members can admit ill loved ones to the hospital.

Depending on state law, a guardian may be appointed and given authority to consent to hospitalization. As Richard Boldt (2015) explains, "In a number of states, the law is clear that a guardian may not consent to the ward's admission to a psychiatric hospital, thus requiring the use of the state's involuntary civil commitment process. . . . In other states, it is clear that a guardian may provide the necessary consent for voluntary admission. In a third group of states, the guardian may consent so long as the ward also consents or, in some jurisdictions, does not object. In a fourth group of states, the guardian's authority to arrange for voluntary inpatient care depends on the guardian obtaining specific court authorization, although the substantive standard and procedural requirements for securing such an order may differ from those that govern involuntary commitment" (pp. 2–3).

With mentally ill, intellectually disabled, and elderly persons, there is always the danger that unscrupulous family members, "friends," or caretakers will seek to place them in institutions and make off with their property. Richard Boldt (2015) notes, "It is, perhaps, because of the coercive features present within many voluntary mental hospital admissions that state law generally imposes restrictions on the practice that are not ordinarily present in the case of voluntary hospital admission for other healthcare services. State laws typically contain detailed provisions setting out the process by which an individual may elect to enter an inpatient mental health treatment facility, the criteria under which that application for admission is to be assessed by hospital personnel, and the rights and restrictions (particularly on requesting discharge from the hospital) that apply once the voluntary patient is admitted" (pp. 10–11).

ADVANCE DIRECTIVES

An advance directive is a legal document, signed while a person is competent, setting forth the person's wishes for medical care if he or she becomes incompetent. In some states, a directive is called a power of attorney for health care decisions. Advance directives are often used to help with end-of-life decisions. State laws vary on the details of advance directives.

Individuals with mental illness can use a psychiatric advance directive. Beanne Sheetz (2007) describes this option:

> The directive can take several forms. One type, the instructional directive, allows individuals to provide directions about treatments that they would or would not like to receive while they are incapable of making treatment decisions. A second type, a proxy directive, permits individuals to appoint an agent to make decisions for them while they are incapacitated. Another type, the hybrid directive, contains elements of both instructional and proxy directives. A fourth type, the Ulysses directive, is most pertinent to individuals with episodic and insight-impairing issues . . . because it enables them prospectively to bind themselves to treatment and override, in advance, their refusals during acute episodes of their illnesses. (p. 403)

Judy Clausen (2014) further explains Ulysses directives. "A Ulysses arrangement authorizes doctors to treat the patient during a future episode when the patient lacks capacity even if the episode causes the patient to refuse treatment at that time. A patient who enters a Ulysses arrangement essentially requests doctors to ignore the patient's illness-induced refusals" (p. 4).

CONCLUSION

Freedom to come and go—our physical liberty—is a cherished American value, enshrined in the Declaration of Independence, with its unalienable rights to "Life, Liberty and the pursuit of Happiness," and in Walt Whitman's poem "Song of the Open Road," where he wrote:

> Afoot and light-hearted I take to the open road,
> Healthy, free, the world before me,
> The long brown path before me leading wherever I choose.
>
> Henceforth I ask not good fortune, I myself am good fortune,
> Henceforth I whimper no more, postpone no more, need nothing,
> Done with indoor complaints, libraries, querulous criticisms,
> Strong and content I travel the open road.

Yet, as much as we value our freedom, we understand that mental illness sometimes robs people of the ability to care for themselves. In rare cases, mental illness renders sufferers a danger to others. In such unfortunate circumstances, society makes the value judgment that the patient must lose the right to come and go at will and to submit temporarily to care by mental health professionals. The goal is not to punish, but to protect and heal the individual, so that his or her freedom can be restored with all deliberate speed.

To conclude, civil commitment plays an important role in the response to interpersonal violence. Practice in this important field is provided mainly by mental health professionals, assisted by the legal system.

Part IV

Clinicians and Courts

Part IV focuses on clinicians' involvement with the courts. Chapter 8 discusses testifying in court, and Chapter 9 addresses expert testimony. Both Chapters 8 and 9 devote considerable attention to cross-examination. Chapter 10 analyzes confidentiality and privilege. Finally, Chapter 11 focuses on professional malpractice and ethical violations that can lead to ethics complaints and lawsuits.

8

Testifying in Court

This chapter outlines the rules and practices governing witness testimony, which plays a central role in civil and criminal litigation. The rules are contained in evidence codes, the best known of which is the Federal Rules of Evidence, commonly referred to as the FRE. Although the FRE applies only in federal court, most states have adopted the FRE for use in state court. The few states that do not have the FRE (e.g., California) have rules very similar to the FRE.

Mental health, medical, and child protective services (CPS) professionals often testify in court, and for many of these professionals, the thought of testifying is often stressful. With this in mind, the aims of this chapter and Chapter 9 are to (1) explain how testifying unfolds; (2) demystify the process, especially that of cross-examination; and (3) help professionals feel comfortable—or at least less uncomfortable—testifying.

COMPETENCE TO TESTIFY

A witness is a person who takes an oath to testify truthfully, and who provides information that is relevant in a legal case. All witnesses must be competent to testify. The elements of testimonial competence are (1) a capacity to observe, (2) a sufficient memory capacity to recall events, (3) an ability to communicate, (4) an understanding of the difference between truths and lies, and (5) an appreciation of the duty to tell the truth in court.

The rules of evidence assume that everyone has these capabilities. Thus, FRE 601 provides, "Every person is competent to be a witness. . . . " In practice, issues of testimonial competence arise only when testimony is offered from children or adults with a mental disability or dementia.

Attorneys may try to prevent a child witness from testifying by arguing that the child is incompetent. If legitimate concerns arise about a child's understanding of the difference between truths and lies, or of the duty to tell the truth, the judge holds a hearing called a competency examination (Myers, 2016). The judge and attorneys ask the child questions to determine whether the child possesses the capacity to testify. Most children as young as 4 have the necessary capacity and can demonstrate that capacity when they are questioned by experienced professionals (see Lyon & Saywitz, 1999). Thomas Lyon and Karen Saywitz have produced helpful, research-based materials on questioning young children about testimonial competence (see Lyon, 2014; Lyon & Saywitz, 1999; Saywitz & Camparo, 2014).

HOW TESTIMONY UNFOLDS

There are three phases of witness testimony: direct examination, cross-examination, and redirect examination. During direct examination, the witness tells the judge or jury what the witness knows about the case. Direct examination is followed by cross-examination, during which the cross-examining, or opposing, attorney may try to poke holes in the witness's testimony. The last phase is redirect examination, during which the witness has an opportunity to clarify issues that were raised during cross-examination.

For additional treatment of testifying in court, you may wish to consult the excellent books by Thomas Gutheil (2013), Allan Barsky (2012), and Stanley Brodsky (1999).

Direct Examination

The attorney who asked (or subpoenaed) the witness to testify begins the questioning with direct examination. The purpose of direct examination is to allow the witness to convey to the jury or judge relevant factual information. The direct examiner asks nonleading questions and elicits the story from the witness in relatively small snippets. For example, an attorney questioning a police officer on direct examination might proceed as follows:

Q: What was the first thing you did when you arrived at the accident scene?

A: I parked my patrol car to protect the scene from traffic.

Q: What did you do next?

A: I saw that there were two badly damaged cars in the intersection, so I got out of my car and went to each car to see if anyone was injured inside.

Q: What did you observe in the first car?

A: Inside the first car was an older gentleman, who appeared unconscious.

Q: And in the other car?

A: There was nobody in the other car.

Q: What did you do next?

A: I contacted dispatch and asked that an ambulance and fire rescue be sent.

Observe how the attorney extracted the story one piece at a time. The attorney used open-ended, nonleading questions. It would be improper for the attorney to ask the police officer, "Tell us about the accident," or "Tell the jury about your investigation." Such questions are considered objectionable because they call for the witness to provide a narrative.

The choppy form of direct examination, with its short, partial answers, can seem stilted and artificial, but there is a reason for the approach. If a witness is given free rein to provide a narrative, that is, to "tell us everything you know about the case," there is too great a chance the witness will blurt out inadmissible information the jury should not hear. For example, a witness invited to "tell the whole story" might include inadmissible hearsay. The witness might say, "And then she said that the victim told her that her Aunt Sally told her not to tell anyone." Although the judge can instruct the jury to disregard the inadmissible hearsay, and the judge can "strike" it from the record, the bell has already been rung. It is difficult for jurors to pretend they haven't heard inadmissible statements. To reduce the likelihood inadmissible evidence is revealed during direct examination, a witness's story is brought out in manageable chunks that allow attorneys to monitor the testimony and to have some control over what is said.

Cross-Examination

When a direct examiner finishes questioning a witness, he or she says, "No further questions" or "Your witness," and the cross-examination phase begins. The opposing attorney has the right to cross-examine the witness. Cross-examination frequently causes the greatest stress for witnesses.

Chapter 1 explained that our system of litigation is adversarial. Each side presents its strongest case, and attempts to undermine the other side's evidence, including its witnesses. The U.S. Supreme Court captured the essence of the adversary system in *In re Gault* (1967), in which the Court wrote, "Truth will emerge from the confrontation of opposing versions and conflicting data" (p. 21). Cross-examination is the primary tool attorneys use to challenge the other side's "data." Evidence scholar John Wigmore (1904/1974) once wrote, "Cross-examination is beyond any doubt the greatest legal engine ever invented for the discovery of truth" (§ 1367). Although judges have the authority to limit cross-examination that is unnecessarily aggressive, embarrassing, or wasteful of time, cross-examiners are given broad latitude.

Cross-examination is not always negative or confrontational. If a cross-examiner believes a witness might provide information favorable to the cross-examiner's client, the cross-examiner may remain positive, even friendly. Cross-examiners understand that a witness is unlikely to volunteer helpful information if the witness feels attacked.

Redirect Examination

Cross-examination is followed by redirect examination. The purpose of redirect examination is simple: Repair the damage. If doubts and questions arose during cross-examination, the witness can explain during the redirect phase. If the cross-examiner refused to allow the witness to clarify answers, an explanation can emerge during redirect. If the witness's credibility is called into question on cross-examination, during redirect, the witness can offer an explanation.

Impeachment

A cross-examiner who challenges or attacks a witness engages in impeachment. Similar to a carpenter who has a toolbox containing essential tools (hammers, saws, drills, screwdrivers), a cross-examiner has a toolkit of essential impeachment tools, which are described next.

Prior Inconsistent Statements

The use in court of a witness's prior inconsistent statements was discussed in Chapter 2, in the context of domestic violence cases. This section provides further information on impeachment with prior inconsistent statements.

During direct examination, a witness says one thing. The cross-examiner knows that, at an earlier time, the witness said something different: a prior inconsistent statement. A cross-examiner may confront such a witness with his or her prior inconsistent statement. In a car accident case, for example, the cross-examination might look like this:

Q: Mr. Mellow, you testified a few minutes ago, on direct examination, that the light was red, didn't you?

A: Yes.

Q: Now, Mr. Mellow, not long after the accident, you were sitting in a bar with your friend Bert, isn't that so?

A: That's right.

Q: And while you were sitting in the bar, you and Bert were talking, and the subject of the accident came up in conversation, didn't it?

A: Yes.

Q: And at that time, while discussing the accident with Bert, you said, "The light was green," didn't you?

The witness can admit or deny the inconsistency. If he admits it, the attorney has impeached his credibility. Mr. Mellow can't keep his story straight. But what if Mellow says, "That's not true. I never said any such thing to Bert." What is the cross-examiner to do? One possibility is to put Bert on the witness stand and have Bert repeat Mr. Mellow's statement made at the bar. The rules on whether Bert can testify are intricate and are beyond the scope of this introduction to impeachment.

Contradiction

The idea of contradiction is simple: The cross-examiner tries to get the witness to contradict (change) something the witness said on direct or cross-examination. For example, on direct the witness said, "The light was red." The cross-examiner tries to get the witness to admit that the light might have been yellow. If the witness agrees, she contradicts herself, undermining her credibility.

Impeachment with a Prior Conviction

A cross-examiner may impeach a witness by confronting the witness with the fact that he or she has been convicted of certain crimes. A cross-examiner might ask, "Isn't it true, Mr. Mellow, that 2 years ago, in this county, you were convicted of perjury?" The idea behind such impeachment is that a person who has been convicted of a crime is not a truthful person and should not be believed. The rules governing impeachment with convictions vary from state to state.

Impeachment with a Witness's Prior Lies

In most states, a cross-examiner is allowed to ask a witness about the witness's prior lies. For example, when cross-examining Mr. Mellow, the attorney might say, "Mr. Mellow, isn't it a fact that 2 years ago, you cheated on your taxes?" When the jury learns of Mr. Mellow's untruthful acts, they may think twice about believing his testimony.

Bias

A witness may be impeached with evidence that the witness is biased for or against a party to the litigation. For example, suppose Mr. Mellow is testifying for Ms. Jones in a contract case. Mr. Mellow gives testimony favorable to Ms. Jones. The cross-examiner asks, "Mr. Mellow, isn't it true that you and Ms. Jones are lovers?" This question is proper because it explores the witness's possible bias in favor of Ms. Jones.

Faulty Memory

A cross-examiner may ask questions to show that a witness's memory is imperfect. Some cross-examiners deliberately ask questions about peripheral details of events in an attempt to show weaknesses in memory.

Defects in Opportunity to Observe

A cross-examiner may cast doubt on whether an eyewitness had a good opportunity to see or hear what the witness described on direct examination. Suppose Mr. Mellow testifies in a car accident case as follows, "I was standing outside my office when I saw the defendant's car go by at a high rate of speed, just before the accident." The cross-examiner asks the following questions:

Q: Mr. Mellow, the night of the accident was dark and stormy, wasn't it?

A: That's true.

Q: When the car went past your office, it was after 10:30 at night, isn't that right?

A: True.

Q: It was dark, wasn't it?

A: Yes.

Q: There are no street lights near your office, are there?

A: That's right.

Q: Your office is about 100 feet from the road, isn't it?

A: About that distance, yes.

Q: Mr. Mellow, it was raining very hard at the time, wasn't it?

A: Yes.

Q: Rain coming down that hard would have made it challenging to see clearly, wouldn't you agree?

A: No, not really.

Q: Thank you, Mr. Mellow. I have nothing further.

The cross-examiner is trying to plant the idea that Mr. Mellow didn't get a good look at the car. Maybe it wasn't the defendant's car! Maybe Mr. Mellow could not tell, in the dark, from that distance, and through driving rain, how fast the car was going.

SECRETS OF CROSS-EXAMINATION

In addition to these impeachment tools, there are a number of techniques, or trade secrets, of cross-examination. Although as a trial lawyer and law professor, I probably shouldn't reveal the trade secrets of the cross-examiner's art, knowing about these techniques may be helpful if you are confronted with them in court.

Controlling the Witness

The key to a successful cross-examination is controlling the witness, by which I mean, controlling what the witness says through a series of leading questions. A leading question is a suggestive question, or one that suggests the answer the questioner desires. Some questions are highly leading. For example, "The car went through the red light, isn't that right?" Other questions suggest, in a milder way, the desired answer.

Unlike the attorney conducting a direct examination, who is supposed to ask nonleading questions, the cross-examiner may ask all the leading questions he or she likes. Indeed, some attorneys almost never ask nonleading questions on cross-examination.

The cross-examiner seeks to control the witness with leading questions that limit the witness's answers to yes or no. If the witness tries to explain, the cross-examiner interrupts and says, "Please answer yes or no." If the witness persists, the cross-examiner might ask the judge to admonish the witness to answer the lawyer's questions. The cross-examiner's goal is to elicit information favorable to the attorney's client, while limiting the witness's opportunity to explain.

If you experience this technique as a witness, you may find it frustrating. Remember, however, the cross-examiner has a job to do, and that job is *not* to give you an opportunity to repeat what you said on direct examination.

Sometimes, a lawyer's yes/no question can't be answered with a simple yes or no. In such cases, it is appropriate to say, "It is not possible to answer with a simple yes or no. May I explain myself?" If the correct answer is "maybe," say so. Judges often permit witnesses to explain. If the judge limits you to yes or no answers, take the advice of Stanley Brodsky (1999): "When the court limits what you can explain, neither panic nor become angry or defensive; rather, testify as confidently and accurately as you can within those restraints" (p. 9). Keep in mind too that after cross-examination, there is redirect examination, when the attorney who asked you to testify has the opportunity to clarify your testimony. The attorney on redirect might ask, "You recall that during cross-examination, the attorney limited you to yes or no answers. Would you like to explain?"

Preparing for the Closing Argument

On TV, you often see dramatic cross-examinations that catch the witness in a blatant lie and force the confession, "You got me. I did it!" Such dramatic results are seldom seen in actual courtrooms. Rarely does cross-examination utterly destroy a witness's credibility. Indeed, a poorly conducted cross-examination can hurt a cross-examiner's case by giving a witness further opportunities to provide damaging testimony. I advise my law students, "You can't win your case on cross-examination, but you sure can lose it."

The goal of the cross-examiner, especially in jury trials, is generally not to score a direct hit on a witness. Rather, the goal is to poke a few small holes in the witness's testimony and to raise a few doubts about the witness's credibility. Those holes are deliberately left unfilled, and those doubts are intentionally left festering until the closing argument, when the attorney reminds the jury of the holes in the witness's testimony and the lingering doubts about his or her credibility. As part of the closing argument, the attorney might say, "In light of all this, ladies and gentlemen, you should not believe the witness's testimony. Give the witness's testimony no weight at all. It doesn't deserve any."

Do you remember the cross-examination of Mr. Mellow, who described seeing the defendant's car speed past his office at night? When the cross-examiner was trying to undermine Mr. Mellow's credibility, the examiner did not ask the logical last question. The examiner did not say, "So, Mr. Mellow, you didn't really get a good look at the car, did you?" If the attorney asks that question, Mr. Mellow may give an answer that the attorney does not want the jury to hear. Thus, the cross-examiner simply raises the possibilities that Mr. Mellow misidentified the car or overestimated its speed, and waits until his or her closing argument, when Mr. Mellow is safely off the witness stand, and the attorney has the final word with the jury. At that time, the attorney says, "Ladies and gentlemen, you recall that Mr. Mellow testified that my client's car went past his office at a high rate of speed. But ladies and gentlemen, you should not put much stock in Mr. Mellow's testimony. Mr. Mellow admitted that it was a dark and stormy night. It was after 10:30 at night. There were no streetlights to help Mr. Mellow see in the dark. His office is a full 100 feet from the street. It was raining hard, and the rain would have impaired Mr. Mellow's view of any car passing by on the street. You recall that other evidence shows that my client's car is black. In these circumstances, Mr. Mellow could very easily have been completely wrong about whose car it was. And given the conditions, he was in no position to judge the speed of whoever's car it was that passed. I'm sure Mr. Mellow was trying his best to be truthful, but you should not believe his testimony. Not because he lied, but because he didn't have the opportunity to see what he says he saw."

Here is another example of a cross-examiner planting the seeds of doubt for the closing argument. The witness is a physician who is part of a multidisciplinary child abuse team. The doctor testified for the prosecutor, describing a child's injuries. The defense attorney questions the doctor as follows:

Q: Now, Doctor, you are employed by Children's Hospital, isn't that correct?

A: Right.

Q: At the hospital, you are a member of the multidisciplinary team that investigates allegations of child abuse, isn't that right?

A: The team performs medical examinations and interviews. We do not investigate. The police investigate. But yes, I am a member of the team.

Q: Your team regularly performs investigative examinations and interviews at the request of the prosecuting attorney's office, isn't that right?

A: Yes.

Q: When you complete your investigation for the prosecutor, you prepare a report for the prosecutor, don't you?

A: A report and recommendation is prepared and placed in the child's medial record, as part of that record. Upon request, the team provides a copy of the report to the prosecutor and, I might add, to the defense.

Q: After your team prepares its report and provides a copy to the prosecutor, you often come to court to testify as an expert witness for the prosecution in child abuse cases, isn't that right, Doctor?

A: Yes.

Q: Do you usually testify for the prosecution, rather than for the defense?

A: Correct.

Q: In fact, would I be correct in saying that you always testify for the prosecution, and never for the defense?

A: I am willing to testify for the defense, but so far I have always testified for the prosecution.

Q: Thank you, Doctor. I have no further questions.

The cross-examiner seeks to portray the doctor as biased in favor of the prosecution. However, the cross-examiner does not ask, "So, doctor, isn't it true that because of your close working relationship with the prosecution, you are biased in favor of the prosecution?" The defense attorney knows the answer is "No," so the cross-examiner simply plants the idea of bias, and then, when it is time for the closing argument, reminds jurors of the doctor's close working relationship with the prosecution—"A relationship, ladies and gentlemen, that is just a little too cozy."

During redirect examination, the prosecutor might say, "Doctor, in light of the defense counsel's questions about your responsibilities as a member of the child abuse team, are you biased in favor of the prosecution?" The doctor can set the record straight.

Don't Ask a Question Unless You Know the Answer

To avoid unpleasant surprises, cross-examiners try to avoid asking questions when they don't know the answer. What you don't know *can* hurt you. Of course, this is not always possible. Sometimes, a cross-examiner has little choice but to ask questions without knowing the answer.

To appreciate why cross-examiners try to avoid questions for which they don't know the answer, consider a case from an unlikely source. William S. Gilbert, who rose to enormous fame when he teamed up with Arthur Sullivan to write Victorian-era comic operas, including *H.M.S. Pinafore*, *The Pirates of Penzance*, and *The Mikado*. Before Gilbert met Sullivan, he was an English barrister with a less than stellar legal career. In his first trial, Gilbert defended a woman accused of stealing purses, scarves, and other items. The police officer who arrested the woman described how he discovered a stolen purse in the defendant's pocket. Mustering up his courage, Gilbert cross-examined the police officer in an effort to show that the defendant was on her way to a prayer meeting and that she had a bible in her pocket. Hoping to elicit information about the bible, Gilbert asked the officer, "Did you find anything else in her pocket?" To which the officer replied, "Yes," he found other stolen purses as well as stolen scarves! Not surprisingly, the woman was convicted. Apparently, she had some choice words for her attorney as she was led off to jail. The obvious moral of the story is: Don't ask a question unless you know the answer.

Avoid Asking Witnesses "Why" or "How" Questions

Recall that one of the goals of cross-examination is controlling the witness. Control is exerted through asking leading questions and limiting the witness's ability to clarify. The moment a cross-examiner asks a witness "why" or "how" something happened, the examiner relinquishes control to the witness. The witness is in the driver's seat.

Master the Facts

The skilled cross-examiner masters the facts of the case and shapes his or her questions to emphasize the facts favoring the cross-examiner's client. To avoid being manipulated, a witness must know the facts as well as, or better than, the cross-examiner. A witness who fumbles the facts loses some credibility.

Abraham Lincoln, Cross-Examiner

Before he became president, Abraham Lincoln was an accomplished trial lawyer. In 1857, a young man named Duff Armstrong was involved in a fight that resulted in a man's death. Armstrong was charged with murder, and Armstrong's mother hired Lincoln to defend her son. The prosecution offered the testimony of Charles Allen, who swore that he saw Armstrong hit the victim on the head. Although the fight occurred near midnight, and Allen was 150 feet away, he testified that he could see clearly because the moon was shining directly overhead. On his cross-examination, Lincoln asked several times how it was that Allen could see the fight. Allen was all too happy to remind Lincoln that the moon shone brightly overhead. Then, Lincoln confronted Allen with a page from an 1857 almanac that stated that, at the time of the fight, the moon was low in the sky. Allen was caught in a lie. His testimony crumbled, and Armstrong was acquitted.

Think of Lincoln's technique as setting a trap for the unwary witness. The lawyer lures the witness into the trap with seemingly innocuous questions that lead the witness in a particular direction. Once the attorney commits the witness to a position, the lawyer—in this case, Honest Abe—confronts the witness with the contradictory evidence.

OBJECTIONS AT TRIAL

When an attorney attempts to admit testimony or evidence that the opposing attorney believes is inadmissible, the opposing attorney objects, "Your honor, I object. The question calls for inadmissible hearsay." Failure by the opposing attorney to promptly object forfeits any argument that the judge should exclude the evidence. The most common objections are described below.

Leading Questions

As mentioned previously, the attorney conducting a direct examination is not supposed to ask leading questions, especially about critical issues. His or her opponent can object to leading questions in this phrase—"Objection, your honor, leading the witness." However, judges usually allow leading questions on direct examination of children and adults who experience difficulty in testifying.

Calls for a Narrative

As I pointed out earlier, an attorney conducting a direct examination is supposed to draw out the witness's testimony bit by bit, with nonleading questions. It is objectionable to ask, "Tell the jury about the accident," or "Tell us what happened."

Irrelevant Evidence

Irrelevant evidence is inadmissible, and questions about irrelevant matters are objectionable. This objection is not very common because attorneys generally don't offer evidence that has nothing to do with the case.

Asked and Answered

On direct examination, an attorney is not supposed to ask the same question repeatedly. If an attorney repeats a question that the witness has already answered, the opposing counsel can say, "Your honor, I object, asked and answered." A cross-examiner is given more leeway to repeat questions.

Assumes Facts Not in Evidence

The purpose of questioning witnesses is to elicit information. It is objectionable for an attorney to ask a question that assumes the truth of facts when there is no evidence in the court record of those facts. The classic example is, "When did you stop beating your wife?" when no evidence of beatings has been received. The proper sequence of questions would be:

Q: Did you ever beat your wife?

A: Yes.

Q: Did you stop beating her?

A: Yes.

Q: When did you stop beating your wife?

Argumentative Question

An argumentative question is not really a question; it is a statement by an attorney in the form of a question. As the California Supreme Court stated in *People v. Chatman* (2006), "An argumentative question is a speech to the jury masquerading as a question. The questioner is not seeking to elicit relevant testimony. Often it is apparent that the questioner does not even expect an answer. The question may, indeed, be unanswerable" (p. 384).

Compound Question

A compound question asks more than one question, and is objectionable. An example is "Did you go to the store and did you go to the movie theater?" Upon objection, the judge may instruct the attorney to reword a compound question into separate questions.

Unresponsive Answer

A witness is supposed to answer the question asked by an attorney, and not venture into new topics. If the witness's answer is not responsive to the question, an objection can be lodged. Either attorney can object that a witness's answers are unresponsive.

Evidence Objections

An attorney may object on a broad range of evidence issues. Some examples include: "Objection, hearsay," "Objection, failure to authenticate," "Objection, violates the best-evidence rule," "Objection, improper impeachment," "Objection, violates the rule against character evidence."

"What Do I Do When an Attorney Objects?"

If an attorney objects during your testimony, stop talking and let the judge rule on the objection. It is not your responsibility to know whether an objection is proper. If the lawyers argue about the objection, you can take a moment to relax. When the judge rules on the objection, the questioning resumes.

CONCLUSION

In your clinical career, you may never testify in court, or the courtroom may become a familiar place. In any event, it is important for clinicians to understand what transpires in court, how testimony unfolds, and something of the techniques and strategies employed by attorneys. If you are called to testify, the material in this chapter, I hope, should help you through the process.

9

Expert Testimony

Testimony by expert witnesses is often crucial in many civil and criminal trials. Most readers of this book have the knowledge and experience to provide expert testimony. The goal of this chapter is to equip you with the information you need to be an effective expert witness.

Before delving into a discussion of expert testimony, it is important to understand the difference between expert witnesses and lay witnesses. A lay witness is someone who saw or heard something that is relevant to a case, and who testifies in court about what he or she knows. An expert witness is a person who has special knowledge, skills, education, or training that helps jurors to understand technical, clinical, or scientific issues that the jurors are not equipped to comprehend. For example, a jury needs assistance from an expert to understand the autopsy details of a dead baby, the significance of DNA evidence, the impact of auditory hallucinations on a person's thinking, a defendant's claim of insanity when she pulled a trigger, the requirements for psychiatric hospitalization, and so on.

When professionals testify, they do not always do so as experts. In some cases, a professional testifies as a lay witness. For example, suppose a child discloses sexual abuse to a nurse. The nurse might testify as a lay witness to repeat the child's disclosure. In another case, the nurse might testify as an expert. In some cases, professionals provide lay *and* expert testimony.

The law governing expert testimony is found in the rules of evidence. Most readers are not terribly interested in evidence rules. Yet, the rules provide a good framework to discuss expert testimony, and, for that reason, the first part of the chapter is organized around evidence rules.

Before discussing the rules, it's important to understand that expert testimony typically takes one of three forms: (1) an opinion, (2) an answer to a hypothetical question, or (3) a lecture to help the jury understand a clinical or technical issue. These forms of expert testimony are discussed below, following a description of opinion testimony from lay witnesses.

OPINION TESTIMONY FROM LAY WITNESSES

Occasionally, one hears the statement "Lay witnesses are not allowed to give opinions." That is not true; lay witnesses offer opinions all the time. The important point to bear in mind is that lay witnesses should, as much as possible, limit their testimony to factual information that is within their personal knowledge. The more specific, factual, and detailed a lay witness's testimony, the better. If some of a lay witness's testimony takes the form of opinion, that is okay. The Federal Rule of Evidence (FRE) 701 sets the parameters for opinion testimony from lay witnesses. The Rule provides:

> If a witness is not testifying as an expert, testimony in the form of an opinion is limited to one that is: (a) rationally based on the witness's perception; (b) helpful to clearly understanding the witness's testimony or to determining a fact in issue; and (c) not based on scientific, technical, or other specialized knowledge within the scope of Rule 702. [Rule 702 deals with expert testimony.]

Judges allow opinions from lay witnesses on a broad range of subjects. For example, a lay witness could testify that a person appeared ill, in pain, injured, drunk, or sober. Examples of opinion testimony from lay witnesses are instructive. The Florida Court of Appeal's decision in *Bush v. State* (2002), involved Munchausen syndrome by proxy, inflicted by a mother. When the child was finally rescued, the child's health improved dramatically. The court ruled that it was proper for a lay witness to describe the child's improved health following her rescue. The court noted, "A lay witness may describe a person's physical appearance using opinions that do not require special skill, so long as the opinions are based upon observations of the witness. . . . Here, the lay witness did not testify that Jennifer seemed 'healthier,' which would have been improper because [the lay witness] did not know Jennifer during her care with [the mother]" (pp. 119–120). If the lay witness *had* known Jennifer before *and* after her rescue, the witness could have testified that Jennifer appeared healthier.

In *Hicks v. State* (2009), the defendant had an argument with his 72-year-old mother, grabbed an ironing board, and hit her with it multiple times. The defendant claimed he acted in self-defense when his mother came at him with a knife. An experienced police officer investigated the case and testified as a lay witness regarding the insignificant nature of wounds on the defendant. The defense objected that expert testimony was needed to describe the defendant's injuries. Disagreeing, the Mississippi Court of Appeals ruled that it was proper for the officer to describe the defendant's injuries.

A lay witness may describe a person's state of mind, for example, happy, sad, depressed, or frightened. In *People v. Acosta* (2014), for example, the defendant was caught in the act of inappropriate conduct with a child. The child's father angrily confronted the defendant. It was proper for the father to testify that the defendant was "very guilty-looking."

May a lay witness offer an opinion that a person seemed insane or out of touch with reality? Clearly, a lay witness can describe a person's behavior and testify to statements the person made. In *People v. Clark* (1988), the defendant walked into a church, drew a gun, and robbed parishioners. At Clark's robbery trial, it was proper for parishioners to describe the defendant's behavior during the robbery. The Michigan Court of Appeals wrote, "The testimony of lay witnesses may be competent evidence of a defendant's mental illness" (p. 178).

A lay witness can also attest that a person appeared to be mentally ill, provided the lay witness has known the person a substantial time. Thus, in *Ex Parte Milteer* (1990), the Alabama Supreme Court wrote, "Generally, the testimony of a lay witness on the issue of sanity is competent and admissible where the lay witness has known the defendant for a long period of time" (p. 1000). In *Milteer,* the prosecutor offered lay testimony from two people who had brief contact with the defendant. The witnesses stated that the defendant appeared sane. Allowing these opinions was an error because the witnesses did not know defendant well enough to form such an opinion.

To summarize, many aspects of mental illness require expert testimony. Basic observations about a person's conduct, however, often fall within the competence of lay witnesses.

There are limits on opinion testimony from lay witnesses. Obviously, a lay witness must not offer expert testimony. In *State v. Duran*

(2014), for example, a trial judge committed reversible error by allowing a forensic interviewer who testified *as a lay witness* to opine, "A majority of children she interviewed delayed in disclosing sexual abuse" (p. 208). Testimony on how children disclose abuse, and, in particular, delayed disclosure, is the bailiwick of experts, not lay witnesses. An experienced forensic interviewer might qualify as an expert on disclosure, but the interviewer in *Duran* testified as a lay witness, not an expert.

WHO MAY PROVIDE EXPERT TESTIMONY?

In litigation involving interpersonal violence, expert testimony is provided by psychiatrists, physicians, nurses, psychologists, social workers, laboratory technicians, and other professionals. Rule 702 of the FRE describes who qualifies to provide expert testimony:

> A witness who is qualified as an expert by knowledge, skill, experience, training, or education may testify in the form of an opinion or otherwise if: (a) the expert's scientific, technical, or other specialized knowledge will help the trier of fact to understand the evidence or to determine a fact in issue; (b) the testimony is based on sufficient facts or data; (c) the testimony is the product of reliable principles and methods; and (d) the expert has reliably applied the principles and methods to the facts of the case.

To qualify as an expert, a professional must possess sufficient "knowledge, skill, experience, training, or education." A professional need not be the foremost authority on a subject to provide expert testimony. Nor must a professional understand every nuance of a subject. It is not necessary for the expert witness to be a published author; indeed, most expert witnesses do not have any published works.

Before a professional may testify as an expert, the judge must be satisfied that the professional is qualified. The normal procedure is for the attorney offering the professional's testimony to first put the professional on the witness stand and ask questions about his or her education, training, and experience. The questioning normally takes place in open court, with the jury present. The opposing attorney has the right to question the witness in an effort to persuade the judge that the person is not an expert, although in most cases, there is no challenge to the expert's qualifications.

Expert testimony is allowed when an expert can help the jury comprehend technical, clinical, or scientific issues. The subject of an expert's testimony does not have to be completely beyond the ken of the jury. Often, an expert adds depth and clarity to subjects that are somewhat familiar to jurors. On the other hand, if the jury is adequately equipped to decide an issue without assistance, expert testimony is inadmissible. In *State v. Willis* (2004), for example, the Washington Supreme Court ruled that jurors do not need expert testimony to help them understand that young children are suggestible.

BASES FOR EXPERT TESTIMONY

Expert witnesses base their testimony on a broad range of facts and data. In the medical and mental health fields, experts rely on many sources of information, including interviews of the individual, discussions with others, consultation with other experts, psychological and medical tests, research in the literature, and written documentation, including hospital records and police reports. The rules of evidence permit experts to formulate court testimony based on the types of facts and data experts rely on in their normal, day-to-day clinical work outside the courtroom. FRE 703 states:

> An expert may base an opinion on facts or data in the case that the expert has been made aware of or personally observed. If experts in the particular field would reasonably rely on those kinds of facts or data in forming an opinion on the subject, they need not be admissible for the opinion to be admitted. But if the facts or data would otherwise be inadmissible, the proponent of the opinion may disclose them to the jury only if their probative value in helping the jury evaluate the opinion substantially outweighs their prejudicial effect.

Rule 703 specifies that experts may base their opinions on information that is *not* admissible in evidence, so long as other professionals in the expert's field rely on such information. In the medical and mental health arenas, experts routinely rely on hearsay that might not be admissible in court. Written hearsay includes clinical records, test results, and documents prepared by the police department and social services agencies. Verbal hearsay includes the patient's "history." A mental health or medical professional acts properly when the professional bases expert testimony on such hearsay.

Although an expert's opinion may be based on inadmissible evidence, including inadmissible hearsay, Rule 703 notes, "But if the facts or data would otherwise be inadmissible, the proponent of the opinion may disclose them to the jury only if their probative value in helping the jury evaluate the opinion substantially outweighs their prejudicial effect." If an attorney objects to an expert disclosing inadmissible evidence that the expert considered in preparing to testify, the judge balances the importance of the inadmissible evidence to a proper understanding of the expert's testimony, against the possibility that the jury will place too much emphasis on the inadmissible evidence. Depending on what the judge views as more important, he or she may prohibit the expert from disclosing to the jury some or all of the inadmissible evidence that supports the expert's testimony. The expert testimony is still admissible; only the inadmissible evidence that supports the testimony is kept from the jury. On the other hand, the judge may conclude that the jury needs to hear the inadmissible evidence in order to gain a full understanding of the expert's opinion.

OPINIONS ON ULTIMATE ISSUES

In every case, there is a legal distinction between ultimate facts and ultimate legal issues. The ultimate facts are the facts that one side must prove to win its case. Suppose, for example, that Sue broke into a house in order to steal. Sue is charged with burglary, which is the breaking and entering of the dwelling house of another at night with the intent to commit a felony therein. The ultimate facts are: (1) breaking, (2) entering, (3) the dwelling house of another, (4) at night, and (5) with the intent to commit a felony inside the dwelling. In a burglary case, lay witnesses could testify to the ultimate facts required for conviction.

In a rape prosecution, the crime is defined as sexual intercourse accomplished by force and against the will of the victim. Penetration is an element of the crime and is an ultimate fact that can be attested to by either the victim and/or an expert witness.

The ultimate legal issue in both the burglary and rape cases is whether the defendant is guilty or innocent. Lay or expert witnesses may testify to ultimate facts, but *not* to ultimate legal issues such as guilt or innocence. Thus, an expert should not venture an opinion on whether the defendant in a criminal case is guilty or innocent. Nor should an expert express an opinion on *who* committed a crime. Determining guilt, innocence, and the identity of the person who committed a crime is a matter for the jury to decide, not experts.

FRE 704 deals with testimony on ultimate legal issues. The Rule states:

(a) An opinion is not objectionable just because it embraces an ultimate issue.
(b) In a criminal case, an expert must not state an opinion about whether the defendant did or did not have a mental state or condition that constitutes an element of the crime charged or of a defense. Those matters are for the trier of fact alone.

In other words, Rule 704(a) allows witnesses—lay and expert—to testify regarding ultimate facts. Rule 704(b) has a direct bearing on expert testimony from mental health professionals, especially in cases involving the insanity defense, and was discussed in Chapter 2.

THE REASONABLE CERTAINTY STANDARD FOR EXPERT TESTIMONY

When eliciting an expert's opinion, attorneys commonly ask, "Doctor, do you have an opinion, based on a reasonable degree of certainty, about whether Ms. Jones was mentally ill?" In *People v. Gilmore* (1995), for example, an expert testified, "to a reasonable degree of medical and psychiatric certainty that defendant was mentally ill and legally insane at the time of the alleged offense" (p. 60). The expert testimony in *Gilmore* illustrates the so-called "reasonable certainty" standard: An expert must be reasonably certain that the opinion is correct (see *Cooper v. Takeda Pharmaceutical America, Inc.*, 2015).

The rules of evidence do not *require* experts to testify based on a standard of reasonable certainty. Yet, attorneys so often ask questions in which the language of reasonable certainty is used that an understanding of the meaning of the term is helpful. Unfortunately, no one knows the meaning of reasonable certainty. Jeff Lewin (1998) explored the development of "reasonable certainty," and concluded: "Although judges expect, and sometimes insist, that expert opinions be expressed with 'reasonable medical certainty,' and although attorneys ritualistically intone the phrase, no one knows what it means!" (p. 380).

Expert witnesses do not have to be completely certain that their opinion is correct. The Iowa Supreme Court observed in *State v. Tyler* (2015), "There is no requirement that the expert be able to express an opinion with absolute certainty" (p. 153). At the same time, experts cannot speculate or guess. The California Court of Appeal wrote in *Pedeferri v. Seidner Enterprises* (2013), "Where an expert bases his conclusion upon assumptions which are not supported by the record, . . . his conclusion has no evidentiary value and should be excluded" (p. 375).

In a similar vein, the California Court of Appeal wrote in *Cooper v. Takeda Pharmaceuticals America, Inc.* (2015), "Courts are to ensure that opinions are not speculative, based on unconventional matters or grounded in unsupported reasoning" (p. 83). Thus, experts may not guess, but, at the same time, they do not have to be 100% certain they are right. Reasonable certainty lies somewhere between guesswork and certainty—closer to the latter.

Not only does the standard of reasonable certainty have no clear meaning, the phrase can cause confusion because it is a legal term, not a term employed in medicine or mental health. Glenn Bradford (2001) comments, "Many lawyers and judges believe the phrase is a medical term of art. Physician commentators, however, have described the phrase as a legal term of art" (p. 137). Norman Poythress (1982) wrote, "I've always had a pretty healthy skepticism about phrases like 'reasonable medical certainty.' . . . Left undefined, there is a risk that lay jurors will think that the opinions are somehow an outgrowth of quasi-objective, scientific investigation" (p. 41). Gary Melton and his colleagues (2007) observe, "There is a danger that, because of the law's preference for certainty, experts will over-reify their observations and reach beyond legitimate interpretations of the data" (p. 11).

In the final analysis, it would probably be wise to jettison the reasonable certainty standard. Some courts have (see *State v. DeLeon,* 2014). For now, however, many attorneys continue asking, "Do you have an opinion, based on a reasonable degree of certainty, whether ______________________?"

Because reasonable certainty has no clear meaning, a more useful way to think about the expert testimony you may give in court is to ask: In formulating my opinion, did I consider all the relevant facts? Do I have an adequate understanding of pertinent clinical and scientific principles? Did I use methods of assessment that are appropriate, reliable, and valid? Are my inferences, assumptions, and conclusions reasonable and defensible? If you can answer these questions to your satisfaction, you can feel confident in your testimony, or, reasonably certain, if you like.

The concept of reasonable certainty should not be confused with the burden of proof. The burden of proof is the level of certainty by which a jury must be persuaded by the evidence that is presented by the party with the burden of proof. The law that applies to a case determines which side has the burden of proof. Three burdens of proof are used (1) beyond a reasonable doubt, (2) preponderance of the evidence, and (c) clear and convincing evidence.

The "beyond a reasonable doubt" standard is used in criminal cases and is the most difficult burden to meet. A prosecutor has the burden of proof to prove the defendant guilty beyond a reasonable doubt. Most civil litigation uses the less demanding "preponderance of the evidence" standard. Under this standard, the party that shoulders the burden of proof need only convince the jury that it is more likely than not that the party should win. The third burden of proof, the "clear and convincing evidence" standard, is reserved for a small number of civil cases in which the stakes are particularly high, including termination of parental rights and involuntary psychiatric hospitalization. In civil commitment proceedings, the government must convince the judge by clear and convincing evidence that the patient is mentally ill and a danger to himself or others.

Burdens of proof are legal concepts that are not reducible to simple percentages. Yet, a measure of insight is afforded by comparing beyond a reasonable doubt to 95% certainty, preponderance of evidence to 51% certainty, and clear and convincing evidence to 75% certainty.

As just discussed, in many courts, experts must be reasonably certain that their opinions are correct. It is important to understand that the certainty needed for expert testimony does *not* vary with the type of litigation. Experts do not have to be more certain in criminal cases, in which the burden of proof is highest, than in civil cases. Regardless of the type of litigation—criminal or civil—experts should ensure the correctness of opinions.

Occasionally, attorneys ask experts whether they are certain of their opinion beyond a reasonable doubt or by a preponderance of the evidence. An accurate response to such a question is, "Counsel, when I reach an opinion, I do not employ the legal concept of burden of proof. Burdens of proof are legal constructs and are not used in psychology. Instead, I use clinical and scientific principles to reach my opinion. In reaching my opinion, I took all the steps I could to ensure that my opinion is correct. I am reasonably certain of my opinion, and, by reasonably certain, I mean I am confident my opinion is correct."

Before we leave the topic of reasonable certainty, take a moment to enjoy a case in which an expert witness clearly got the better of an attorney. In *Gagon v. Lemoyne Sleeper Co.* (2009), the following exchange occurred between a lawyer and a doctor:

Q: Doctor, what's your definition of "reasonable certainty," as you use it?

A: I don't use it.

Q: You don't use it?

A: That's a legal term.

Q: But you don't . . . You don't know what it means in the legal context?

A: No, but if you tell me what it means, I'll tell you if I think that that's what I think.

SCIENTIFIC EVIDENCE

When expert testimony is based on scientific or technical principles—especially principles that are unproven or novel—the attorney opposing the expert may ask the judge to hold a hearing to determine whether the scientific or technological knowledge underlying the proposed expert testimony is valid and reliable. Such hearings are called *Frye* or *Daubert* hearings, after two famous cases, *Frye v. United States* (1923) and *Daubert v. Merrell Dow Pharmaceuticals, Inc.* (1993).

The *Frye* case, decided in 1923 by the Court of Appeals for the District of Columbia, dealt with an early version of the polygraph. The court ruled that expert testimony based on novel scientific principles cannot be admitted in evidence until the principles are generally accepted as reliable by the scientific community, that is, until the principles pass the admittedly fuzzy line that separates novelty from general acceptance. This test for the reliability of scientific evidence is called the general acceptance test or, simply, *Frye*.

During a *Frye* hearing, expert testimony is offered concerning the validity and reliability (i.e., general acceptance) of the disputed scientific principle. If the judge finds that the principle is generally accepted, the expert testimony is allowed. However, if the judge finds that the principle underlying the expert testimony is not generally accepted as reliable or valid, the judge excludes the testimony.

For most of the 20th century, *Frye* was the dominant test for evaluating novel scientific evidence. Yet, over the years, *Frye* has been criticized. The basic criticism was that *Frye*'s requirement of general acceptance excludes expert testimony based on scientific or technological concepts that have not achieved general acceptance, but that are nevertheless sufficiently reliable for use in court. Criticism of *Frye* culminated in the U.S. Supreme Court's 1993 decision in *Daubert v. Merrell Dow Pharmaceuticals, Inc.*, in which the Court rejected *Frye* and replaced it with a broadened test for scientific evidence.

As is true with *Frye,* under *Daubert,* an attorney can object that expert testimony is based on unreliable scientific principles or techniques, and he or she can request a hearing—called a *Daubert* hearing. Unlike *Frye,* in which the only issue was general acceptance, a judge conducting a *Daubert* hearing considers *all* the evidence shedding light on reliability and validity. The judge considers whether the scientific principles underlying the proposed expert testimony have been subjected to testing by the scientific method. Has the principle been scrutinized by peer review and publication? Is there an established error rate when the principle or technique is used? Are there standards governing use of the principle? Finally, borrowing from *Frye,* is the principle generally accepted as reliable in the scientific community? A scientific principle or technique that has yet to achieve general acceptance may nevertheless be sufficiently reliable/valid under *Daubert* to gain admission in court.

The *Daubert* decision concerned expert testimony based on science. Following *Daubert,* there was uncertainty about whether *Daubert* applied to expert testimony that combines scientific knowledge and professional judgment and interpretation. Thus, does *Daubert* apply to much of the expert testimony provided by physicians and mental health professionals? In 1999, the Supreme Court answered in the affirmative in *Kumho Tire Company, Ltd. v. Carmichael* (1999). The Court ruled, "*Daubert*'s general holding . . . applies not only to testimony based on scientific knowledge, but also to testimony based on technical and other specialized knowledge" (p. 141).

The Supreme Court's rulings in *Daubert* and *Kuhmo* are binding only on the federal courts, and do not compel the states to abandon *Frye.* As of 2017, however, most states had jettisoned *Frye* in favor of *Daubert.* States retaining *Frye* include California, Illinois, New Mexico, and Washington.

In the vast majority of cases involving expert testimony, there is no *Frye* or *Daubert* hearing. A qualified expert testifies on the witness stand, is cross-examined, and that is the end of it. *Frye* or *Daubert* hearings arise only in exceptional cases.

A few states (e.g., Arizona, California) have a rule that *Frye/Daubert* does not apply to expert testimony in the form of opinion. In *Logerquist v. McVey* (2000), for example, the Arizona Supreme Court wrote, "To put it simply, *Frye* is inapplicable when a qualified witness offers relevant testimony or conclusions based on experience and observation about human behavior for the purpose of explaining that behavior" (p. 123).

The premise supporting this rule is that jurors are not likely to be misled or overimpressed by opinion testimony. Jurors, so the theory goes, can evaluate the worth of expert opinion, especially with the aid of cross-examination. By contrast, jurors may be awestruck or blindsided by machines, devices, and techniques that profess to be based on science, and that purport to yield definitive answers to complex questions. Jurors and cross-examining lawyers are not well equipped to peer into "little black scientific boxes" to determine whether they yield valid and reliable data. Out of concern that jurors will be too impressed by questionable science, courts in these states limit *Frye/Daubert* to expert testimony based on novel scientific principles, machines, devices, and techniques.

The problem with the approach employed in Arizona and California is that opinion testimony can be just as misleading, inaccurate, obtuse, invalid, and unreliable, and just as likely to blindside a jury, as anything emerging from the scientific version of a little black box. Moreover, there is little reason to believe cross-examining attorneys are better at dissecting opinion testimony than testimony based on scientific devices or techniques. If the primary concern is protecting juries from "junk science," the best approach is to apply *Frye/Daubert* to any expert testimony of dubious validity or reliability, whether in the form of opinion or a little black box.

PREPARATION IS THE KEY

Preparation is the key to effective expert testimony. You cannot be too well prepared. It is appropriate and ethical to meet with the attorney who asks you to testify. Go over your testimony and discuss questions and answers. Often, experts help lawyers refine questions or add angles the attorney did not think of.

Should you communicate with the opposing attorney? This is a matter of judgment and varies from case to case and expert to expert. You should know, however, that if you refuse to communicate with an attorney, don't be surprised if, during cross-examination, the attorney asks, "Isn't it true, Dr. X, that I called your office to discuss this case with you, and you refused to talk to me?" With this in mind, you may want to discuss with the attorney who asks you to testify about the wisdom of talking to opposing counsel.

You probably have a résumé or curriculum vitae (CV). If you testify frequently, it is a good idea to edit your CV into a one-page court résumé summarizing your qualifications to testify as an expert.

EXPERTS ARE EDUCATORS, NOT ADVOCATES

Attorneys advocate. Experts don't, or at least, shouldn't. Your job is not to win the case, but to help the jury or judge understand clinical, scientific, or technical issues. Avoid giving the impression you are an advocate for one side. The American Psychological Association's (2013) "Specialty Guidelines for Forensic Psychology" state, "When offering expert opinion to be relied upon by a decision maker, . . . forensic practitioners strive for accuracy, impartiality, fairness, and independence. . . . [F]orensic practitioners strive to be unbiased and impartial. . . . This guideline does not preclude forceful presentation of the data and reasoning, upon which a conclusion or professional product is based" (Guideline 1.02, pp. 8–9).

DIRECT EXAMINATION OF EXPERT WITNESSES

Once the judge approves a professional as an expert witness, testimony begins with direct examination. As mentioned earlier, an expert's direct testimony typically takes one or more of the following forms: an opinion, an answer to a hypothetical question, or a lecture providing technical or clinical information to the jury.

Opinion is the most common form of expert testimony. For example, an expert might claim that a child experienced abusive head trauma. An expert might testify that an interviewer asked too many suggestive questions while questioning a child. An expert might describe the psychological examination of a sex offender, and give an opinion on the risk the offender will recidivate. An expert might say, "In my opinion, the victim was vaginally penetrated."

Less often than an expert is asked for an opinion, he or she is asked a hypothetical question. The attorney describes a hypothetical set of facts that parallel the facts of the case on trial. Then, the expert is asked for an opinion about the hypothetical facts. The jury applies the expert's opinion about the *hypothetical* facts to the *actual* facts of the case.

Many attorneys avoid hypothetical questions. The hypothetical question can seem stilted and artificial, leaving the jury to wonder, "Why is the lawyer asking about a hypothetical case? Why doesn't the lawyer ask about *this* case?" Because the rules of evidence allow experts to opine about the facts of the case on trial, many attorneys prefer the direct approach over the circuitous route of a hypothetical question.

Experts are more likely to encounter hypothetical questions during cross-examination than in direct examination. The cross-examiner may try to weaken the expert's opinion by asking about a hypothetical set of facts that differs from the facts described by the expert. The cross-examiner then asks, "If the hypothetical facts I have suggested turn out to be true, would that change your opinion?" David Chadwick (1990) observed that it is "common to encounter hypothetical questions based on hypotheses that are extremely unlikely, and the witness may need to point out the unlikelihood" (p. 967). When a cross-examiner asks a far-fetched hypothetical question, the answer might be, "If the facts were as you suggest, my opinion could change, yes. Of course, the facts you suggest were not the facts I observed."

In some cases, the expert limits testimony to a lecture intended to give the jury technical, clinical, or scientific information that it needs to evaluate the evidence in the case. With this form of expert testimony, the expert does not render an opinion. The expert's testimony is limited to educating the jury. This form of testimony is used, for example, in some child sexual abuse cases, when the defense attorney argues that because a child delayed reporting, made inconsistent statements, or recanted, the child cannot be believed. When the defense attacks a child's credibility in this way, judges often allow an expert to help the jury understand that it is not uncommon for sexually abused children to delay reporting, provide partial or piecemeal disclosures, and recant. Equipped with this information, the jury is in a better position to evaluate the child's credibility.

CROSS-EXAMINATION OF EXPERT WITNESSES

The prospect of cross-examination may send shivers down your spine, especially if you are new to testifying. This section covers what a cross-examination looks like in actual trials. Some familiarity with the process can be helpful in reducing stress.

When you testify as an expert, the following guidelines may be useful.

• ***Don't lose your cool.*** The experienced expert refuses to be cajoled, dragged, or tricked into verbal sparring with the cross-examiner. The professional is at all times just that—professional. In light of the aggression of some cross-examiners—aggression that is sometimes laced with error, insinuation, sarcasm, and even ad hominem attacks—it can be difficult to maintain a calm, professional demeanor. Yet, remember, the jury is looking to you for objective guidance and wisdom. The jury wants a strong expert, but not someone who takes the gloves off and fights it out with the cross-examiner. This does not mean that the expert cannot employ strong responses during cross-examination. The expert should express confidence when challenged and should not vacillate or equivocate in the face of attack. On the other hand, the expert should concede weak points and acknowledge conflicting evidence. In short, be reasonable.

• ***Ask for clarification.*** Don't answer a question unless you fully understand it. When in doubt, ask the attorney for clarification. Such a request does not show weakness. After all, if you don't understand a question, it is very likely the jury doesn't either. When a cross-examiner's question is two or three questions combined into one, the other attorney may object that the question is "compound." Absent objection, it is proper to ask the cross-examiner which question the attorney would like answered first.

• ***The cross-examiner tries to undermine your facts, inferences, or conclusions.*** One of the most effective cross-examination techniques with experts is to get the witness to agree to the facts, inferences, and conclusions that support her or his opinion, and then dispute one or more of those facts, inferences, or conclusions. Consider a case in which a psychologist testifies that a sex offender is likely to abuse other children. The cross-examiner begins by committing the expert to the facts and assumptions underlying the opinion. The attorney says, "So, doctor, your opinion is based exclusively on your interview with the subject, your review of the file, and the results of psychological tests, is that correct? And there is nothing else you relied on to form your opinion. Is that correct?" The cross-examiner commits the expert to a specific set of facts and assumptions so that when the attorney disputes those facts or assumptions, the expert's opinion cannot be justified on some other basis.

Once the cross-examiner pins down the basis of the expert's opinion, the examiner attacks the opinion by disputing one or more of the facts, inferences, or conclusions that support it. The attorney might ask a hypothetical question— whether the expert's opinion would change if certain facts were different. The attorney might ask the expert whether other experts could come to different conclusions based on the same facts.

Or rather than attack the expert's facts, inferences, and conclusions during a cross-examination, the attorney may limit cross-examination to pinning the expert down to a limited set of facts, inferences, and conclusions, and then, when the expert has left the witness stand, offer another expert to critique the expert's testimony.

- ***What you said before could come back to haunt you.*** If you testify in a case in January, and are called to testify in a different case in July, an attorney in the July case may have checked your January testimony. In July, if you say something that is inconsistent with your January testimony, be prepared to be confronted with the inconsistency. The California Supreme Court noted in *People v. DeHoyos* (2013), "An expert's testimony in prior cases involving similar issues is a legitimate subject of cross-examination" (p. 123).
- ***"Are you being paid for your testimony?"*** The cross-examiner who asks this question is trying to give the jury the impression you are a hired gun; you will say whatever the person who pays your bill wants you to say. It is proper to be compensated for your time. An answer to the "are you being paid" question is, "I am paid for my time, not my opinion. My opinion is not for sale."

It is not possible within the scope of this book to showcase cross-examinations that apply to clinicians in all mental health, medical, and social work fields. To illustrate what happens during a typical cross-examination, I have created a scenario involving a forensic interviewer, who is a social worker. The techniques and principles of cross-examination used on the interviewer are equally applicable to other professionals.

CASE STUDY: SAMANTHA

Eight-year-old Samantha disclosed sexual abuse to her best friend. Samantha asked her friend not to tell anyone, but the friend, as often happens, told her mother, who, in turn, told Samantha's mom, who called the police. The alleged perpetrator is Samantha's grandfather, who lived in Samantha's home until the abuse was disclosed. The responding police officer talked to Samantha and her mother. The officer had little experience in talking to children and asked Samantha some very leading questions. Samantha did not tell the officer anything. After the officer left, Samantha told her mother, "I don't want to tell the policeman because it's secret." The same day, Samantha was taken to her pediatrician, who also asked some leading questions. In response to the doctor's questions, Samantha said, "Grandpa puts his finger in my tee-tee sometimes, but he stops when I say it hurts." Four days after the initial disclosure, Samantha was interviewed at a child advocacy center (CAC). The interview was video recorded, and was observed by a detective and a CPS social worker. The interviewer, Linda Carter, is a social worker trained in the National Institute of Child Health and Human Development (NICHD) Structured Interview Protocol and in Thomas Lyon's 10-step adaptation of the NICHD protocol. Lyon's 10 steps are set forth next:

1. **Don't Know** instruction.

   "If I ask you a question and you don't know the answer, then just say, 'I don't know.' "
   "So if I ask you, 'What is my dog's name?' What do you say?"
   "OK, because you don't know."
   "But what if I ask you, 'Do you have a dog?' "
   "OK, because you do know."

2. **Don't Understand** instruction.

   "If I ask you a question and you don't know what I mean or what I'm saying, you can say, 'I don't know what you mean.' I will ask it a different way."
   "So if I ask you, 'What is your gender?' What do you say?"
   "That's because 'gender' is a hard word. So I would say, 'Are you a boy or a girl?' "

3. **You're Wrong** instruction.

   "Sometimes I make mistakes or say the wrong thing. When I do, you can tell me that I am wrong."
   "So if I say, 'You are 30 years old,' what do you say?"
   "OK, so how old are you?"

4. **Ignorant Interviewer** instruction.

   "I don't know what's happened to you."
   "I won't be able to tell you the answers to my questions."

5. **Promise to Tell the Truth.**

   "It's really important that you tell me the truth."
   "Do you promise that you will tell me the truth?"
   "Will you tell me any lies?"

6. **Practice Narratives.**

   a. **Like to do/don't like do.**

   "First, I'd like you to tell me about things you Like to do."

   Follow up with Tell Me More questions—for example, "You said you like to play soccer. Tell me more about soccer."

   "Now tell me about the things you Don't Like to do."

   Follow up with Tell Me More questions.

   b. **Last birthday.**

   "Now tell me about your last birthday. Tell me everything that happened."

   Follow Up with What Happened Next? questions—for example, "You said you played in the bouncy. What did you do next?"

7. **Allegation.**

   (If the child discloses abuse, go directly to Allegation Follow-Up. Determine in Advance which allegation questions you will ask.)

   a. **Tell me why I came to talk to you.**

   Or, "Tell me why you came to talk to me."

   "It's really important for me to know why I came to talk to you/you came to talk to me."

   b. **I heard you saw**—for example:

   "I heard you saw a policeman last week. Tell me what you talked about."

   c. **Someone's worried—**for example:

   "Is your mom worried that something may have happened to you? Tell me what she is worried about."

   d. **Someone bothered you—**for example:

   "I heard that someone might have bothered you. Tell me everything about that."

   e. **Something wasn't right**—for example:

   "I heard that someone may have done something to you that wasn't right. Tell me everything about that."

8. **Allegation Follow-Up.**

   "You said that [repeat allegation]. Tell me everything that happened." For example:

   "You said that Uncle Bill hurt your pee-pee. Tell me everything that happened."

9. **Follow up with *Tell Me More* and *What Happened Next* questions.**

   Avoid yes/no and forced-choice questions.

10. **Multiple Incidents.**

    "Did [repeat allegation] happen one time or more than one time?"
    "Tell me everything that happened the time you remember the most . . . ."
    "Tell me everything that happened the first time . . . ."
    "Tell me everything that happened the last time . . . ."
    "Was there another time . . . ?"

It was a busy day at the CAC. One of the interviewers called in sick that morning. The remaining interviewer had a waiting room full of children, and felt rushed. Normally, the interviewer painstakingly goes through Lyon's steps 1 through 6. On that day, however, with so much do to, the interviewer skipped steps 3 (You're Wrong instruction) and 4 (Ignorant Interviewer instruction). At step 7 (Allegation), the interview proceeded as follows:

THE INTERVIEW

Q: Tell me why you came to talk to me today.

A: To tell the truth.

Q: The truth about what?

A: About what happened.

Q: Remember, I don't know what happened to you, so I need for you to tell me what happened.

A: I don't want to get Grandpa in trouble. I don't want to talk about it.

Q: I know this can be hard. I talk to lots of kids, and sometimes they tell me things that are hard to tell. It is OK for you to tell me what happened to you.

A: Do I have to?

Q: It is up to you, Samantha, but, like I said, I talk to lots of kids about difficult matters. It is OK to talk here, and to tell the truth. Can you do that?

A: Yes.

Q: Good. What did your grandpa do to you?

A: He touched me in the wrong places.

Q: Tell me more about that.

A: He touched my tee-tee.

Q: Where is your tee-tee? Can you point to your tee-tee?

A: Here (points to her genitals).

Q: And did that happen one time or more than one time?

A: More than one time.

Q: Do you think it happened more than 10 times?

A: Maybe a hundred. I don't remember.

Q: When your grandpa touched your tee-tee, what did he touch you with?

A: His finger.

Q: Were your clothes off or on when he touched you with his finger?

A: On.

Q: Where were you when your grandpa touched your tee-tee?

A: In the family room, but sometimes in my room.

Q: Were you sitting on the couch with him when he touched you?

A: Mostly.

Q: When your grandpa touched your tee-tee with his finger, were his clothes off or on?

A: On.

Q: When your grandpa touched your tee-tee, did he touch you on top of your clothes, or did he touch your bare skin?

A: Sometimes my bare skin.

Q: Tell me how his finger touched your tee-tee.

A: He put his finger in his mouth, then he touched my tee-tee, and sometimes he put his finger in me, and it hurted, and I told him, "Stop, Grandpa, that hurts," and he stopped. And he said, "I'm sorry."

Q: Did grandpa tell you not to tell anyone what he did to you?

A: No, he said, "This is our secret. Can you keep our secret?"

Q: Can you remember, when was the last time he touched your tee-tee?

A: Before he moved.

Q: A long time before he moved, or just before he moved?

A: I can't remember.

Q: Tell me everything you can remember about the last time your grandpa touched your tee-tee.

A: He put his finger in his mouth, and we were watching Sponge Bob, and he put his finger in me and moved his finger in and out, but I pretend I didn't know, and I just watched Sponge Bob and Patrick and they were making something, but it didn't work.

Q: Did that happen in the family room?

A: Yes.

Q: Did you ever see your grandpa's penis?

A: Well, I can't talk about that.

Q: It sounds like you have a secret, is that right?

A: Yes, a special secret.

Q: Who told you to keep a secret?

A: Grandpa.

Q: What did your grandpa say about a secret?

A: He said I can't tell anybody about the snake in his pants, but I know it is really his penis and not a snake.

Q: When did you see his penis?

A: Well, that's what I'm not supposed to tell. That's the secret.

Q: I understand, but it is really important for me to understand what happened to you. So you need to tell the secret, even if it is hard to tell, OK?

A: Well, OK. Sometimes, Grandpa takes out his penis and shakes it up and down. And then he covers it up with a Kleenex and shakes it some more, and then he goes "Ahh Ahh Ahh." And he throws the Kleenex in the toilet, and then we go for ice cream. He always takes me for ice cream after he shakes his penis.

Q: Does anything come out of his penis?

A: No. He pees in the toilet.

Admitting the CAC Interview into Evidence

In Samantha's case, the prosecutor offers the video-recorded interview into evidence. Before a video interview can be used in court, the party offering the recording must persuade the judge that the recording is accurate and has not been edited. Lawyers call this laying a foundation, or authentication. In Samantha's case, the forensic interviewer will lay the necessary foundation. Foundation testimony is not expert testimony.

The following requirements constitute the foundation for the video interview:

1. The person operating the recording equipment was competent to do so.
2. The equipment was in working order and was properly operated.
3. The time, date, and place of recording.
4. The recording has not been edited or altered, unless any edits or alterations are explained.
5. Whether the entire interview is preserved on the recording, and if not, what parts are omitted.
6. The whereabouts of the recording are accounted for from the date of recording until the recording is offered in evidence.
7. The recording accurately reflects the interview.
8. The persons seen and heard on the recording are identified.

The prosecutor's foundation questioning of the forensic interviewer proceeds as follows:

Q: Please state your full name, spelling your last name for the record.

A: Linda Carter, C-A-R-T-E-R.

Q: Ms. Carter, where are you employed?

A: I work as a forensic interviewer at our local child advocacy center, or CAC.

Q: What is a forensic interviewer?

A: My master's degree is in social work. For the past 3 years, I have worked full time at our child advocacy center, interviewing children about possible abuse. The purpose of forensic interviewing is to allow children to describe what may have happened to them, and to do so in a safe environment where questioning is as nonsuggestive as possible.

Q: At the child advocacy center, please tell us the logistics of how interviews are conducted.

A: Sure. We have three interview rooms. Each room has child friendly furnishings. The rooms don't have toys because children can be distracted by toys, but the furniture is child sized. There is a one-way glass in each interview room so that other professionals can watch the interviewing. Each interview room has a highly sensitive microphone built into the wall to pick up what is said in the room. Each room also has video-recording equipment. The video equipment is hidden, although every child is told that the interview is being recorded.

Q: Are you familiar with the equipment used to record interviews?

A: Yes.

Q: Are you trained to use the equipment?

A: Yes.

Q: Please describe your training and experience with the equipment.

A: Sure. I received training on the proper use and maintenance of the video-recording equipment from a technician employed by the company that installed the equipment. It is my responsibility before each interview to check the equipment to make sure that it is working properly. Interviews are digitally recorded on the equipment.

Q: Did you check on the equipment before the interview in this case?

A: Yes. The equipment was operating properly.

Q: Did you activate the equipment before this interview?

A: Yes. I turned on the equipment before the child entered the interview room. The equipment was operating properly. I did sound and video checks, and everything was fine. It is the practice at our CAC to turn on the equipment before the interview begins, and to leave it recording for the entire interview and until the child has left the interview room. That is exactly what happened in this case.

Q: So, if I understand you, the video-recording equipment was operating properly—recording everything—before the child entered the room? And kept recording the entire time?

A: That is right. Every second of the interview, from the time the child walked into the room until she walked out, after it ended, was recorded.

Q: What date, time, and place did the interview occur?

A: August 1, 2017, at 1:30 P.M., at the child advocacy center here in the city.

Q: How long did the interview last?

A: Exactly 30 minutes, from the time the child entered the interview room until the child left the room.

Q: Did you or anyone else interview or question the child outside the interview room on August 1, 2017?

A: No, we make a practice of making sure that all interaction between the child and the forensic interviewer—all questioning—is recorded in an interview room. The child is greeted by a receptionist, but the receptionist does not talk to the child, except to welcome the child.

Q: When the interview you conducted ended, what, if anything, did you do with the recording equipment?

A: Before the child left the interview center, I went to the equipment and checked to make sure the interview was properly recorded. It was. I then said goodbye to the child and her mom. I immediately downloaded the interview onto a DVD and onto the hard drive of the CAC computer. I labeled the interview with the date, time, and child's name, and other pertinent information. I made three copies of the interview, one for you, one for the defense, and one for the file. We have a protocol for storing interviews, and I followed all the steps in the protocol.

Q: Did you bring a copy of the interview with you to court today?

A: Yes.

Q: How are you sure it is the correct interview?

A: Yesterday, I retrieved the DVD from the locked file cabinet where it has been stored since the day of the interview.

Q: Was the interview DVD removed from the locked file cabinet at any time before you got it yesterday?

A: No. Whenever anyone removes a DVD from the file, they have to sign it out, and the sign-out log indicates that no one removed the DVD of this interview from the time I placed it in the file until I removed it yesterday.

Q: Since you obtained the DVD yesterday, has it been in your continuous possession?

A: Yes.

Q: What did you do with the DVD before you brought it to court today?

A: I watched the entire interview to make sure it is the right one, and that nothing has happened to it since the recording.

Q: When you watched the video yesterday, who was on the video?

A: The child in this case and me, the forensic interviewer.

Q: Anyone else?

A: No.

Q: Since the interview was recorded, has the recording been altered or edited in any way?

A: No. The DVD I brought to court today is exactly the same as when the interview was recorded on August 1. It has not been altered or edited in any way.

Q: Is the DVD you have with you today an accurate recording of the entire interview?

A: It is.

Q: Is the recording you have with you today complete?

A: Yes, it shows the entire interview. Nothing has been cut out.

Prosecutor: Your honor, the People offer People's Exhibit number 1 for identification into evidence as People's number 1.

Defense Counsel: No objection.

Court: It will be received.

SHOULD A FORENSIC INTERVIEWER DO MORE THAN LAY THE FOUNDATION FOR A CAC INTERVIEW?

It is clear that forensic interviewers can lay the foundation for CAC interviews. But can forensic interviewers offer more when they testify? Prosecutors sometimes offer testimony from forensic interviewers for the following purposes: (1) to prove that the proper interview technique was employed, (2) to prove that a child's statements and/or behavior are consistent with sexual abuse, or (3) to prove that a child was truthful.

Proving the Proper Interview Technique Was Employed

Everyone agrees that it is proper for a forensic interviewer to lay the foundation to admit a video recording in evidence. However, is it proper for an interviewer to go further during direct examination and to testify that proper interview practices were employed during an interview?

There is a rule of evidence that the credibility of witnesses should not be bolstered or supported until the witness's credibility is impeached—the so-called rule against bolstering witnesses prior to impeachment. What is the purpose of a forensic interviewer testifying that proper interview technique was used? Isn't the purpose to convince the jury to believe the child's statements during the interview? If so, doesn't testimony that proper technique was used violate the rule against bolstering prior to impeachment? Some attorneys would object, on that basis, to testimony that proper technique was used.

If a defense attorney attacks an interview, it is acceptable for a properly qualified interviewer to testify that proper technique was used. How does an attack on an interview occur? It might come as early as the opening statement to the jury, when the attorney tells jurors, "Ladies and gentlemen, you may see a video-recorded interview later in the trial. The evidence will show that the interview was defective in many ways."

Often, the attack comes during the cross-examination of the interviewer. Following such cross-examination, the prosecutor can use redirect examination to give the interviewer an opportunity to explain away issues raised during cross-examination. On redirect, the interviewer might testify that she or he followed the protocol utilized by the interview center, or can explain why any departures from the protocol occurred.

In addition to testimony from the interviewer, the prosecutor may wish to offer rebuttal expert testimony. Such testimony is invited by the attack and is proper.

Should the forensic interviewer who conducted a disputed interview be the one to testify as an expert witness on interviewing? If it is the interviewer her- or himself who is the target of the attack, it feels a bit odd to offer the target as the rebuttal expert. Typically, it is more effective to offer someone else. As well, many otherwise competent forensic interviewers lack the depth of knowledge needed to provide expert testimony on interviewing. Such an expert needs to know more than the protocol used at the interview center. An expert possesses detailed knowledge, based on current research, of child development, including children's memory and suggestibility, the process by which children disclose abuse, fabricated allegations, and the theories behind interviewing. Most forensic interviewers lack this depth of understanding.

Should a Forensic Interviewer Testify That a Child's Statements and/or Behaviors Are Consistent with Sexual Abuse?

Occasionally, a prosecutor asks a forensic interviewer whether a child's interview statements and behaviors are consistent with sexual abuse. The complexity of "consistent with sexual abuse" testimony is analyzed in Chapter 12. Suffice it to say here that such testimony from most forensic interviews is objectionable and should not be allowed. Few forensic interviewers possess the expertise to offer expert testimony on whether a child's statements and/or behavior are consistent with sexual abuse.

Prosecutors occasionally offer testimony from forensic interviewers that, for all intents and purposes, is an opinion that the child was abused. In *Williams v. State* (2007), for example, the Mississippi Court of Appeals approved expert testimony from a forensic interviewer that a child's interview was "consistent with" sexual abuse. This testimony was offered to prove abuse. Yet, there was no indication that the interviewer possessed the expertise required to provide "consistent with" testimony.

In *State v. Douglas* (2009), the South Carolina Supreme Court considered testimony from a victim assistance advocate who regularly interviewed children. The interviewer had attended a 40-hour training session on forensic interviewing, plus follow-up training. She did not have a college degree. The interviewer testified that, based on her interview, she concluded that the child needed a medical evaluation. Although the interviewer did not opine that the child was telling the truth or had been abused, the import of her testimony could not have been lost on the jury. In essence, the interviewer told the jury, "I believed the child had been abused; therefore I referred the child for a medical examination." Such testimony amounted to an indirect opinion that the child was abused. Nevertheless, the South Carolina Supreme Court was convinced that the interviewer's testimony—which the court did not consider expert testimony—was helpful to the jury. It seems to me the court was wrong. The testimony *was* offered to prove abuse. Yet, as in the Mississippi case, there was no proof that the interviewer was competent to provide such testimony.

A forensic interviewer's hunch about abuse should not be presented to a jury as expert evidence. Forensic interviewers are experts on forensic interviewing, not on the psychosocial assessment of child sexual abuse—a task for which most psychiatrists, psychologists, and clinical social workers are not qualified.

Proving a Child Was Truthful

Prosecutors sometimes ask forensic interviewers whether children were truthful during interviews. Judges agree that professionals may not offer an opinion that a child was truthful or credible. Forensic interviewers, like other professionals, have no expertise to determine whether a child told the truth.

CROSS-EXAMINATION OF THE FORENSIC INTERVIEWER

If there are problems with a forensic interview, cross-examination is likely. Cross-examination of forensic interviewers commonly focuses on (1) a failure to follow the interview protocol used by the interviewer's employer; (2) the use of suggestive or leading questions; (3) pressuring the child to answer; (4) not taking "nothing happened" for an answer; (5) mentioning events or people not first mentioned by the child; (6) failing to establish rapport with the child; (7) failing to video record the entire interview; (8) emphasizing that other persons (e.g., parents, police, doctors) questioned the child before the forensic interview, and that these persons are not trained in the dangers of asking suggestive questions; (9) pointing to the literature on children's suggestibility; and (10) alignment between the interviewer and law enforcement.

No two cross-examiners are the same. Some are more aggressive than others. Some like to go on fishing expeditions in the hope of catching the forensic interviewer in an error. Some attorneys like to hear themselves talk, even if their questions bore or alienate the judge or jury, or give the witness another opportunity to damage the cross-examiner's client. Personally, I'm a minimalist. My cross-examination style leans toward "less is more." I am not suggesting that my approach is superior—after all, cross-examination is an art, not a science. The following cross-examination is in the "less is more" category: my cross-examination of the forensic interviewer who interviewed Samantha follows:

CROSS-EXAMINATION BY MR. MYERS

Q: Good morning, Ms. Carter. Thank you for being here this morning.

A: Good morning.

Q: I want to ask you a few questions. You testified in response to the prosecutor's questions that you are trained in the use of Dr. Lyon's 10-step interview protocol. Is that right?

A: Correct.

Q: Ms. Carter, I hand you what has been marked as Defense Exhibit 3 for identification. Please take as much time as you need to review this short document. Your honor, may the record reflect that I am also handing Exhibit 3 to the prosecutor?

Court: The record will so reflect.

Q: Does the Court have a copy?

Court: Yes.

Q: Ms. Carter, have you had enough time to read the document?

A: Yes. I am familiar with this. It is Dr. Lyon's 10-step interview protocol.

Q: Is the copy you are holding complete and accurate?

A: Yes.

Q: Your honor, I offer Defense Exhibit 3 for identification into evidence as Defense Exhibit 3.

Prosecutor: No objection.

Court: It is received.

Q: Your honor, I request permission to hand Defense Exhibit 3 to the jury for their inspection. I have copies for each juror.

Prosecutor: That's fine, your honor.

Court: Proceed, counsel.

Q: Thank you, your honor. Now, Ms. Carter. You interviewed the child in this case, correct?

A: Yes.

Q: Based on your training as a forensic interviewer, do you agree that it is important at the beginning of interviews of children to establish certain ground rules for the interview?

A: Yes.

Q: In fact, do you agree that numbers 1 through 6 of Dr. Lyon's 10-step interview protocol are basically ground rules for the interview?

A: Yes.

Q: Let's take a look at step number 1, the "Don't Know instruction." The purpose of that instruction is to help the child understand that if you ask a question that the child doesn't know the answer to, the child has permission to say, "I don't know, is that right?

A: Right.

Q: Step number 1 is important because research and experience tell us that children will sometimes answer adult's questions even if they don't know the answer, is that right?

A: Yes.

Q: And you use the "Don't Know instruction" to give the child practice saying, "I don't know," is that correct?

A: Correct.

Q: When you interviewed Samantha, did you use the "Don't Know instruction" with her?

A: Yes.

Q: Moving on to step number 2, the "Don't Understand instruction," the purpose of this instruction is to help the child understand that if they don't understand one of your questions, the child has permission to say, "I don't understand," isn't that right?

A: Yes.

Q: Step number 2 is important because research and experience tell us that children will sometimes answer an adult's question even if they don't understand the question, isn't that right?

A: Yes.

Q: When you interviewed Samantha, did you use the "Don't Understand instruction" with her?

A: Yes.

Q: Moving on to step number 3, the "You're Wrong instruction," the purpose of this instruction is to help the child understand that if you, the interviewer, say something that is wrong, the child can correct you, isn't that right?

A: Right.

Q: Step number 3 is important because research and experience tell us that children are sometimes reluctant to correct adults who make mistakes, isn't that right?

A: Right.

Q: When you interviewed Samantha, you did not ask her the "You're Wrong instruction," did you?

A: No, I didn't because . . .

Q: Thank you, Ms. Carter, you have answered my question. You didn't ask Samantha the "You're Wrong" question. Ms. Carter, the "You're Wrong" question is part of Dr. Lyon's 10-step interview protocol, isn't it?

A: Yes.

Q: When you interview children, you try to follow the protocol, don't you?

A: Yes.

Q: But when you interviewed Samantha that day, you did not follow step 3 of the protocol, did you?

A: No, I was in a hurry.

Q: Let's move on to step number 4, the "Ignorant Interviewer instruction." The purpose of this instruction is to help the child understand that you, the interviewer, don't know what happened to the child, right?

A: Yes.

Q: The "Ignorant Interviewer instruction" is based on research and experience that teaches us that children often think adults already know what happened, isn't that right?

A: Correct.

Q: It is important for the child to know that you don't know what happened, do you agree?

A: Yes.

Q: When you interviewed Samantha, you did not ask her the "Ignorant Interviewer" question, did you?

A: No.

Q: The Ignorant Interviewer instruction is part of the 10-step protocol, isn't it?

A: Yes.

Q: But you did not ask the Ignorant Interviewer question, did you.

A: No, I didn't.

Q: So, of the first six instructions in Dr. Lyon's 10-step protocol, your interview of Samantha omitted two of the six, isn't that right?

A: Correct.

Q: Ms. Carter, when you did the interview, you were aware that prior to your interview, Samantha had spoken with a police officer, right?

A: I was aware of that.

Q: Isn't it a fact that the police officer asked Samantha some suggestive questions about abuse?

A: That is true.

Q: When you did the interview, you were aware that Samantha had been questioned by her pediatrician, weren't you?

A: Yes.

Q: The pediatrician asked Samantha some suggestive questions about abuse, isn't that right?

A: That is my understanding.

Q: Ms. Carter, children, like adults, are sometimes suggestible, isn't that true?

A: Yes.

Q: Indeed, a large body of research indicates that children Samantha's age are sometimes suggestible, isn't that right?

A: Yes.

Q: It is possible, isn't it, that suggestive questions like those asked by the police officer and the doctor might have contaminated Samantha's memory, isn't it?

Prosecutor: Objection, the question is vague and calls for speculation.

Defense Attorney: Your honor, the witness has admitted that she was aware that the police officer and the doctor asked some suggestive questions. As a forensic interviewer, Ms. Carter has the training needed to say whether suggestive questions can contaminate a child's memory.

Prosecutor: Your honor, Ms. Carter has not been qualified to testify as an expert on suggestibility. If defense counsel wants to call her as an expert, the defense can call her during its case-in-chief and qualify her as an expert.

Court: I will sustain the objection.

Q: Now, Ms. Carter, referring to your interview of Samantha, you have in your possession a verbatim transcript of the interview, right?

A: That's right. I have it right here.

Defense Attorney: Your honor, by stipulation with the prosecutor, I ask the court's permission to give the jurors copies of the interview transcript so they can follow my questioning.

Prosecutor: That's right, your honor, we have no objection.

Court: Very well.

Q: Now, Ms. Carter, I want to direct your attention to the following question you asked of Samantha. You asked her, "What did your grandpa do to you?" right?

A: Yes, I asked that question.

Q: Up to that point in the interview, Samantha had not said her grandfather had done anything to her, had she?

A: Well, no, I don't agree with you. She said she didn't want to talk about what he had done. That implies he had done something.

Q: Her statement may imply something, but up to that point, she had not actually described anything that her grandfather had done, had she?

A: Not in so many words.

Q: Well, Ms. Carter, let's not mince words. Let's be precise. Up to that point, she had not described anything that her grandfather had done, had she?

A: No.

Q: With your question, you were the first one to introduce into the interview the idea that the grandfather had done anything to her. Isn't that right?

A: All I asked was what did he do. I was not specific.

Q: Ms. Carter, your question clearly suggests that he did something. You asked, "What did your grandpa do to you?" That question clearly suggests that he did something, doesn't it?

A: I guess so.

Q: And it was you who were the first to suggest, by your question, that something happened, isn't that right?

A: Yes.

Q: Isn't it true that when interviewing children, the interviewer isn't supposed to be the first one to introduce facts?

A: That is generally true, but not always.

Q: As a general rule, though, the information should come first from the child rather than from the interviewer, isn't that right.

A: As a general rule, yes.

Q: But in this case, you were the first to suggest that the grandfather did something, isn't that so?

A: I suppose so.

Q: So, you broke the general rule, didn't you?

A: I don't believe so, no.

Q: A little later in the interview, you asked, "Were you sitting on the couch with him when he touched you?," right?

A: That is correct.

Q: Samantha had not mentioned that it happened on the couch, had she?

A: No, but she said it happened in the family room.

Q: But it was you who first introduced the fact that it happened on the couch, isn't that so?

A: True.

Q: A little further in the interview, you asked, "Did grandpa tell you not to tell anyone what he did to you?"

A: That's right.

Q: Your question suggested what the grandfather did. Your question was suggestive, wasn't it?

A: Not really suggestive.

Q: Isn't it true that in your training as a forensic interviewer, you are taught that questions that begin with the word "did" are often suggestive?

A: That is true sometimes, but not always.

Q: And you asked a question that began with "did," didn't you?

A: Yes.

Q: A little further on in the interview, you asked another "did" question. You asked, "Did you ever see grandpa's penis?" Right?

A: I did ask that question.

Q: Up to that point in the interview, Samantha had not mentioned anything about her grandfather's penis, had she?

A: No.

Q: You were the first to use the word "penis," isn't that right?

A: That's correct.

Q: When you introduced the idea of a penis, you did it with a question that begins with the word "did," didn't you?

A: Yes.

Q: And you testified a minute ago that in your training as a forensic interviewer, you are trained that questions beginning with "did" can be suggestive, right?

A: Sometimes.

Q: So, not only were you the first to introduce the idea of genitalia into the interview, you did it with a suggestive question, didn't you?

A: I don't think it was a suggestive question.

Q: That question violated two fundamental principles of forensic interviewing. First, the question violated the principle that the interviewer is not supposed to introduce facts that the child has not already mentioned, isn't that so?

A: That is not the way I see it.

Q: Second, the question violated the principle that the interviewer should avoid suggestive questions, isn't that also true?

A: OK.

The purpose of my cross-examination was not to score a direct hit on Ms. Carter's interview of Samantha. Her mistakes were minor. The purpose of my questions was to raise a few doubts about the interview; to plant the idea that suggestive questions, combined with failing to follow all the steps in the protocol, may have caused Samantha to provide inaccurate information. During the closing argument, I'll remind the jury of the glitches in the interview and ask the jurors to discount Samantha's credibility.

There are other aspects of the interview that could be challenged. For example, the interviewer asked quite a few yes/no questions. Also, the interviewer did not ask very many follow-up questions such as, "Tell me more about that." These two issues are partly artifacts of the fact that the transcript is artificially short in order to fit into the book. The actual interview would be longer and would (hopefully) contain fewer yes/no questions and more opportunities for the child to expand on answers.

CROSS-EXAMINATION USING A LEARNED TREATISE

An expert witness can be cross-examined with quotations from books and articles. The rule of evidence on this point is Rule 803(18) of the FRE. The rule states:

> Statements contained in a treatise, periodical, or pamphlet [can be admitted in evidence] if:
>
> (A) the statement is called to the attention of an expert witness on cross-examination or relied on by the expert on direct examination; and
>
> (B) the publication is established as a reliable authority by the expert's admission or testimony, by another expert's testimony, or by judicial notice.
>
> If admitted [in evidence], the statement may be read into evidence but not received as an exhibit.

Consider Stephanie Gomez, a psychologist, who testifies for the prosecution that 6-year-old Jenny's symptoms and behaviors are consistent with child sexual abuse. On cross-examination, the defense counsel proceeds as follows:

Q: Dr. Gomez, your testimony a few minutes ago was that the child's symptoms and behaviors are consistent with sexual abuse, is that right?

A: Correct.

Q: Is it fair to say that when you say consistent with sexual abuse, you mean that the symptoms and behaviors tend to prove sexual abuse?

A: Yes.

Q: Is it your testimony that mental health professionals, such as yourself, can examine a child's symptoms and behaviors and draw conclusions that the symptoms and behaviors tend to prove sexual abuse?

A: Not in every case, by any means, but in some cases, yes.

Q: Doctor, I now hand you what has been marked for identification as Defense Exhibit 10, and I will ask you, have you ever seen this before?

Defense Counsel: May the record reflect that I am also handing a copy to the prosecutor?

Court: The record will so reflect.

A: Yes, I am familiar with this article in the professional literature.

Q: How is it that you are familiar with it?

A: Well, I had read the article years ago, and then, you sent me a copy of it about a month ago, and asked me to read it.

Q: Are you familiar with the first author of the article, Dr. Gary Melton?

A: Yes, Dr. Melton is a psychologist, and a leading authority on forensic psychology.

Q: Do you recognize Dr. Melton as an authority on psychological evaluation of children for sexual abuse?

A: Yes.

Q: Please tell the jury what you are holding; the article I called Defense Exhibit 10.

A: This is an article from the psychological literature titled "Psychologists' Involvement in Cases of Child Maltreatment" published in the *American Psychologist* in 1989. The authors are Gary Melton and Susan Limber.

Q: Are you familiar with the journal *American Psychologist*?

A: Yes, it is one of the American Psychological Association's flagship journals.

Q: Is *American Psychologist* peer reviewed?

A: Yes.

Q: Now, directing your attention to the sentence I highlighted in yellow, at page 1230 of the article, please read that sentence to yourself.

A: OK.

Q: Have you read the sentence?

A: Yes.

Q: That sentence says, and here I am quoting Dr. Melton, "Under no circumstances should a court admit the opinion of an expert about whether a particular child has been abused." Do you agree with Dr. Melton?

A: Well, I respect his opinion, but . . .

Q: I've asked you a yes or no question. Do you agree with what Dr. Melton wrote?

A: I can't really answer with a simple yes or no because the answer is complicated. May I explain?

Q: We will talk about your reasoning, but first I want an answer. Do you agree with Dr. Melton?

A: Not completely.

Q: Do you agree that Dr. Melton takes the position he does because, in his judgment, mental health professionals such as yourself have no particular expertise in determining whether a child was sexually abused?

A: That does appear to be his position.

Q: And you recognize him as a leading authority on forensic psychology and child sexual abuse, right?

A: The fact that he is highly regarded does not mean he is always right.

Q: But Dr. Melton's position is that professionals like you can't determine whether a child was sexually abused; you agree that that is his position, don't you?

A: Yes, as far as I know.

Prosecutor: Objection, your honor, I don't believe my colleague has laid the necessary foundation to use a learned treatise.

Defense Counsel: I disagree. The doctor's answers to my questions establish the foundation to use the article under the learned treatise rule. First, I directed her attention to the article on cross-examination. Second, the doctor recognized the publication as a reliable authority. Third, the doctor recognized Dr. Melton as an authority on the subject. This satisfies the foundation for Rule 803(18).

Court: Overruled.

Q: Dr. Gomez, I hand you what has been marked for identification as Defense Exhibit 11, and ask you, have you seen this before? I am also handing a copy to the prosecutor.

A: Yes, this is an excerpt from a book on forensic psychology, written by Dr. Melton and his colleagues.

Q: How are you familiar with the book?

A: It is a leading treatise on forensic psychology. I own the book, and I use it in my practice.

Q: I guess it is fair to say, then, that you recognize the book as authoritative on forensic psychology.

A: Certainly.

Q: And it is the same Dr. Gary Melton, who is the first author of this book, who wrote the article we discussed a few minutes ago?

A: Correct.

Q: Are you familiar with the other authors?

A: Yes, they are also experts.

Q: Now doctor, please tell the jury the name of the book.

A: Sure. It is *Psychological Evaluations for the Courts: A Handbook for Mental Health Professionals and Lawyers,* Third Edition, published in 2007, by Guilford Press.

Q: Is Guilford a respected publisher of books on psychology?

A: Absolutely.

Q: Directing your attention to page 516, do you see the sentence highlighted in yellow?

A: Yes.

Q: By the way, prior to trial, did I ask you to review this sentence?

A: Yes, you sent me a packet of materials, and asked that I review them because you wanted to ask me questions about them in court.

Q: The sentence states, and I quote, "Although clinical intuition may be useful in guiding treatment planning, it is insufficient as a basis for determining whether maltreatment may have occurred." Do you agree that in that sentence, Dr. Melton is saying that clinical judgment is not sufficient to determine whether a child was abused?

A: That is not my interpretation of the text, no.

Q: But that is a fair interpretation of Dr. Melton's position, isn't it?

A: Again, that is not the way I read that sentence.

Q: I want to ask you about another sentence, also marked in yellow, this one on page 516. Do you see that sentence?

A: Yes.

Q: On page 516, Dr. Melton writes, "There is no reason to believe that clinicians' skill in determining whether a child has been abused is the product of specialized knowledge." Do you agree that it is Dr. Melton's position that mental health professionals such as yourself cannot determine with reasonable certainty whether particular children have been sexually abused?

A: I believe that it his position. I just don't agree with him.

Q: But it is his position, right?

A: Yes.

Q: Also on page 516, there is a third passage highlighted in yellow. Do you see that sentence?

A: Yes.

Q: And there, Dr. Melton writes, "The determination of whether abuse or neglect occurred is a judgment requiring common sense and legal acumen, but it is outside the specialized knowledge of mental health professionals." Thus, according to Dr. Melton, mental health professionals like you have no specialized knowledge that allows you to determine whether a child was abused, right?

A: That is his position.

Q: Doctor, are you familiar with a psychologist named Steve Herman, PhD?

A: Yes.

Q: Is Dr. Herman a professor of psychology at the University of Hawaii?

A: Yes.

Q: Do you recognize Dr. Herman as an authority on the psychological evaluation of children for sexual abuse?

A: He is one of the main contributors to the literature on that subject, and I am familiar with his work.

Q: Do you recognize him as an authority on the topic?

A: Yes.

Q: I hand you now—and I'm also handing a copy to the prosecutor—a document that is marked Defense Exhibit 12 for identification. Do you recognize the document?

A: Yes. This is an article by Dr. Herman published in 2005 in the journal *Law and Human Behavior.* I will add that this is an excellent peer-reviewed journal.

Q: Have you read the article?

A: I read it when it was first published, and I reread it in preparation for my testimony and at your request.

Q: Directing your attention to page 90, on that page, Dr. Herman writes, quoting, "There is a widespread (but not universal) consensus among experts in the field that decisions by clinicians to either substantiate or not substantiate uncorroborated sexual abuse allegations currently lack a firm scientific foundation and that such opinions may be based on little more than a clinician's subjective opinion or hunch that abuse did nor did not occur." Do you agree or disagree with his statement?

A: I think it is necessary to examine the basis for what he is saying.

Q: Doctor, I understand, and I respect your opinion, but I asked a yes or no question. Do you agree or disagree with Dr. Herman's statement?

A: I can't answer with a simple yes or no, I'm sorry.

Q: Very well, but you agree with me that the quote I read is Dr. Herman's position, right?

A: Right.

Q: Doctor, are you familiar with a book published in 2009 and edited by psychologists Kathryn Kuehnle and Mary Connell titled *The Evaluation of Child Sexual Abuse Allegations: A Comprehensive Guide to Assessment and Testimony,* published by John Wiley?

A: Yes. It is an important contribution to the literature.

Q: Have you read the book?

A: I own the book, and I have read it cover to cover.

Q: I hand you and the prosecutor Defense Exhibit 13 for identification, and ask if you recognize the document?

A: Yes, this is Chapter 1 of the book by Kuehnle and Connell.

Q: Are you familiar with the three authors of Chapter 1?

A: I am most familiar with the work of Dr. David Faust.

Q: Is Dr. Faust an authority on the subject discussed in Chapter 1?

A: Yes.

Q: The title of Chapter 1 is, and I quote, "Methods for the Identification of Sexually Abused Children: Issues and Needed Features for Abuse Indicators." Directing your attention to the highlighted sentence on page 4, do you see that sentence?

A: Yes.

Q: Please read the highlighted sentence, and I want to ask you a couple of questions. Have you had time to read it?

A: Yes, and I reviewed it before coming to court.

Q: Dr. Faust and his colleagues write, "Such evaluations rest mainly on unverified methods or conjecture that almost certainly at times increase, rather than decrease, error." When Dr. Faust says "evaluations," he means evaluations for possible sexual abuse performed by mental health professionals such as yourself, isn't that right?

A: Yes.

Q: And Dr. Faust's position is that such evaluations rest mainly on unverified methods, right?

A: That is what he said.

Q: He is saying that when a mental health professional determines that a child's symptoms and behavior are consistent with sexual abuse, that determination is based on unverified methods, isn't he?

A: I suppose so, but I don't agree.

Q: You are free to disagree, but I am asking, it is Dr. Faust's position that such determination is based on unverified methods, right?

A: Right.

Q: Also regarding such determinations, it is Dr. Faust's position that such determinations rest mainly on conjecture, guesswork, right?

A: That is his opinion.

Q: Finally, it is Dr. Faust's position that mental health evaluations sometimes lead to increased errors, isn't that so?

A: Yes.

Prosecutor: Your honor, I object. There is all sorts of professional literature, much of which disagrees with the literature offered by the defense. How long is this parade of articles going to last?

Court: Well, counsel, that's not really an objection. You will have your opportunity to offer articles of your choosing, if you like. The defense has the right to do what it is doing. Overruled. How many more articles do you intend to offer counsel?

Defense Counsel: Just one more, your honor.

Court: Very well. You may proceed.

Q: Doctor, I hand you now, and I'm also handing it to the prosecutor, what has been marked Defense Exhibit 14 for identification. Are you familiar with this?

A: Yes. This is an article you sent me.

Q: Are you familiar with the author, Professor John Myers?

A: I know of Professor Myers. He's a law professor who writes on child abuse issues. I've read some of his work, including this article.

Q: The article was published in 2010 in the University of California, Davis, *Journal of Juvenile Law and Policy,* right?

A: Yes.

Q: Do you recognize Professor Myers as an expert on the evaluation of children for possible sexual abuse?

A: No. He is a lawyer, not a mental health professional. I guess maybe he's an expert on the law related to child abuse, but he is not an expert on psychological evaluation of children.

Prosecutor: Your honor, I object to any reference to Myers's article. The witness does not recognize him as an expert.

Defense Counsel: Your honor, during my case, I will offer expert testimony that Professor Myers is recognized as an authority on evaluation of children for possible child sexual abuse. That expert testimony will satisfy the requirements of Rule 803(18). I ask the court to allow me to proceed with my cross-examination, with my promise to the court that, at the proper time, I will establish Professor Myers's expertise.

Court: With that promise in mind, you may proceed. Objection overruled, for the time being.

Q: Professor Myers's article is titled "Expert Testimony in Child Sexual Abuse Litigation: Consensus and Confusion," right?

A: Correct.

Q: On your direct testimony today, you testified that the child's symptoms and behaviors are consistent with sexual abuse, right?

A: That is my opinion, yes.

Q: Directing your attention to page 40 of Professor Myers's article, do you see the first highlighted portion?

A: Yes.

Q: And at that point on page 40, he writes, "Despite the tendency of courts to admit "consistent with" testimony, there are three problems with such testimony." So, it is his opinion that there are problems with "consistent with" testimony, right?

A: That is his position.

Q: Professor Myers concludes that because of what he calls the shortcomings of "consistent with" testimony, and I quote him, "Such testimony should be excluded unless the proponent addresses two issues during the expert's direct examination. First, the expert should explain why the symptoms tend to prove sexual abuse. It is simply not enough to state that a child's symptoms are consistent with sexual abuse. Second, the expert should explain the impact of symptom frequency and population size on probative value. Only when explanations of symptom frequency and population size are added to "consistent with" testimony is the jury equipped with the information it needs to give "consistent with" testimony its proper weight. Absent this information, "consistent with" testimony is inherently misleading." Do you agree with him?

A: The issues he raises are legitimate.

Q: During your direct examination, you did not mention symptom frequencies, did you?

A: I wasn't asked to, but I can do that if asked.

Q: During your direct examination, you did not discuss population sizes, did you?

A: Again, I'm happy to do that now, if you like.

Q: That's not my question. During your direct testimony, you did not discuss population sizes, did you?

A: No.

Q: It is Professor Myers's opinion that without a discussion of population sizes and symptom frequencies, testimony like the testimony you gave—"consistent with" testimony—is inherently misleading. That is his position, right?

A: Correct.

Q: And again, when you testified, you didn't mention population sizes or symptom frequencies, did you?

A: No. Would you like me to go into it now?

Q: That won't be necessary.

When you are called to testify, and are confronted with books or articles from the medical or psychological literature, recall that you are allowed to say, "I have not read that article. I will be happy to comment, if I am given an opportunity to read the entire article. But I can't comment on one sentence from a lengthy article without studying the whole thing."

The best preparation for this type of cross-examination is to be familiar with the relevant literature and to discuss the literature with the attorney who asked you to testify. Finally, remember, after the cross-examination there is the redirect examination, purpose of which is to repair the damage.

CONCLUSION

The legal system depends on clinicians to provide expert testimony. It is not an exaggeration to say that without such testimony, the law would be crippled in its capacity to protect victims and ensure justice.

10

Confidentiality and Privilege

Relationships between clinicians and clients require confidentiality. The American Medical Association's (2007) *Code of Ethics* emphasizes the importance of confidentiality:

> The information disclosed to a physician by a patient should be held in confidence. The patient should feel free to make a full disclosure of information to the physician in order that the physician may most effectively provide needed services. The patient should be able to make this disclosure with the knowledge that the physician will respect the confidential nature of the communication. The physician should not reveal confidential information without the express consent of the patient, subject to certain exceptions which are ethically justified because of overriding considerations. (Ethics Opinion 5.05—Confidentiality)

The confidentiality requirement is also true for the other helping professions.

Ask yourself, if you seek help from a psychotherapist, will you reveal your deepest secrets if the therapist is free to discuss your case on the 6 o'clock news? If a teenage girl wants birth control, might she cancel her appointment if she learns the doctor will call her parents? If Sam is charged with a crime, will he feel safe telling his lawyer *all* the details if he believes police can compel the lawyer to repeat what he said in the privacy of the lawyer's office? Without confidentiality, these professional relationships are nipped in the bud. By contrast, when professionals promise confidentiality, relationships blossom in an atmosphere of trust. Confidentiality is indispensable for success.

Before we dive into the deep end of confidentiality, consider three vignettes. Each story raises different aspects of confidentiality.

CASE STUDIES

THE PROSECUTOR SUBPOENAS RECORDS ON MARIA

Paula is the Executive Director of a nonprofit domestic violence center. The center runs a shelter for victims of domestic violence and has a counseling service. Recently, Paula received a subpoena demanding that she disclose to the local prosecutor whether a woman named Maria Jiminez ever received therapy at the center, and, if she had, to disclose her clinical record.

There are two kinds of subpoenas: A subpoena for testimony, sometimes referred to with the Latin term, *subpoena ad testificandum,* requiring a person to testify, and a *subpoena duces tecum,* which requires the disclosure of records. The subpoena Paula received was a *subpoena duces tecum.*

Maria is currently in jail, awaiting trial on a charge of murder. She shot her husband while the two were at home. Maria's defense attorney plans to offer expert testimony that Maria was a victim of chronic domestic violence at the hands of her husband, and that she killed in self-defense. The prosecutor disputes the self-defense claim and will argue that Maria was not a victim of domestic violence. The prosecutor wants access to Maria's records at the domestic violence center for two reasons. First, if Maria never contacted the center, then the prosecutor will argue that her failure to contact the center is evidence she was never abused. If she had been abused, so the argument goes, she would have gone to the center for help. Thus, the prosecutor wants to find out whether Maria was ever a client at the center. Second, if Maria was a client at the center, the prosecutor wants to read her clinical file to see if it contains information that can be used against Maria in court.

How should Paula respond to the subpoena? A subpoena is a court order, and it cannot be ignored. Yet, not all subpoenas are valid (American Psychological Association Committee on Legal Issues, 2016). Of particular importance, a subpoena does not override privileges like the psychotherapist–client privilege, which is discussed later in the chapter. If Maria received counseling, her clinical record is privileged. If Maria contacted the center in the past, the very act of contacting the center may be privileged. Suppose Maria never contacted the center. Could the *lack of contact* with the center possibly be confidential? That's a tough one.

DID HE FALL OR JUMP?

Juan was a young attorney at a large law firm in the city. Late one night, Juan either jumped or fell to his death from the window of his office on the 36th floor of the Acme Building. No one saw what happened. There was no suicide note. The window in Juan's office opens wide enough for someone to fit through. Juan's widow, Natalie, has sued the owner of the Acme Building. Natalie's "wrongful death" lawsuit claims that Juan fell out his office window when he tried to push the window open. Natalie claims the window was not working properly, and the owner of the building was negligent in failing to repair the window. The owner of the Acme Building says the window was working properly, and that Juan committed suicide by opening the window and jumping out. If Juan committed suicide, Natalie cannot sue the owner of the building.

In the year before his death, Juan received psychotherapy and pharmacological treatment for depression from Beth, a psychiatrist. Leading up to the trial, the attorney for the Acme Building issued a *subpoena ad testificandum* for Beth's testimony. The attorney wants to put Beth on the witness stand and ask her about Juan's depression, and whether he was suicidal. Natalie's attorney files a motion to quash the subpoena for Beth's testimony. Natalie's attorney argues that Beth should not testify because all communications between Juan and Beth are covered by psychotherapist–client and physician–patient privileges.

A judge will decide whether to grant Natalie's motion to quash the subpoena for Beth's testimony. If you were the judge, how would you rule? Should Beth testify, or should the motion to quash the subpoena be granted based on privilege?

"WHAT HAPPENED AT WORK TODAY?"

After a long day at the office, millions of couples greet each other with, "What happened at work today?" If one or both of the couple is a mental health, medical, social work, or legal professional, is the professional free to discuss everything that occurred at the office? For example, in my work as a lawyer, clients have told me things—some quite shocking—that I'd love to share with my wife. But can I reveal to her what clients told me in confidence? I mean, if I can't tell my wife, who can I tell? The answer is: No one, not even her.

CONFIDENTIALITY DEFINED

Before discussing confidentiality, let's define it. The dictionary defines confidentiality as "private" or "secret." The HIPAA Privacy Rule, which applies to many readers of this book, and which is discussed subsequently, employs the following legalistic definition: "Confidentiality means the property that data or information is not made available or disclosed to unauthorized persons or processes" (45 *Code of Federal Regulations* [CFR] § 164.304). Probably the best definition of confidentiality is, "It's none of your business."

At the outset of therapy, mental health professionals discuss confidentiality and its limits (American Psychological Association, 2010a; *Ethical Principles of Psychologists and Code of Conduct,* Standard

4.02(a) and (b)). Professionals providing services on the Internet, or through other electronic means, must inform clients of possible risks to privacy (Standard 4.02(c)).

For information on the many ethical and legal issues raised by the emerging field of telehealth and electronic recordkeeping, see Baker and Bufka (2011) and Devereauz and Gottlieb (2012).

SOURCES OF CONFIDENTIALITY

There are five primary sources of confidentiality. First, there is the commonsense idea that some information is private. You don't need laws or ethics codes to tell you that certain information should not see the light of day; "It's none of your business." Second, ethics codes of professional organizations put meat on the bones of confidentiality. Third, clients have privacy rights guaranteed by the Constitution. Fourth, every state and the federal government have complex laws governing confidentiality (e.g., the HIPAA Privacy Rule). Fifth, in legal proceedings, confidential communications between clients and certain professionals are protected from disclosure by evidentiary privileges, such as the psychotherapist–client privilege and the physician–patient privilege.

Ethics Codes

The ethics codes of the helping professions emphasize confidentiality. For example, the American Psychological Association's (2010a) *Ethical Principles of Psychologists and Code of Conduct* states, "Psychologists respect the dignity and worth of all people, and the rights of individuals to privacy, confidentiality, and self-determination" (General Principle E, p. 4). To implement General Principle E, Ethical Standard 4.01 provides that psychologists have a "primary obligation to take reasonable precautions to protect confidential information" (p. 7).

The National Association of Social Workers' (2008) *Code of Ethics* remarks, "Social workers should respect clients' right to privacy. . . . Social workers should protect the confidentiality of all information obtained in the course of professional service" (Ethical Standard 1.07(a) and (c)).

According to the *Code of Ethics for Nurses* of the American Nurses Association (2015), "The nurse has a duty to maintain confidentiality of all patient information" (Provision 3, Interpretive Statement 3.1, p. 9). For decades, new nurses have taken the Florence Nightingale Pledge, which states, in part, "I will do all in my power to maintain and elevate the standard of my profession, and will hold in confidence all personal matters committed to my keeping and all family affairs coming to my knowledge in the practice of my calling."

Medical students take the Hippocratic Oath, written in the fifth century B.C.E. by the father of medicine, Hippocrates (or one of his students). The original oath provided, "Whatever, in the course of my practice, I may see or hear . . . , whatever I may happen to obtain knowledge of, if it be not proper to repeat it, I will keep sacred and secret. . . . " The Hippocratic Oath lives on. Today's *Code of Medical Ethics* of the American Medical Association (2007) states,

> The information disclosed to a physician by a patient should be held in confidence." (Opinion 5.05—Confidentiality)

Lawyers share the commitment to confidentiality. The American Bar Association's (2016) *Model Rules of Professional Conduct* state, "A lawyer shall not reveal information relating to the representation of a client" (Rule 1.6(a)—Confidentiality of Information). The seriousness of the responsibility is emphasized by a California law that provides, "It is the duty of an attorney to maintain inviolate the confidence, and at every peril to himself or herself, to preserve the secrets of his or her client" (California Business and Professions Code § 6068(e)(1)).

Constitutional Law

The U.S. Constitution does not mention a right of privacy or confidentiality. In decisions spanning more than a century, however, the U.S. Supreme Court has interpreted the Constitution to guarantee citizens limited rights to privacy vis-à-vis the government. Thus, in 1973, the Court predicated a woman's right to abortion on privacy (*Roe v. Wade*, 1973).

Every state has a state constitution. The constitutions of five states—Alaska, California, Florida, Hawaii, and Montana—expressly mention a right to privacy. Florida's Constitution notes, "Every natural person has the right to be let alone and from governmental intrusion into the person's private life . . . " (Florida Constitution Art. 1, § 23). The California Constitution stipulates, "All people are by nature free and independent and have inalienable rights. Among these are enjoying and defending . . . privacy" (California Constitution, Art. 1, § 1). Although constitutions in other states don't specifically mention privacy, judges interpret state constitutions to protect privacy.

Federal and State Laws

Every state has complex laws governing the confidentiality of records. Any effort to describe the specifics of confidentiality law in all 50 states would be extremely lengthy, would be immediately out of date, and would put you to sleep. There is one law, however, a federal regulation called the HIPAA Privacy Rule, which has such a pervasive impact nationwide that it is worth studying HIPAA in some detail (see the *Code of Federal Regulations*, Title 45, Part 164).

The HIPAA Privacy Rule protects the confidentiality of health and mental health information. The Rule is broad, protecting all "individually identifiable health information." HIPAA applies to most health and mental health professionals in the United States. Professionals and entities covered by HIPAA are called "covered entities." The Privacy Rule requires covered professionals to ensure the confidentiality, integrity, and availability of all electronic health information. In addition, professionals must take reasonable steps to protect against threats to the security of electronically stored health information (e.g., protect against hacking).

The HIPAA Privacy Rule is too complex to describe in full detail. The highlights are summarized below.

- ***Consultation and training.*** HIPAA respects the time-honored tradition of professionals consulting each other about cases. HIPAA understands that supervisors discuss cases with trainees (45 CFR § 164.506(a)).

- ***Client access.*** Clients have the right to inspect and copy their health information (45 CFR § 164.502(a)(2)). A "personal representative" is a person who is legally authorized to make health care decisions for a client. If a client has a personal representative, the representative has the right to inspect and copy health information.

- ***The client may authorize disclosure.*** Professionals cannot disclose protected health information without proper authorization (45 CFR § 164.508(a)). Clients may authorize the release of health information covered by HIPAA. Professionals may obtain client consent to use or disclose health information in order to carry out treatment and obtain payment (45 CFR § 164.506(b)).

• ***Disclose the minimum.*** When professionals disclose health information, HIPAA requires a release of the minimum amount of information needed to accomplish the purpose of the release.

• ***Requirements for valid authorization to disclose.*** To be valid, an authorization for disclosure must (1) describe the information to be disclosed; (2) state who is authorized to disclose; (3) state to whom disclosure is authorized; (4) describe the purpose of the disclosure ("At the request of the individual" will suffice); (5) specify the date, or an event, at which authorization ends; (6) contain the signature and date by the person authorizing disclosure; (7) contain a statement that the client can revoke the authorization; and (8) be written in plain language. The client must be given a copy of the signed authorization.

• ***The client can revoke authorization.*** A client can revoke authorization to disclose health information (45 CFR § 164.508(b)(iii) and (5)).

• ***HIPAA rule on children and adolescents.*** As a general matter, parents have the right to inspect their child's health records, communicate with professionals about their child's care, and authorize release of their child's health information (45 CFR § 164.502(g)(3)(i)).

Privacy rights for adolescents are somewhat more complex. In a legal sense, a teenager is still a "child." Thus, parents can talk to professionals treating the "child." At the same time, state laws allow teenagers to consent to certain medical and mental health care, without parental involvement. When these laws apply, HIPAA specifies that parents do not have the right to a teenager's medical information (45 CFR § 164.502(g)(3)(i)(A) and (B)).

HIPAA gives licensed health care professionals the authority to exercise their judgment to decide, in individual cases, that parents should be denied access to a child's health care information (45 CFR § 164.502(g)(3)(ii)(C)). A professional may deny parental access to a child's medical record when the professional reasonably believes a parent has neglected or abused the child, or when allowing parental access could endanger the child, and allowing access is not in the child's best interest (45 CFR § 164.502(g)(5)(i)(A), (B), (ii)).

HIPAA specifies that parents can sign "an agreement of confidentiality," in which parents agree to respect the confidentiality of communications between a professional and a child (45 CFR § 164.502(g)(3)(i)(C)). In practice, most mental health professionals who work with children—particularly adolescents—insist that parents respect the privacy of communications between therapist and child.

• ***The rule for psychotherapy notes.*** The HIPAA Privacy Rule has special protections for psychotherapy notes, which the Rule defines as notes recorded in any medium by mental health professionals documenting or analyzing the contents of conversations during private therapy sessions, group sessions, or joint or family therapy, "that are separated from the rest of the individual's medical record" (45 CFR § 164.502). The federal Department of Health and Human Services (12/28/2000) described the justification for added protection for psychotherapy notes: "The rationale for providing special protection for psychotherapy notes is not only that they contain particularly sensitive information, but also that they are the personal notes of the therapist intended to help him or her recall the therapy discussion and are of little or no use to others not involved in the therapy. Information in these notes is not intended to communicate to, or even be seen by, persons other than the therapist" (Federal Register, vol. 65, p. 82623). Not even the patient has the right to inspect psychotherapy notes (45 CFR § 164.524(a)(1)).

Psychotherapy notes do not include "medication prescription and monitoring, counseling session start and stop times, the modalities and frequencies of treatment furnished, results of clinical tests, and any summary of the following items: Diagnosis, functional status, the treatment plan, symptoms, prognosis, and progress to date" (45 CFR § 164.501).

Many mental health professionals organize client files to keep psychotherapy notes in separate files. Doing so surrounds this highly sensitive information with added protection from disclosure; for example, an insurance provider cannot demand access to psychotherapy notes.

Disclosure of psychotherapy notes requires a separate release, signed by the client (45 CFR § 164.508(a)(2)). A separate release is not required to use psychotherapy notes for training and supervision (45 CFR § 164.508(2)(i)(B)). A court may order disclosure of psychotherapy notes (*In re Jonathan C.*, 2015). It should be added, however, that judges are aware of the extraordinary sensitivity of psychotherapy notes, and it is often possible to persuade a judge not to reveal the notes. For example, the judge might require the therapist to testify, but order that the psychotherapy notes remain confidential.

• ***Disclosures for judicial proceedings.*** A professional may release health information in response to a court order (45 CFR § 164.512(e)). As well, release of information is permitted in response to a subpoena or discovery request, so long as the party seeking the release meets certain requirements (45 CFR § 164.512(e)).

• ***HIPAA does not forbid attorneys from contacting treating professionals.*** An attorney may contact a patient's health care provider. Of course, HIPAA and other laws limit what, if anything, the provider may say to an attorney. In *Caldwell v. Chauvin* (2015), the Kentucky Supreme Court wrote, "We conclude that no law inhibits [attorneys] from seeking . . . interviews with the opposing party's treating physicians. But the disclosure of medical information during those . . . meetings is controlled by HIPAA. For disclosure to be permitted, the [attorney] must first obtain a court order authorizing disclosure in a voluntary . . . interview" (p. 143).

Alcohol and Drug Abuse Patient Records

Federal law requires added confidentiality for patient records of alcohol and drug abuse treatment in "any federally assisted alcohol and drug abuse program" (42 CFR § 2.3(a)). It is a crime to improperly disclose such records (42 CFR § 2.4). It violates the law even to disclose that a person is a patient (42 CFR § 2.13(c)). The client may consent to release of patient information (42 CFR § 2.31). Federal law also allows reports of suspected child abuse (42 CFR § 2.12(c)(6)), and a court may order a disclosure of records. Information may be disclosed in emergencies.

Evidentiary Privileges

This section discusses evidentiary privileges. The word "evidentiary" is used because privilege law is part of the law of evidence. As you may recall from earlier chapters, evidence law governs what and how evidence is used in court. For example, evidence law prescribes the rule against hearsay. Evidence law determines what witnesses can say, and who qualifies to testify as an expert witness. The rules of evidence define evidentiary privileges.

Evidentiary privileges apply only in legal proceedings. Five evidentiary privileges are described here: psychotherapist–client privilege; physician–patient privilege; attorney–client privilege; clergy–penitent privilege; spousal privileges; and clergy–penitent privilege. Nearly all states have these evidentiary privileges, and some states have more. California, for example, adds a sexual assault counselor–victim privilege (California Evidence Code § 1035.8) and a domestic violence counselor–client privilege (California Evidence Code § 1037.5).

In *People v. Rivera* (2015), the New York Court of Appeals described the benefits of privileges:

> The privilege serves several objectives: it encourages unrestrained communication between a patient and his or her medical provider so that the patient may obtain diagnosis and treatment without fear of embarrassment over potential disclosure; it encourages physicians to be forthright in recording their patients' confidential information; and it protects patients' reasonable privacy expectations against disclosure of sensitive personal information. (p. 261)

With the exception of the spousal privileges, the privileges analyzed here share the same elements: (1) a client or patient; (2) a professional who is covered by privilege law; (3) communication between the client/patient and the professional; and (4) an expectation that the communication will not be disclosed.

Evidentiary privileges are the close kin of ethical duties of confidentiality. Both spring from the importance of privacy in professional relationships. How do they differ? First, evidentiary privileges apply only in legal proceedings. By contrast, ethical duties of confidentiality apply everywhere—at the office, a restaurant, a professional conference, *and* in legal proceedings.

The following example illustrates the distinction between evidentiary privilege and the ethical duty of confidentiality. Sarah is a clinical social worker in private practice. Sarah has an ethical duty to protect confidential client information. As well, Sarah is a psychotherapist, who is covered by her state's psychotherapist–client privilege rule. Sarah is treating Beth for depression. After work, Sarah and her friend, Ruth, are enjoying a meal. During dinner, is Sarah free to discuss Beth's case with her friend? Of course not. Does the prohibition arise from her ethical duty, the psychotherapist–client privilege, or both? The answer is, Sarah's duty to maintain confidentiality over dinner is based on her ethical duty, and has nothing to do with privilege. Evidentiary privileges apply only in legal proceedings, not over dinner.

How is a "legal proceeding" defined for the purposes of evidentiary privilege? Clearly, proceedings in court (e.g., testimony) are legal proceedings. In addition, a pretrial deposition is a legal proceeding. A subpoena that requests production of privileged records occurs in a legal proceeding.

A second difference between privilege and ethical duty is breadth of coverage. Ethical duty covers all information on a client, including administrative information about the client, as well as communications during therapy. Privileges apply only to confidential communications in the course of a professional relationship. It should be added that a number of courts hold that the patient's name is privileged.

A third distinction between privilege and ethical duty is that in legal proceedings, privileged communications have greater protection from disclosure than information covered by the ethical duty of confidentiality. For example, a subpoena typically overrides the ethical duty of confidentiality, but not a privilege. So too in court: When a professional testifies, a question that requires disclosure of ethically protected information must be answered. By contrast, a question that would require revelation of privileged information does not have to be answered.

Psychotherapist–Client Privilege

All states and federal courts have some version of the psychotherapist–client privilege. The privilege protects confidential communications between clients and therapists from disclosure in legal proceedings. The privilege applies in all civil, criminal, and administrative legal proceedings. Communications remain privileged after the therapeutic relationship ends, and the privilege continues after the client dies.

The privilege belongs to the client, not the therapist—in evidence parlance, the client is the "holder" of the privilege. Although the client is the holder of the privilege, the therapist is ethically (and in some states, legally) obliged to assert the privilege whenever privileged information is sought. For example, suppose you are testifying on the witness stand. An attorney asks you a question that you believe requires you to reveal privileged communications with a client. The other attorney might object to the question on the basis of privilege. If an attorney does not raise the issue, you might say, "I prefer not to answer your question because doing so would necessitate disclosure of information I believe is privileged." Your answer alerts the judge and the attorneys to the privilege issue. The judge will decide whether you have to answer the question.

When a therapist believes that someone is seeking access to privileged information, the therapist should consult the client. A client who is mentally competent may authorize access to privileged information. The therapist should inform the client that once privileged information is disclosed, the privilege generally no longer applies. The professional should discuss with the client the pros and cons of releasing privileged information. Most clients have little understanding of the protection afforded by privilege. If the client wants a privilege respected, the professional may want to consult an attorney and/or encourage the client to do so. Even if the client decides to release privileged information, it may be a good idea to consult an attorney first.

A subpoena does *not* override the psychotherapist–client privilege. Mental health and medical professionals need to understand that although a subpoena should not be ignored, not all subpoenas are valid (American Psychological Association Committee on Legal Issues, 2016). A subpoena that is invalid, or that seeks privileged communications, can be quashed by filing a motion to quash.

Although a subpoena should not be ignored, a mental health professional can get in trouble for *obeying* a subpoena! Consider psychologist Polly Rost. Rost supervised a trainee who provided therapy to a child. The child had recurring headaches from a fall at a community center. The child's mother sued the community center. The attorney for the community center sent a subpoena to Rost for the child's treatment records. Rost sent the records. Although the mother had previously authorized release of records to the *child's* attorney, there was no permission to release records to the community center or its attorney. Rost did not contact the mother or her attorney for permission to release the records.

Rost was officially reprimanded for disclosing confidential records without proper authorization. The court that reviewed the reprimand wrote, "Rost had a duty to either obtain written permission to release the records from [the child's parent] or challenge the propriety of the subpoena before a judge. Rost did neither. Instead, she unilaterally gave [the child's] records to [the community center attorney] without consulting with [the child's parent] or [the parent's] attorney. . . . The language of [the governing ethical principles] unambiguously prohibits this type of conduct." The court approved the reprimand. Thus, Polly Rost got in trouble for complying with a subpoena (*Rost v. State Board of Psychology*, 1995)!

As mentioned earlier, a subpoena overrides the ethical duty of confidentiality, although a subpoena does not override privileges. The American Psychological Association Committee on Legal Issues (2016) takes the position that a subpoena is "generally not sufficient to warrant a disclosure of confidential information" (p. 1) unless the subpoena is followed by a court order requiring disclosure. I am not sure that is correct, at least in some states. To be sure of the law in your state, it is best to consult an attorney before complying with a subpoena.

Physician–Patient Privilege

Most states have a physician–patient privilege. The U.S. Supreme Court has not approved the physician–patient privilege for federal criminal trials.

The patient is the holder of the physician–patient privilege. As is true with the psychotherapist–client privilege, a physician is ethically (and in some states legally) obliged to assert the privilege on behalf of the patient (American Psychological Association Committee on Legal Issues, 2016). The physician–patient privilege covers confidential communications between doctor and patient. Also within the privilege is information the doctor observes while examining a patient (*Cole v. Panos,* 2015).

In some states, the physician–patient privilege does not apply in criminal cases. By contrast, as noted earlier, the psychotherapist–client privilege does apply in criminal litigation. A few states have a nurse–patient privilege.

Attorney–Client Privilege

The attorney–client privilege is the oldest evidentiary privilege. The client is the holder of the privilege. It may surprise you to learn that mental health and medical professionals are sometimes covered by the attorney–client privilege (see *Neuman v. State,* 2015). This happens when when a mental health or medical professional is hired or court-appointed to assist an attorney in preparing for a trial. The California Court of Appeal observed in *Elija W. v. Superior Court* (2013), "When a psychotherapist is appointed [by a judge] to assist defense counsel, he or she is obligated to maintain the confidentiality of the client's communications not only by the psychotherapist–client privilege but also by the lawyer–client privilege."

Spousal Privileges

States have two spousal privileges: (1) spousal testimonial privilege and (2) spousal confidential communications privilege.

Under the testimonial privilege, one spouse can refuse to testify against the other. For example, if wife is accused of bank robbery, her husband can refuse to testify against her. The prosecutor cannot force the husband to take the witness stand and testify against his spouse.

The testimonial privilege also holds that a spouse *may* testify against the other if he or she wishes, but cannot be forced to do so. Thus, if the husband is willing to testify against his wife at her bank robbery trial, he may do so, and the wife cannot prevent him from taking the witness stand.

The confidential communications privilege protects private communications between spouses, and is similar, in this respect, to the other privileges discussed here. To continue with the bank robbery case, if the husband is willing to testify against his wife, he can take the witness stand, but the wife can assert the confidential communications privilege to keep him from revealing private conversations between them.

An important exception to the confidential communications privilege relates to domestic violence and child abuse. Generally, when one spouse is prosecuted for domestic violence or child abuse, the privilege does not apply.

Clergy–Penitent Privilege

Most states have a clergy–penitent privilege for confidential communications between religious leaders and persons seeking spiritual guidance. The most well-known situation covered by the clergy–penitent privilege is the Catholic confessional. The privilege does not apply to every communication with a clergy person, There must be a spiritual component to the communication.

A Child as Privilege Holder

The psychotherapist–client and other privileges, such as attorney–client privilege, apply when the client is a child. Normally, a child's parents assert the child's privilege. When a conflict exists between the parents and child, however, another adult decides issues related to privilege. In *L.A.N. v. L.M.B.* (2013), the Colorado Supreme Court ruled that in juvenile court proceedings involving young children, the child's guardian ad litem holds the child's privilege. In California juvenile court proceedings, an abused or neglected child's court-appointed attorney coholds privileges with the child (Cal. Welfare & Institutions Code § 317).

WAIVER, FORFEITURE, AND INAPPLICABILITY OF PRIVILEGES

A privilege can be waived by failing to assert it (see *United States v. Babarinde,* 2015). Generally, voluntary disclosure of privileged information to outsiders waives privilege. It is possible, however, to disclose confidential and/or privileged information for limited purposes, and such disclosure is not considered a general waiver. Clearly, waiving or forfeiting privileges is complicated and requires input from an attorney.

Patient–Litigant Exception

When a patient or client sues another person, and seeks to recover money damages for physical or mental injury, the person sued, called the defendant, has a right to prove that he or she did not cause the injuries. The defendant may seek access to the plaintiff's confidential/privileged medical or psychological records to prove that the plaintiff's injuries pre-existed the incident that forms the basis of the lawsuit (e.g., car accident). The patient–litigant exception to confidentiality and privilege states that when a person intentionally puts his or her physical and/or mental condition at issue in a lawsuit by seeking money from a defendant, the defendant may have a right to access records. The plaintiff's decision to sue forfeits the claim to privacy.

The law in many states provides that the defendant cannot be the one who triggers the patient–litigant exception by putting the plaintiff's mental or physical condition at issue. The initiative must come from the plaintiff. In *Koch v. Cox* (2007), for example, the court wrote, "A plaintiff does not put his mental state in issue merely by acknowledging he suffers from depression, for which he is not seeking recompense; nor may a defendant overcome the privilege by putting the plaintiff's mental state in issue" (p. 391). At the same time, however, when a party's mental or physical condition is central to the outcome of a case, the law generally allows judges to balance the need for relevant information against the harm caused by disclosure of privileged information.

The patient–litigant exception sometimes arises in contested child custody litigation. One parent seeks access to the other parent's mental health records in an effort to persuade a judge that the children will be harmed by the parent's mental problems. States take different approaches to this issue (Amundsen, 2015). In some states, judges generally rule that a decision to fight for custody does not automatically make a parent's mental condition a subject of dispute (see *Kinsella v. Kinsella,* 1997; *Manela v. Superior Court,* 2009; *M. M. v. L. M.,* 2012). In other states, judges are more sympathetic to the argument that parents should have access to privileged records that might shed light on what is best for children. In all states, judges have the authority to balance a parent's desire to maintain the confidentiality of psychological information against the need to ensure that children are safe.

Complaint against a Professional

Suing a professional for malpractice, or filing an ethics complaint against a professional, waives confidentiality and privilege to the extent necessary for the professional to prepare a defense against the claims (see *Koch v. Cox,* 2007). Disclosure of confidential or privileged information may be essential to establish that proper care was provided.

A DANGEROUS PATIENT

When a psychotherapist believes that a client poses a danger to others or herself, the law allows the therapist to reveal privileged communications to protect the client or others (see *Walden Behavioral Care v. K.I.*, 2015). California law, for example, observes, "There is no [psychotherapist-client privilege] if the psychotherapist has reasonable cause to believe that the patient is in such mental or emotional condition as to be dangerous to himself or to the person or property of another and that disclosure of the communication is necessary to prevent the threatened danger" (Cal. Evid. Code § 1024).

Liability for failing to warn third parties of a dangerous patient—known as the *Tarasoff* duty—is discussed more fully in Chapter 11.

Reporting Laws

Laws that require professionals to report suspected child abuse, elder abuse, and other matters, override confidentiality and privilege (Pomerance, 2015). Generally, however, reporting laws do not completely abrogate confidentiality. Rather, confidentiality is lifted only for so much information as is required to fulfill the reporting duty. Information that is not essential for the report remains protected. When a reporting law requires disclosure, the professional should reveal the minimum that is required to comply with the law. Reporting laws are discussed in Chapter 11.

CONFIDENTIALITY AND PRIVILEGE IN FORENSIC EVALUATIONS

When a judge orders a person evaluated by a mental health professional, and the professional is expected to prepare a report for court, expectations of confidentiality differ markedly from those protected by the psychotherapist–client privilege. With a court-ordered evaluation, privileges typically do not apply because there is reduced or no expectation of confidentiality.

The forensic evaluator discusses the limits of confidentiality with the client (see the American Psychological Association's [2013] *Specialty Guidelines for Forensic Psychology,* Guideline 6.01). The American Academy of Psychiatry and the Law's (2005) *Ethics Guidelines for the Practice of Forensic Psychiatry* provide, "Respect for the individual's right of privacy and the maintenance of confidentiality should be major concerns when performing forensic evaluations. Psychiatrists should maintain confidentiality to the extent possible, given the legal context. Special attention should be paid to the evaluee's understanding of medical confidentiality. A forensic evaluation requires notice to the evaluee and to collateral sources of reasonably anticipated limitations on confidentiality." The academy recommends informing clients that the professional is not the client's "doctor" or "therapist."

Courts sometimes order people to participate in counseling or psychotherapy. For example, psychotherapy may be a condition of probation. In juvenile court, parents who maltreat children may be ordered into treatment. When therapy is court ordered, the psychotherapist–client privilege generally applies. The California Supreme Court observed in *People v. Gonzales* (2013) that, although the privilege applies, a therapist may provide the court with general, nonintrusive information, such as whether the client regularly attends and participates in therapy sessions.

APPLY WHAT YOU HAVE LEARNED

To Commit, or Not to Commit—That Is the Question

When Ramiro was 7, he contracted spinal meningitis, which caused lifelong intellectual deficits. Although Ramiro was not intellectually disabled, according to the current legal standard, he was close, with an IQ between 65 and 71. When Ramiro reached adulthood, he lived with his mother, received SSI disability payments, and made extra money by collecting cans for recycling and mowing lawns. At age 20, Ramiro was convicted of his first sex offense when he hugged a 5-year-old who lived at a home where he mowed the lawn. He had an erection. Two years later, at another home where he mowed the lawn, the mother of a 7-year-old child observed Ramiro touching the child's bottom and crotch, over her clothes. When the mother confronted Ramiro, he said it "looked easy," that he didn't know how to "do sex" with women, and that he "got hot" when he looked at the child. Ramiro got his second conviction. Seventeen years elapsed before Ramiro's next conviction, this time for rubbing the genital area of a 4-year-old. For this offense, Ramiro was sentenced to a long prison term.

Years later, Ramiro was released from prison on parole. A condition of Ramiro's parole was that he attend outpatient psychological treatment as directed by his parole agent. Ramiro entered therapy with a psychologist. While on parole, Ramiro was in and out of jail for minor parole violations unrelated to children. He struggled to avoid alcohol, which was another condition of his parole. Ramiro was fitted with a GPS tracking device, and was told not have any contact with children. His parole agent monitored the GPS and, at one point, discovered that Ramiro had recently been at a park with a playground. When the parole officer called Ramiro for an explanation, Ramiro said he was at his mother's house. The officer could hear children in the background. The officer arrested Ramiro for being near children and for drinking.

While Ramiro sits in jail for the parole violations, the district attorney files a petition to civilly commit Ramiro as a sexually violent predator. The district attorney issues a subpoena for all of Ramiro's treatment records with the treating psychologist. Ramiro's attorney files a motion to quash the subpoena, arguing that Ramiro's treatment records are protected by the psychotherapist–client privilege.

In a case involving civil commitment for alleged sexual violence, should the psychologist–client privilege apply to deny the government access to privileged communications? Or is the public interest in protecting children sufficiently strong to override the privilege? What do you think?—*People v. Gonzales,* 296 P.3d 945 (Cal. 2013)

Analysis: The California Supreme Court upheld the psychotherapist–client privilege.

CONFIDENTIALITY AND PRIVILEGE IN COUPLE, FAMILY, AND GROUP THERAPY

Therapists are ethically obliged to protect confidentiality; clients are not. This obligation can create issues in couple, group, and family therapy. Therapists should explain the importance of confidentiality and encourage family and group members to respect the privacy of the group. Gerald Koocher and Jessica Daniel (2012) offer this advice, "[G]roup leaders cannot unconditionally promise group members confidentiality. . . . [I]t is important to remind group members frequently about the importance of confidentiality, not just at the beginning of the group" (vol. 2, p. 35).

The psychotherapist–client privilege applies in couple, group, and family therapy. Normally, when a third person who is not a client is present during therapy, communications are not privileged. Courts agree, however, that couple, group, and family therapy members are not "third persons" for this purpose (see *Farrell L. v. Superior Court,* 1988). The Minnesota Supreme Court observed in *State v. Andring* (1984):

> [W]e conclude that the medical privilege must be construed to encompass statements made in group psychotherapy. The participants in group psychotherapy are not casual third persons who are strangers to the psychiatrist/psychologist/nurse–patient relationship. Rather, every participant has such a relationship with the attending professional, and, in the group therapy setting, the participants actually become part of the diagnostic and therapeutic process for co-participants. . . .
>
> An interpretation which excluded group therapy from the scope of the psychotherapist–patient privilege would seriously limit the effectiveness of group psychotherapy as a therapeutic device. This would be particularly unfortunate because group therapy is a cost-effective method of psychotherapy in that it allows the therapist to treat a number of patients at the same time. It is also more effective with some patients, who, upon hearing other people reveal their innermost thoughts, are less reluctant to reveal their own . . . Because the confidentiality of communications made during group therapy is essential in maintaining its effectiveness as a therapeutic tool, . . . [w]e hold that the scope of the physician–patient medical privilege extends to include confidential group psychotherapy sessions where such sessions are an integral and necessary part of a patient's diagnosis and treatment. (p. 133)

DISCLOSURE OF CONFIDENTIAL AND PRIVILEGED INFORMATION

This section summarizes the law and practice governing the disclosure of confidential and privileged information.

Client Authorization

A competent adult client can authorize the release of confidential or privileged information. The American Psychological Association's (2010a) *Code of Ethics* provides, "Psychologists may disclose confidential information with the appropriate consent of the . . . individual client/patient . . . , unless prohibited by law" (Standard 4.05(a)). In a similar vein, the National Association of Social Workers' (2008) *Code of Ethics* states, "Social workers may disclose confidential information when appropriate with valid consent from a client or a person legally authorized to consent on behalf of a client" (§ 1.07(b)).

Unauthorized disclosure of confidential or privileged information can result in discipline (see Chapter 10). In *Sugarman v. Board of Registration in Medicine* (1996), for example, Dr. Sugarman was retained by a mother in a high-conflict custody case, with allegations of sexual abuse against the father. The judge imposed a gag order. Dr. Sugarman violated the order by releasing a psychological evaluation and holding a press conference. In upholding discipline, the Massachusetts Supreme Judicial Court found that the doctor undermined public confidence in the integrity of the medical profession. The doctor's conduct violated the family's privacy and her ethical duties as a psychiatrist. The doctor was also wrong to opine about a person she had not evaluated. In addition to professional discipline, such conduct could result in a malpractice lawsuit.

Disclose the Minimum Necessary

When a professional discloses confidential information—with client consent or because the law requires disclosure—the professional should disclose only so much as is dictated by the situation. The National Association of Social Workers' (2008) *Code of Ethics* advises, "In all instances, social workers should disclose the least amount of confidential information necessary to achieve the desired purpose; only information that is directly relevant to the purpose for which the disclosure is made should be revealed" (Ethical Standard 1.07(c)).

Disclosure Required by Law or a Court Order

A professional may release confidential information when the law requires disclosure. An ethics opinion from the American Medical Association maintains, "When the disclosure of confidential information is required by law or court order, physicians generally notify the patient. Physicians should disclose the minimal information required by law, advocate for the protection of confidential information, and, if appropriate, seek a change in the law" (see HIPAA, 45 CFR § 164.512(a)). In *In re A.M.* (2014), the Iowa Supreme Court grappled with the application of a mother's psychotherapist–patient privilege in the context of juvenile court proceedings to protect her children. The Supreme Court was "mindful of the importance of confidentiality to mental health treatment. . . . Requiring a therapist to testify without the patient's consent will have a chilling effect on mental health treatment" (p. 377). At the same time, however, the court recognized the overriding importance of protecting children from abuse and neglect. Balancing these competing interests, the court concluded that Iowa law required the mother's therapist to testify in juvenile court and to answer questions requiring disclosure of privileged communications.

Reporting Laws

Every state has laws requiring professionals to report suspected child maltreatment to a child protective services or law enforcement agency. Most states have similar laws requiring reports of elder abuse and neglect. (For a discussion of ethical issues in reporting elder abuse, see Zeranski & Halgin, 2011.) Doctors are required to report certain wounds. Reporting laws override confidentiality and privilege. The HIPAA Privacy Rule specifies that professionals may disclose protected health information in order to comply with the duty to report suspected maltreatment (45 CFR § 164.512(b)(ii)).

In addition to disclosures mandated by reporting laws, HIPAA allows the disclosure of health information on victims when disclosure is required by law, the victim agrees to disclosure, and the professional believes that disclosure is needed to prevent harm to the victim or others (45 CFR § 164.512(c)). A professional may disclose on behalf of a victim who is incapable of authorizing disclosure, if a government official states that the protected health information is not intended to be used against the victim, and that the information is immediately necessary for an ongoing investigation (45 CFR § 164.512(c)(1)(B)). The victim should be informed, unless doing so would endanger the victim (45 CFR § 164.512(c)(2)).

Tarasoff Duty to Warn

The California Supreme Court's decision in *Tarasoff v. Regents of the University of California* (1976), discussed in Chapter 11, imposes a duty on psychotherapists to warn potential victims of dangerous clients. The *Tarasoff* duty overrides confidentiality and privilege.

Professional Consultation

By long tradition, professionals discuss confidential information when they consult about cases (see American Psychological Association *Code of Ethics,* 2010a, Standard 405(b)). When the consultant is not the therapist's immediate supervisor, it is generally not necessary to reveal the client's identity. The American Psychological Association *Code of Ethics* states, "When consulting with colleagues, (1) psychologists do not disclose confidential information that reasonably could lead to the identification of a client/patient . . . with whom they have a confidential relationship unless they have obtained the prior consent of the person . . . or the disclosure cannot be avoided, and . . . (2) they disclose information only to the extent necessary to achieve the purpose of the consultation."

Emergencies

In emergencies, it is sometimes essential to reveal confidential information. The HIPAA Privacy Rule authorizes emergency disclosure that serves the client's interests (HIPAA, 45 CFR §§ 164.510(b)(3); 164.512(j)). The National Association of Social Workers' (2008) *Code of Ethics* states, "The general expectation that social workers will keep information confidential does not apply when disclosure is necessary to prevent serious, foreseeable, and imminent harm to a client or other identifiable person."

Law Enforcement Requests

Law enforcement agencies are allowed to obtain access to certain confidential information (see HIPAA, 45 CFR 164.512(f)(3)). Although it is a good practice to cooperate with law enforcement, unthinking responses to police requests for confidential or privileged information are unwarranted. What exactly are the police seeking? Will releasing the information harm a client? Would it be better to ask the police to get a subpoena or court order for the information, than to turn over it over in response to a request? Should the client be consulted before releasing information? (Usually, yes.) Would it be a good idea to talk to an attorney? If the client has an attorney, perhaps the attorney should be informed of the police request. There is no one-size-fits-all response to police requests for records.

Voluntary Disclosure

When a competent patient voluntarily or willingly discloses to outsiders some or all of a privileged communication, any privilege is generally waived (see *In re Clergy Cases,* 2010). But what is the meaning of voluntary" or "willing" disclosure? Not all voluntary disclosures waive all privileges. Moreover, clinicians are well advised to operate on the assumption that privileged information remains privileged until a judge says otherwise. It is not the clinician's job to determine when a client has "willingly" or "voluntarily" disclosed privilege information, waiving privilege. If you have questions, seek legal advice.

Protective Order

If confidential or privileged information is disclosed in legal proceedings, it may be advisable to ask a judge to issue a protective order to limit the disclosure on sensitive information (American Psychological Association Committee on Legal Issues, 2016). For example, a judge may order clinical records sealed or may order that records be disclosed only to certain persons.

Mental Health and Medical Professionals Who Testify Should Consult an Attorney before Taking Client Records to Court

When a professional takes confidential or privileged records to court, and uses the records to refresh his or her memory while testifying, the opposing attorney has a right to read the records and ask about them (Federal Rule of Evidence 612).

If the professional does not take such records to court, but reads them in preparation for testifying, the opposing attorney may ask, "Did you review the client's clinical record before coming to court today?" If the answer is "Yes," the attorney may ask the judge to require the professional to obtain the records so the lawyer can cross-examine him or her about them. The judge has discretion in requiring the professional to comply with the attorney's request.

Mental health professionals are advised to consult an attorney about reviewing confidential and privileged records in preparation for testimony and about taking these records to court.

CASE STUDIES REVISITED

Let's return to the cases outlined at the beginning of the chapter, beginning with the prosecutor's subpoena for records on Maria. Recall that the prosecutor wanted to know if Maria was ever a client of the domestic violence center.

THE PROSECUTOR SUBPOENAS RECORDS ON MARIA

Maria's was an actual case from my practice. I represented the domestic violence center, and I filed a motion to quash the prosecutor's subpoena based on the psychotherapist–client privilege. In my motion, I argued that any records on Maria were privileged, including any record that she had—or hadn't—received services from the center. In the end, the prosecutor, who is a fine attorney, didn't put up a fight, and the issue "went away."

DID HE FALL OR JUMP?

Remember Juan, the young attorney who either jumped or fell to his death from his office in the Acme Building? The sad facts of Juan's death are drawn from a New York case (*Prink v. Rockefeller Center, Inc.*, 1979). The state's highest court ruled that the lawsuit triggered the patient–litigant exception to privilege. The court wrote, "By bringing or defending a personal injury action in which mental or physical condition is affirmatively put in issue, a party waives the privilege" (p. 316).

"WHAT HAPPENED AT WORK TODAY?"

You've come home from a long day seeing clients, and you've heard some amazing stories. When you walk in the door, your partner says, "Hi. What happened at work today?" What do you say? My guess is that this ethical dilemma confronts every professional who deals with clients. On one hand, the answer should be easy: You can't reveal confidential information to your partner any more than you can to your barista at Starbucks. But is that realistic? Don't most of us tell our spouses or partners more than we should? I'm not saying I do—that's confidential!

CONCLUSION

Confidentiality is at the heart of clinical work. Yet, complete privacy cannot be guaranteed because competing values are at work that, in some cases, necessitate disclosure. A complex labyrinth of laws and ethical guidelines strive to strike the proper balance between privacy and revelation.

11

Malpractice and Ethical Violations

This chapter discusses the unpleasant subject of professional malpractice and violations of ethics rules. The odds are small that you will ever be sued for malpractice or have an ethics complaint filed against you. Yet, medical and mental health professionals who work with victims of interpersonal violence, or who treat offenders, understand the level of emotion involved, and the likelihood that clients will be embroiled in civil or criminal litigation. Given the often volatile nature of the work, a basic knowledge of malpractice and ethical lapses has become increasingly necessary.

The word "malpractice" combines the words "mal" and "practice." In Latin, "mal" means bad. Thus, malpractice literally means bad practice. Claims of malpractice are usually based on accusations of negligence. We introduced the concept of negligence in Chapter 2 on crimes and defenses. We revisit it here. The American Law Institute publishes *Restatements* of the law in various areas (e.g., contracts, property, torts). The third *Restatement of Torts* defines negligence as follows: "A person acts negligently if the person does not exercise reasonable care under all the circumstances" (§ 3.)

The elements of negligence in the context of malpractice are: (1) the professional owed a duty of care to the client, (2) the professional breached the duty of care, and (3) the breach caused harm to the client. Another way to describe malpractice based on negligence is to say that a professional's conduct fell below the standard of care required for professionals in that discipline.

In malpractice litigation, expert testimony is normally required to establish that the practice of the accused professional fell below the standard of care. In rare cases, malpractice is so obvious that expert testimony is not required. As the Louisiana Court of Appeals reasoned in *Elledge v. Williamson* (2014), "Plaintiff is generally required to produce expert testimony in a medical malpractice action to establish the applicable standard of care and to determine whether that standard was breached, except where the negligence is so obvious that a lay person can infer negligence without the counsel of expert testimony" (p. 438).

Medical and mental health professionals owe a duty of care to patients and clients. At the same time, these professionals are not guarantors of success. Thus, they are generally not liable when a course of treatment is not effective. As the court found in *Park v. Kovachevich* (2014), "Liability is imposed only if the doctor's treatment decisions do not reflect his or her own best judgment, or fall short of the generally accepted standard of care" (p. 81). Errors in judgment, as well as mistakes, are not typically malpractice. The standard of care does not demand perfection.

MALPRACTICE LIABILITY FOR PSYCHOTHERAPY

Psychotherapy treatment is seldom a basis for malpractice liability. There are many theories and techniques of psychotherapy. A wise therapist does not guarantee success. Liability could attach if a professional restricts treatment to talking, in the face of evidence that something else is needed. For example, if a competent psychotherapist would realize that a client's symptoms point to an organic disorder—for example, dementia or a brain tumor—the therapist could be held liable for a failure to apprehend the client's condition and make the proper referral. Thus, in *Deasy v. United States* (1996), the plaintiff was a disabled veteran. He successfully sued two VA medical centers because VA psychiatrists failed to refer him for treatment of edema, a buildup of fluid in the body.

A therapist might be liable for continuing talk therapy when a reasonable professional would understand that the client has decompensated to the point of needing hospitalization.

There is one area of psychotherapy, as practiced by a small number of therapists in the 1980s and 1990s, that led to lawsuits. Therapists were accused of using highly suggestive techniques to implant false memories of childhood sexual abuse (see, e.g., *Johnson v. Rogers Memorial Hospital,* 2005).

CLINICAL AND FORENSIC ROLES IN MENTAL HEALTH

Clinical practice and forensic practice are typically incompatible. Samuel Knapp and Leon VandeCreek (2006) advise, "Psychologists should avoid mixing treatment and forensic relationships" (p. 166). The American Psychological Association's (2013) "Specialty Guidelines for Forensic Psychology" state, "Providing forensic and therapeutic psychological services to the same individual or closely related individuals involves multiple relationships that may impair objectivity and/or cause exploitation or other harm" (Guideline 4.02.01).

What is forensic practice? According to the American Psychological Association's (2013) "Specialty Guidelines," "Forensic psychology refers to professional practice by a psychologist working within any subdiscipline of psychology (e.g., clinical, developmental, social, cognitive) when applying the scientific, technical, or specialized knowledge of psychology to the law to assist in addressing legal, contractual, and administrative matters." Clearly, conducting a court-ordered psychological evaluation to determine whether a criminal defendant is competent to stand trial or is insane is forensic practice. When a mental health professional conducts a child custody evaluation for family court, the professional is practicing forensically. Knapp and VandeCreek (2006) explain, "Any time psychologists write letters recommending custody or visitation arrangements, they are making a custody recommendation" (p. 167). Rebecca Weiss and Barry Rosenfeld (2012) provide useful guidance on cross-cultural issues in forensic assessment. Jorge Varela and Mary Conroy (2012) delve into professional competencies in forensic practice. Jennifer McLaughlin and Lisa Kan (2014) discuss test usage in forensic practice.

What is *not* forensic practice? Being aware of the forensic implications of therapy does not transform clinicians into forensic practitioners. Nor does testifying, unless the testimony focuses squarely on psycholegal issues. Reporting suspected child abuse is not forensic practice. The fact that a client has been ordered into therapy by a judge does not render therapy forensic.

PROFESSIONAL BOUNDARIES

A boundary separates clients from therapists. The boundary is not a hierarchical one in which one is superior to the other; rather, clients and therapists are on an equal footing. The boundary is intended to preserve the differing roles of client and therapist.

That boundary is permeable, of course. And not all boundary crossings are unethical or improper. For example, in the right circumstances, a therapist may decide to cross the boundary by self-disclosing some aspect of his or her life (see Knapp, Handlesman, Gootlieb & VandeCreek, 2013). In another situation, if a therapist's child is on the same sports team as the client's, and the adults interact when their children are competing at games, there is no ethical lapse.

DUAL RELATIONSHIPS

In the literature on ethics and psychotherapy, no issue garners more attention than dual relationships, or, as they are also called, multiple relationships. Ofer Zur (2007) defines dual relationship as "any situation in which multiple roles exist between a therapist and a client" (p. 21). The American Psychological Association's (2012) *Code of Ethics* gives the following definition:

> A multiple relationship occurs when a psychologist is in a professional role with a person and (1) at the same time is in another role with the same person, (2) at the same time is in a relationship with a person closely associated with or related to the person with whom the psychologist has the professional relationship, or (3) promises to enter into another relationship in the future with the person or a person closely associated with or related to the person. (Ethical Standard 3.05(a))

Examples of dual relationships include providing psychotherapy to a friend or family member; having a sexual relationship with a client; engaging in business with a client; and switching from a therapeutic to a forensic role.

Zur (2007) clarifies the distinction between dual relationships and boundary crossings:

> It is important to differentiate between boundary crossings such as therapeutic touch, clinically driven self-disclosure, home visits, and gift exchanges, which do not entail a secondary relationship and those associations that involve dual relationships. Therapists in the former situations operate exclusively in their clinical capacity and, therefore, these situations are not considered dual relationships. For the same reasons, attending a client's wedding or self-disclosing for clinical reasons rather than social ones does not constitute social or other dual relationships. However, if self-disclosure or attending the

> client's wedding takes place in the course of a social relationship or as part of a community relationship between the therapist and client, it constitutes a dual relationship. Incidental, chance encounters between therapists and clients outside the therapy room that are not part of a social, collegial, or business connection do not constitute dual relationships. (pp. 21–22)

Not all dual relations are unethical. Thomas Nagy (2011) observes, "Not every multiple-role relationship is unethical, but when a psychologist's objectivity and competence are compromised, the psychologist may find that personal needs and ambitions surface, diminishing the quality of his or her work" (p. 37).

Mental health professionals should think twice before entering dual relationships. As the American Psychological Association's (2012) *Code of Ethics* cautions:

> A psychologist refrains from entering into a multiple relationship if the multiple relationship could reasonably be expected to impair the psychologist's objectivity, competence, or effectiveness in performing his or her functions as a psychologist, or otherwise risks exploitation or harm to the person with whom the professional relationship exists. Multiple relationships that would not reasonably be expected to cause impairment or risk exploitation or harm are not unethical. (Ethical Standard 3.05(a))

Knapp and VandeCreek (2006) advise, "Psychologists need not develop rigid stances, but they should use their clinical judgment to determine when such boundary crossings may be therapeutically indicated" (p. 76).

Using the Informed Consent Process to Inform about Boundaries and Dual Relations

As part of the informed consent process, clients should be informed about the importance of boundaries and the nature of potential dual relationships.

Self-Disclosure

Experts have different opinions regarding the propriety of self-disclosure in psychotherapy. Some therapists have a rigid policy against it; others are less absolute. The debate is ongoing.

Touch

Touch is powerful, and the decision to touch or hug a client deserves forethought. In many, but not all cases, a brief, compassionate pat on the hand or shoulder is proper and comforting.

Sex with a Client

It is unethical for a mental health professional to have sex with a current client (*Kirchmeyer v. Phillips,* 2016). As the National Association of Social Workers' (2008) *Code of Ethics* affirms, "Social workers should under no circumstances engage in sexual activities or sexual contact with current clients, whether such contact is consensual or forced" (Ethical Standard 1.09(a)). According to the American Psychiatric Association's (2015) *Commentary on Ethics in Practice,* "Sexual behavior with patients is unethical. Further, even the possibility of a future sexual or romantic relationship may contaminate current clinical treatment. Therefore, sexual activity not only with current, but also with former patients is unethical" (Topic 3.2.6).

In *Leon v. Ohio Board of Psychology* (1992), the Ohio Supreme Court ruled that waiting 7 months after treatment ended to begin a sexual relationship was not sufficient to avoid discipline. The court wrote, "It takes no citation of authority to safely state that sexual relations between any professional and a client or immediate ex-client are universally prohibited by the ethical regulations of practically every profession" (p. 687). In some states, sex with clients is not only unethical, it is criminal. When it comes to sex with former clients, the American Association for Marriage and Family Therapy (2012) states that a minimum of 2 years should elapse after therapy ends (Principle 1.5).

Having sex with a client is virtually always malpractice. Knapp and VandeCreek (2006) note, "Courts have traditionally viewed sexual relationships with patients as grounds for malpractice" (p. 890). In *L.L. v. Medical Protective Company* (1984), a woman hired a psychiatrist to help her with "difficulty maintaining healthy interpersonal relationships, particularly with men" (p. 457). During therapy, the psychiatrist had the patient orally copulate him. The patient sued for malpractice. In *Disciplinary Counsel v. Bunstine* (2013), a lawyer was suspended for a year after soliciting sex from a client in a child custody case. The lawyer had offered to "make other arrangements" for payment of fees, which included instructing the client to answer her door naked.

INFORMED CONSENT

A client must consent to any medical or psychological treatment before treatment begins. The National Association of Social Workers' (2008) *Code of Ethics* affirms, "Social workers should provide services to clients only in the context of a professional relationship based, when appropriate, on valid informed consent" (Ethical Standard 1.03(a)). The American Psychiatric Association's (2015) *Commentary on Ethics in Practice* notes, "Psychiatrists should recognize the importance of informed consent for assessment or treatment as an essential means to recognition of and respect for the patient's autonomy and personhood" (Topic 3.2.4). Consent is only valid if it is informed. Treatment without informed consent can constitute malpractice.

To ensure that consent is informed, the client should be apprised of (1) the nature and limits of the proposed treatment, (2) the likelihood of successful treatment, (3) the risks and benefits of treatment, (4) the side effects, (5) the alternatives to the proposed treatment, (6) the client's right to refuse or terminate treatment, and (7) the extent and limits of confidentiality. Regarding confidentiality, Samuel Lustgarten (2015) advises, "Informed consent should incorporate a method for securing, protecting, and handling data. . . . It is important that an informed consent document properly explain, justify, and present accurate risks to data storage and communication. Should an expectation for phone, text, and/or e-mail communication be established, it is important to inform clients of the increased risk and methods for reducing leaks. In the interest of client privacy and autonomy, it may be appropriate to suggest pen and paper if worries about privacy concerns are present" (p. 159).

A discussion of the side effects of medicines is an important part of informed consent. Some medicines used to treat mental illness, for example, have powerful side effects, which can be permanent. The most well-known side effect of certain antipsychotic drugs is tardive dyskinesia. Sheldon Gelman (1984) describes tardive dyskinesia: "The tongue, mouth, and chin are common sites of tardive dyskinesia: the tongue sweeps from side to side, the mouth opens and closes, and the jaw moves in all directions. Fingers, arms and legs may display comparable movements; swallowing, speech or breathing can be affected as well" (p. 1742). Patients who developed tardive dyskinesia have sued mental health providers (see *Barclay v. Campbell,* 1986; *Deen v. Pounds,* 2011).

When a court orders a client to have a mental health evaluation, informed consent may not be necessary. Nevertheless, the professional informs the client of the elements of informed consent and helps the client understand whether, and to what extent, the client can refuse an evaluation. When a person is not competent to consent to treatment, another person may be appointed to consent on his or her behalf (e.g., a guardian or conservator). In some cases, consent is obtained from a judge.

Informed consent is not required in emergency situations in which an individual needs immediate care, but is incapable of consenting, perhaps because he or she is unconscious.

Normally, children cannot consent to medical or mental health care, and parental approval is needed. States generally allow minors to consent to certain medical procedures without parental involvement. Gerald Koocher and Jessica Daniel (2012) caution, "Never take the word of one parent that they have sole legal custody or that the other parent has agreed. In such cases, always ask to see the custody agreement and attempt to talk with the other parent to confirm agreement" (vol. 2, p. 11).

States allow teenagers to consent to some types of care, especially regarding reproductive health and mental health counseling. For example, in California, a minor age 12 or older may consent to mental health care. The teen's parents can be involved unless the provider determines parental involvement would be inappropriate (Cal. Family Code § 6924). A teenager can consent to medical care related to the prevention and treatment of pregnancy (Cal. Family Code § 6925). He or she also can consent to treatment of sexually transmitted infection (Cal. Family Code § 6926). Finally, a minor who is the victim of rape or sexual assault may consent to medical care and the collection of medical evidence regarding the offense (Cal. Family Code § 6927, 6928). Similar laws exist in other states.

DISCLOSURE OF CONFIDENTIAL AND/OR PRIVILEGED MATTER

Professionals can be sued for improperly disclosing confidential and/or privileged records. In *David D. v. Luzio* (2013), for example, the plaintiff was a minor who had sexually abused a younger child. The minor was brought before the juvenile court, where he was evaluated by mental health professionals. Later, the mental health professionals devised a mock trial based on the juvenile court case. The professionals conducted the mock trial to help other mental health professionals understand juvenile court. Apparently, during performances of the mock trial, the offending minor's name, and that of the other child, was revealed. The minors sued. Although the suit was unsuccessful because the minors did not prove damages, the case illustrates the importance of keeping confidential information, including names in a legal case, confidential.

Another interesting case is *Gracy v. Eaker* (2002). A married couple consulted a mental health provider for help with marital difficulties. According to the couple, during individual sessions with the therapist, each of them disclosed to the therapist, *in confidence,* extremely private information that had never been revealed to the other spouse. The therapist then revealed this information to the other spouse. The couple sued the therapist for emotional distress caused by disclosing the information. The Florida Supreme Court ruled the case could go forward to a trial.

In Arkansas, a nurse disclosed confidential patient information to her husband, who then threatened to reveal the information (Wood, 2016). The nurse and her husband were indicted in federal court for conspiracy to violate HIPAA. The nurse pleaded guilty.

Consider also *Pachowitz v. LeDoux* (2003), in which Katherine, a volunteer emergency medical technician (EMT) for the fire department, and other EMTs responded by ambulance to a 911 call at Julie's home, where they found her unconscious. After transporting Julie to the hospital, Katherine told her friend that she had taken Julie to the hospital for a possible overdose. Julie sued Katherine for invasion of privacy, and won.

SUICIDE

No area of mental health practice poses a greater risk of being sued than patient suicide. The New Jersey Supreme Court wrote in *Komlodi v. Picciano* (2014) "A psychiatrist treating a suicidal patient may have a duty to protect the patient from self-harm" (p. 1247). Suicide-related cases generally involve (1) suicide of a hospitalized patient, (2) suicide after a patient is released from the hospital, and (3) suicide of an outpatient.

Suicide of a Hospitalized Patient

Mental health professionals owe a duty of care to hospitalized patients to take reasonable steps to prevent suicide (*In re P.W.*, 2016). In *Kockelman v. Segal* (1998), the California Court of Appeal wrote, "a hospital owes its patients a duty of protection and must exercise such reasonable care as the patient's known condition might require" (p. 500).

Suicide of a Recently Discharged Patient

When a recently discharged patient commits suicide, dies in some other way, or kills someone, the next of kin sometimes argue that the discharge decision was negligent. In *Kozlovski v. Altapointe Health Systems, Inc.* (2015), for example, a young man named Jeffrey Brown had a long history of serious mental illness, running away from home, and committing violent acts. Jeffrey attacked his father and was involuntarily hospitalized. Following treatment, the hospital staff agreed that Jeffrey met the requirements for discharge, and he was released to a group home. A few days later, Jeffrey left the group home and was struck and killed by a car. His family sued the group home and the psychiatrist who was in charge of Jeffrey's treatment in the state hospital. The court ruled in favor of the psychiatrist, pointing out that there was no evidence that the doctor did anything wrong in discharging Jeffrey. The court acknowledged the competing interests that mental health professionals must balance when deciding to discharge a patient:

> [Mental health professionals] owe a duty to the general public not to release a civilly committed patient until his treatment has been completed and he is no longer a threat to public safety and order. However, [mental health professionals] have a concomitant duty to the patient. The [professionals] must provide their patient a treatment program that achieves the purposes of confinement under the least restrictive conditions. They must provide him with immediate and long-range treatment goals; and, if he fulfills those goals or no longer requires hospitalization in accordance with the standards for commitment, they must release him. (p. 449)

The Alabama Supreme Court ruled that the psychiatrist had immunity from liability because she exercised reasonable judgment in balancing the competing interests, and in discharging Jeffrey to the group home.

Another "discharge" case, *Squeo v. Norwalk Hospital Association* (2015), concerned Stephen, who was suicidal. His mother called the police, and Stephen was taken to a hospital for psychiatric evaluation. The following morning, a professional at the hospital telephoned Stephen's parents and informed them that their son would soon be released from the hospital because he did not appear to be suicidal. Within hours, Stephen returned to his parents' home and hung himself from a tree, where his parents discovered him. The parents sued the professional and the hospital. The Connecticut Supreme Court ruled that, in the right circumstances, surviving family members can sue in such cases.

See also *Jacoves v. United Merchandising Corp.* (1992) in which a 20-year-old committed suicide not long after being discharged from a hospital.

Suicide of an Outpatient

It is easy to make the case that medical and mental health professionals must take reasonable steps to protect hospitalized patients from self-harm. Hospital staff has considerable control over inpatients. However, should the duty to protect extend to outpatients, over whom they have very little, if any, control? In *Kockelman v. Segal* (1998), the California Court of Appeal said yes. The court wrote, "California courts have recognized that psychiatrists owe a duty of care, consistent with standards in the professional community, to provide appropriate treatment for potentially suicidal patients, whether the patient is hospitalized or not. There is no reasonable basis [to distinguish between inpatients and outpatients]. Indeed, it would seem almost self-evident that doctors must use reasonable care with *all* of their patients in diagnosing suicidal intent and implementing treatment plans" (p. 501).

The *Haar v. Ulwelling* (2007) case had a different outcome. Eric Haar was receiving treatment from a psychologist for bipolar disorder. Haar also had five office visits with Dr. Ulwelling, a psychiatrist. Dr. Ulwelling prescribed medications. Haar expressed dissatisfaction with Dr. Ulwelling, and Haar's mother suggested he get a new doctor. Haar missed two office visits with Dr. Ulwelling. He was hospitalized, and was treated by a different psychiatrist. Haar killed himself a month later. Haar's parents sued Dr. Ulwelling, claiming he had a duty to prevent their son's suicide. The trial judge ruled that Dr. Ulwelling had no duty to prevent Haar's suicide, and the New Mexico Court of Appeals affirmed, writing:

> Under the circumstances, we see no affirmative duty, much less a right, on the part of Defendant to have intervened in the ongoing treatment by the other mental health care providers, treatment that Haar chose and continued with to the exclusion of Defendant and without having sought Defendant's assistance in any regard. Haar showed no interest in maintaining any semblance of a physician-patient relationship with Defendant. We therefore think it is unreasonable to place upon Defendant a requirement that he have imposed his views or treatment recommendations on Haar [or his new doctors] for the purpose of

> guarding against Haar's suicide. Further, under circumstances such as those in the present case, we are concerned about the consequences of burdening therapists generally with such a requirement. . . .
>
> The once-existing special relationship and ability to control Haar's treatment disintegrated as a result of Haar's failure . . . to seek Defendant's assistance in any regard and Haar's having chosen other mental health providers to handle his treatment and medication. (p. 73)

THE DUTY TO PROTECT THIRD PERSONS FROM A DANGEROUS PATIENT

Generally, the law does not impose a duty on people to protect other people from dangerous or criminal acts committed by third persons. However, the law *does* impose a duty to protect when "a special relation exists between the actor and the third person, which imposes a duty upon the actor to control the third person's conduct" (*Restatement of Torts, Second* § 315(a)). A "special relation" exists between mental health providers and clients. As a result, in some cases, providers must take prudent steps to protect third persons from dangerous clients.

Consider Ruth's dilemma. In September, Ruth, a psychotherapist in private practice, began treating 22-year-old Sean, a university student, for depression. Sean's parents arranged for him to get help because he has long suffered from depression, he is failing his classes, and he seldom sets foot outside his dorm room. Ruth had weekly sessions with Sean, and, after five sessions, he began disclosing worrisome fantasies about shooting fellow students and professors. Sean told Ruth that he spent many hours on his computer reading about campus shootings. Ruth concluded that Sean was deeply depressed and needed medication. She discussed medication with Sean, but he resisted, telling Ruth, "I hate the way that stuff makes me feel. My parents forced me to take medication when I was a kid, but I won't do it anymore." Ruth asked Sean about his fantasies, and he said, "It is just fantasy; not reality; like a video game. I'm not going to hurt anyone." Ruth asked if Sean had access to a gun. He said, "No." In further sessions, Ruth determined that Sean's depression was worsening and was taking on psychotic features. Sean continued ruminating about shooting students and professors, especially his physics professor, who Sean said, "really has it in for me. He hates me. He has his teaching assistant follow me."

What should Ruth do? Should she contact Sean's parents? Should she contact university administrators or the police? How about the university health service? Should she call the physics professor and his teaching assistant and warn them about Sean? If Ruth contacts anyone, what information should she disclose? If she decides to contact other people, should Ruth inform Sean of her plan?

The leading court decision on the duty to warn third parties of dangerous clients is the California Supreme Court's decision in *Tarasoff v. Regents of the University of California* (1976), in which the court ruled that psychotherapists have a duty to warn potential victims of dangerous clients. The court wrote, "[O]nce a therapist does in fact determine, or under applicable professional standards reasonably should have determined, that a patient poses a serious danger of violence to others, he bears a duty to exercise reasonable care to protect the foreseeable victim of that danger. While the discharge of this duty of due care will necessarily vary with the facts of each case, in each instance the adequacy of the therapist's conduct must be measured against the traditional negligence standard of the rendition of reasonable care under the circumstances" (p. 442). Failure to warn potential victims is malpractice.

A duty to warn arises only when a patient threatens a third person. In *Dunnigan v. Silva* (2005), James Prather was civilly committed to a psychiatric hospital. Upon his release, he killed his wife and daughter, and then took his own life. Surviving family members sued a doctor and the hospital for failing to inform the victims that James was released. The defendants prevailed because there was no evidence that James had made threats against his wife and daughter.

Professional organizations have recognized the duty to warn. For instance, an ethics opinion from the American Medical Association (2007) states, "When a patient threatens to inflict serious physical harm to another person or to him or herself and there is a reasonable probability that the patient may carry out the threat, the physician should take reasonable precautions for the protection of the intended victim, which may include notification of law enforcement authorities."

The *Tarasoff* duty to warn overrides claims of confidentiality and privilege. According to the California Supreme Court in *Tarasoff*, "The public policy favoring protection of the confidential character of patient–psychotherapist communications must yield to the extent to which disclosure is essential to avert danger to others. The protective privilege ends where the public peril begins" (p. 442). In a similar vein, the Colorado Supreme Court remarked in *People v. Kailey* (2014), "We hold that if a mental health treatment provider believes, using his or her professional judgment, that statements made by a patient during a therapy session threaten imminent physical violence against a specific person or persons—and accordingly trigger the provider's 'duty to warn'—the patient's threatening statements are not protected by the psychologist–patient privilege" (p. 91).

The *Code of Ethics* of the National Association of Social Workers (2008) grapples with *Tarasoff* as follows: "The general expectation that social workers will keep information confidential does not apply when disclosure is necessary to prevent serious, foreseeable, and imminent harm to a client or other identifiable person" (Ethical Standard 1.07(c)).

Medical and mental health professionals who warn potential victims of a dangerous client cannot be sued for disclosure of confidential information (see *Expose v. Thad Wilderson & Associates,* 2015).

The *Tarasoff* duty to warn is controversial. Donald Bersoff (2014) argued "that *Tarasoff* is bad law, bad social science, and bad social policy" (p. 461). Bersoff and other critics argue that requiring a therapist to breach confidentiality may destroy the therapist's ability to help the patient deal with feelings of anger or violence because the patient cannot reveal those feelings without risking disclosure. Bersoff suggests giving therapists a measure of discretion in whether to disclose. Stephen Huey (2015) goes a step further, arguing, "A better rule would require disclosure of serious violent threats only with a patient's consent. . . . [I]f disclosure could occur only with consent, therapy would be a safe place for them to obtain help" (p. 284). Griffin Edwards (2014) conducted empirical research and concluded that requiring therapists to warn potential victims could actually increase the murder rate!

Those who favor requiring therapists to warn potential victims about dangerous clients argue that although confidentiality is important, human life is more so. If warning potential victims saves lives, the sacrifice of confidentiality is worth the cost. If a patient threatens a therapist, the therapist is permitted to breach confidentiality in the name of self-protection. Shouldn't the same rule apply when a patient threatens others?

About half the states have statutes on the *Tarsoff* duty to warn. The California Legislature codified *Tarasoff* in Civil Code § 43.93, which maintains: "There shall be no monetary liability on the part of . . . a psychotherapist . . . in failing to protect from a patient's threatened violent behavior or failing to predict and protect from a patient's violent behavior except if the patient has communicated to the psychotherapist a serious threat of physical violence against a reasonably identifiable victim or victims." Arizona's law states, "There shall be no cause of action against a mental health provider nor shall legal liability be imposed for breaching a duty to prevent harm to a person caused by a patient, unless both of the following occur: (1) The patient has communicated to the mental health provider an explicit threat of imminent serious physical harm or death to a clearly identified or identifiable victim or victims, and the patient has the apparent intent and ability to carry out such threat. (2) The mental health provider fails to take reasonable precautions" (Arizona Revised Statutes § 36-517.02).

In summary, a professional with a duty to warn takes reasonable precautions by communicating the threat to identifiable victims, contacting law enforcement officials, initiating involuntary civil commitment proceedings, or taking other reasonable steps.

Assuming that a *Tarasoff*-like duty to warn is applicable, and a mental health professional warns a potential victim or calls the police, may the provider also testify in future legal proceedings? The Colorado Supreme Court addressed this question in *People v. Kailey* (2014):

> While virtually all jurisdictions have acknowledged some form of the duty to warn, various jurisdictions have nevertheless strenuously disagreed whether mental health treatment providers can testify about threatening statements made by their patients when these statements have been disclosed pursuant to the duty to warn. For example, in *United States v. Hayes,* 227 F.3d 578, 586 (6th Cir. 2000), the Sixth Circuit Court of Appeals held that even if a mental health treatment provider warns potential victims and law enforcement about a patient's threatening statements, the provider is still barred from testifying about these statements in court. In contrast, in *United States v. Auster,* 517 F.3d 312, 317 (5th Cir. 2008), the Fifth Circuit Court of Appeals held that the testimonial privilege does not bar mental health treatment providers from testifying about threatening statements that the providers disclosed pursuant to their duty to warn.
>
> We conclude that the Fifth Circuit's approach best harmonizes the legislature's sometimes-competing objectives in establishing the psychologist-patient privilege and the duty to warn. Specifically, we hold that threatening statements disclosed pursuant to that duty are not subject to the privilege because (1) such statements are not confidential as a matter of law, and (2) barring them would be inconsistent with legislative intent. (p. 94)

The third *Restatement of Torts* has useful examples of situations in which a duty to warn may arise:

Dr. Jones, a psychiatrist, sees a patient, Todd. During the course of therapy, Todd expresses a desire to harm his former girlfriend, Caroline, who had severed their relationship. Dr. Jones concludes that Todd poses a real risk of acting on his threat. Although Todd does not name his girlfriend in his sessions with Dr. Jones, her name was in Todd's medical records based on an initial history completed when Todd first became a patient of Dr. Jones. Dr. Jones does nothing to notify Caroline or otherwise take steps to protect her. Todd physically harms Caroline, who sues Dr. Jones. Dr. Jones owes Caroline a duty of reasonable care and is subject to liability for Caroline's harm.

Steve, a 14-year-old having adolescent adjustment difficulties, is referred to Dr. Cress, a psychologist. Dr. Cress treats Steve for several months, concluding that Steve suffers from mild depression and deficits in peer social skills. Steve occasionally expresses generalized anger at his circumstances in life but never blames others or gives any other indication that he might act violently, and Dr. Cress has no reason to think that Steve poses a risk of harm to others. Steve hacks his parents to death with a scythe. In this case, Dr. Cress had no duty to Steve's parents and is not subject to liability to the administrators of their estates.

Dr. Strand, a clinical psychologist, becomes aware, during the course of counseling that his patient, Lester, is sexually abusing his 8-year-old stepdaughter, Kelly. Dr. Strand does not communicate this information to Kelly's mother or to appropriate officials of the state Department of Social Services, no does he take any other steps to prevent Lester from continuing his sexual assaults on Kelly. Dr. Strand owes a duty of reasonable care to Kelly and is subject to liability for the harm due to Lester's continuing abuse of her.

Perrin suffers from schizophrenia, which can generally be controlled with medication. However, Perrin intermittently, with no apparent pattern, stops taking his medication. On these occasions he suffers severe delusions and frequently believes that he is under attack by various inanimate objects. Several of these episodes are punctuated by aggressive and threatening behavior that leads Dr. Hillsley, his treating psychotherapist, to believe that Perrin cannot live on his own and poses a significant danger to others unless he continues taking his medication. Dr. Hillsley receives a call from Perrin one Saturday morning, during which it becomes clear that he is not taking his medicine. Perrin requests an immediate office visit and tells Dr. Hillsley that pedestrians on the street are carrying surgical instruments with which to investigate Perrin's brain; Perrin assures Dr. Hillsley that he

> will retaliate in kind at the first provocation. Dr. Hillsley, not wanting to be bothered on the weekend, declines to meet with Perrin to evaluate whether he should be involuntarily committed or to recommend that Perrin seek an evaluation at the local psychiatric hospital. Instead, he suggests that Perrin go home and call his office on a weekday to make an appointment to see him during regular hours. Instead of going home, Perrin grabs Jake, a passerby on the street, and stabs him in the neck. Dr. Hillsley has a special relationship with Perrin and a duty of reasonable care to Jake and others put at risk by Perrin. Dr. Hillsley is subject to liability for Jake's harm. (§ 41, pp. 69–71)

John Monahan (2008) draws on his experience consulting on *Tarasoff* cases to offer the following advice:

> Most of the *Tarasoff*-like cases on which I have worked have faulted clinicians not for making an inaccurate prediction but for failing to gather information that would have made a reasonable effort at prediction possible. There are generally four sources in which relevant information can be found: in the records of past treatment, in the records of current treatment, from interviewing the patient, and from interviewing significant others. In some criminal contexts (e.g., assessments for suitability for release on parole or from insanity commitment) additional records in the form of police and probation reports, arrest records, and trial transcripts may also be available and should be consulted. But in the civil context, these records are generally not available to clinicians. (p. 182)

In *Thapar v. Zezulka* (1999), the Texas Supreme Court rejected the duty to warn, writing, "We refrain from imposing on mental-health professionals a duty to warn third parties of a patient's threats" (p. 636).

Returning to Ruth's dilemma with Sean, the troubled college student, her case makes me happy I'm not a mental health professional! Ruth's is a classic *Tarasoff* duty-to-warn scenario. What should Ruth do? Reasonable minds can differ, but, one thing is sure, Ruth should *not* do nothing. I believe these facts trigger a duty to warn. Ruth should immediately consult colleagues. What form the warning takes will depend on the law in Ruth's state. Ruth should seek legal advice. Everything must be carefully documented. If Ruth reveals confidential or privileged information, she should keep such disclosures to a minimum while, at the same time, ensuring adequate warning. Speaking for myself, I believe protecting people from serious harm or death is more important than confidentiality, so I would err on the side of disclosing enough to make warnings effective.

ABANDONMENT VERSUS TERMINATION OF TREATMENT

Bringing therapy to an end is part of therapy, not an afterthought. Nagy (2011) explains, "Psychologists generally terminate treatment when the client or patient (a) no longer needs the services, (b) is not likely to benefit, or (c) is being harmed by continuing. A fourth situation not mentioned in the Ethics Code would be a judgment call by the therapist that the client or patient is no longer benefiting from the services" (p. 194).

Knapp and VandeCreek (2006) add, "Except when institutional policies state otherwise, psychologists may refuse to treat potential patients for any reason, including their perceived ability to pay for services. Once treatment has started, however, they do not have an unqualified right to terminate unless the treatment is completed; the patient ends the relationship; or the psychologist recommends alternative services and provides termination counseling, unless precluded by the actions of the clients or third-party payers" (p. 196).

Competent termination of treatment looks nothing like abandonment. Knapp and VandeCreek (2006) advise, "Abandonment means termination of a patient when the psychologist knows or should have known that more treatment was needed" (p. 197). The New Jersey Supreme Court defined abandonment in *Marshall v. Klebanov* (2006): "A mental health practitioner abandons a patient by failing to continue to provide service to the patient when it is still needed in a case for which the physician has assumed responsibility and from which the physician has not been properly relieved" (p. 897). It is malpractice to abandon a client when the abandonment harms the client.

THE DUTY TO REPORT CHILD ABUSE AND NEGLECT

Every state requires professionals who interact with children to report suspected child abuse and neglect. The reporting duty applies to social workers, physicians, dentists, nurses, psychologists, counselors, teachers, law enforcement officers, and child care professionals.

The duty to report suspected maltreatment is triggered when a professional possesses the level of suspicion specified in the reporting law. Reporting laws differ slightly in the wording used to describe the triggering level of suspicion. Common phrases include "cause to believe," "reasonable cause to believe," "known or suspected abuse," and "observation or examination that discloses evidence of abuse."

Although the wording of reporting laws differ, the basic thrust of these laws is the same: A report is required when a professional has information that would lead a competent professional to believe maltreatment is likely. Whether the triggering level of suspicion exists depends on the facts of the case, interpreted through the lens of experience and judgment.

Although it is sometimes difficult to determine when the triggering level of suspicion exists, one thing is clear: The reporting law does not require the professional to be certain maltreatment occurred. Reporting is triggered by suspicion, not certainty. A professional who postpones reporting until all doubt is eliminated violates the reporting law. Moreover, a mandated reporter is required to report suspected maltreatment whether or not the professional believes reporting is wise. When maltreatment is suspected, reporting is mandatory, not discretionary.

The reporting law leaves final decisions about whether maltreatment occurred to investigating authorities, not reporters. Mandated reporters should report their suspicions and leave any further investigation to child protective services (CPS) agencies or the police. This does not mean that professionals can ask no questions. Alternatives to maltreatment can be considered. The point is that in-depth investigation and decision making about maltreatment is reserved for CPS and law enforcement officials—not mandated reporters. Once the triggering level of suspicion is reached, the reporter turns the matter over to the authorities.

The intentional failure to report suspected child abuse or neglect is a crime. If a mandated reporter does not report suspected maltreatment—and the child is further abused or killed—the professional may face charges of criminal liability and can be sued for malpractice (*Landeros v. Flood,* 1976). Several states have laws specifically authorizing lawsuits against professionals who willfully fail to report.

In a small number of cases, angry parents have sued medical or mental health professionals who reported suspected maltreatment. Such lawsuits are generally dismissed because the child abuse reporting law gives professionals immunity from civil liability.

CIVIL RIGHTS VIOLATIONS

Occasionally, individuals sue mental health professionals for alleged violations of civil rights. When a jail or prison inmate commits suicide, for example, surviving family members may utilize the federal law found at 42 U.S.C. § 1983 to assert that mental health professionals working for the facility failed to provide proper treatment or supervision (see *Perez v. Oakland County,* 2006). Typically, in such cases, mental health defendants have qualified immunity from liability (see *Miller v. Harbaugh,* 2012; *Comstock v. McCrary,* 2002).

COURT-APPOINTED EXPERTS HAVE IMMUNITY

Professionals appointed by a judge to evaluate an individual, prepare a report, and/or testify, generally have immunity from lawsuits for court-related activities (see *Diehl v. Danuloff,* 2000; *Hathcock v. Barnes,* 2001; *Heisterkamp v. Pacheco,* 2016; *J.S. v. Berla,* 2015; *P.T. v. Richard Hall Community Mental Health Care Center,* 2000). As the court phrased it in *Cooney v. Rossiter* (2009), "Court-appointed experts, including psychiatrists, are absolutely immune from liability for damages when they act at the court's direction. They are arms of the court, much like special masters, and deserve protection from harassment by disappointed litigants, just as judges do" (p. 970). Similarly, the Louisiana Court of Appeals stated in *Faust v. Pesses* (2015), "Louisiana law is clear and unambiguous that a court-appointed expert enjoys absolute immunity from suit for services provided pursuant to that appointment."

Child custody cases in family court can breed incalculable anger. When a mental health professional is appointed by the family court judge to conduct a custody evaluation, the professional typically enjoys absolute immunity from civil liability. In some states, a mental health professional who is not court-appointed lacks absolute immunity. It is not surprising that many mental health professionals will only accept custody cases when they are appointed by the court.

YOUR RIGHT TO BE SAFE

A therapist has no duty to treat a client who poses a danger to the therapist. No one expects you to risk your life to help others. Consider Rachel, a psychotherapist who treated Pam for 3 years for depression and anxiety (*R.D. v. P.M.,* 2011). Rachel ended therapy when Pam became increasingly hostile toward her, screamed obscenities at her, refused to leave her office, and obtained her home address and phone number. Pam made many calls to Rachel's home and office numbers, threatening to stalk her, file complaints against her of abandonment, and claim (falsely) a sexual relationship between them, unless Rachel resumed treatment. Six weeks after therapy ended, Pam confronted Rachel in a stairwell at Rachel's office, begging her to resume therapy. Pam verbally accosted Rachel in the parking lot of the middle school attended by Rachel's daughter. Pam sought to volunteer at the daughter's school even though Pam had no children of her own. What should Rachel do?

Therapists are not ethically or legally required to continue therapy for clients who threaten them. Rachel was justified in ending treatment. As a matter of good practice, Rachel should refer Pam to another therapist. In the actual case on which "Rachel's Dilemma" is based, Rachel obtained a 1-year civil harassment restraining order against Pam. Unfortunately, when the order expired, Pam renewed the harassment, and Rachel was compelled to return to court to renew the restraining order.

Being stalked or harassed is can be terrifying, and sometimes lethal. Understandably, victims often turn to the courts for protection. Before seeking a restraining order, however, I recommend consulting a domestic violence center or an attorney experienced with such matters. Filing legal paperwork can inflame the situation; moreover, it is not easy to get a restraining order. You don't want to seek a restraining order, just to have a judge reject it, handing your stalker or harasser what he or she views as a victory and, possibly, a green light for further misconduct.

Kivisto, Berman, Watson, Gruber, and Paul (2015) conducted survey research on the experiences of psychologists who were being stalked and threatened. Fardin Jussab and Helen Murphy (2015) provide detailed guidance on helping professionals who have been threatened.

CONCLUSION

At the beginning of this chapter, it is pointed out that the odds are small that you will ever be sued for malpractice. The likelihood is slightly higher, although still quite small, that a client will file an ethics complaint against you. Nevertheless, the mere thought of being sued, or accused of ethical lapses, is alarming. Hopefully, this chapter gives you a better idea of how to structure your practice to make a small risk even smaller.

Part V

Proving Interpersonal Violence in Court

Part V consists of two chapters. Chapter 12 focuses on how interpersonal violence is proven in court. Chapter 13 offers some concluding thoughts.

If you managed to stay awake through earlier chapters, you know that *you,* and professionals like you, play an enormously important role in child abuse, domestic violence, rape, stalking, and elder abuse cases. It is the frontline professionals who rescue victims, diagnose and treat them, listen to *and document* their stories, and come to court to testify, who help prove abuse.

12

Proof in Court

It would take volumes to analyze all the aspects of proving interpersonal violence in court. My own book on the subject (Myers, 2016) is more than 1,200 pages, and it just scratches the surface. The purpose of this chapter is to offer an introduction to this complex subject.

PROOF OF DOMESTIC VIOLENCE

Proof of domestic violence depends on the ability and willingness of victims to report the crime, to follow up with the police and prosecutors, to remain steadfast in the resolve to press charges, and to testify in court. The key to success is well-trained and dedicated police officers and prosecutors. But competent police and prosecutors aren't enough. Just as important are the advocates who support victims of abuse through the psychological and legal minefield that awaits them. It is these advocates, many of whom are mental health and social work providers, who keep victims on an even keel. In addition to victim advocates and legal beagles, there are the clinicians who provide therapy to victims of domestic violence.

In addition to the victim's testimony, photographs of injuries sustained by the victim can be used in court and are often powerful and disturbing evidence of abuse. In many cases, the police officer who responded to a 911 call has valuable eyewitness evidence of the immediate aftermath of violence. The victim's statements to the police, family members, and medical professionals at the hospital are hearsay when they are repeated in court; however, the victim's hearsay statements often meet the requirements of the excited utterance exception, the medical diagnosis or treatment exception, or the catchall exception to the rule against hearsay. Anything the perpetrator said that points to guilt is admissible.

The same types of evidence are admissible in both a criminal case and in a civil proceeding seeking a restraining order.

PROOF OF CHILD PHYSICAL ABUSE

Physical child abuse is nonaccidental physical injury. Physical abuse can be a crime as well as a basis to protect children through child protective services (CPS) and juvenile court.

To prove physical abuse, the law relies heavily on expert testimony from physicians. Doctors describe injuries, opine that injuries are not accidental, describe the means used to inflict injury, discuss the degree of force required to injure, and opine on the cause of death.

Adults who hurt children often provide implausible explanations for serious or fatal injuries. Countless children are said to have suffered serious or fatal head injuries by falling off "killer couches" onto carpeted floors. A physician may testify that an adult's explanation is not consistent with a child's injuries.

Battered child syndrome is an accepted medical diagnosis and is therefore not subject to *Frye* or *Daubert* tests. For decades, judges have approved expert testimony on shaken baby syndrome, although there is a movement away from the term *shaken baby syndrome,* and toward *abusive head trauma.* As you know, there is controversy about whether shaking alone can cause serious and fatal injury.

U.S. law permits parents to use "reasonable" corporal punishment. Unfortunately, a great deal of physical abuse is the result of corporal punishment that got out of control. When a parent is charged with physical abuse, the parent may argue that he or she was using reasonable corporal punishment. To determine whether corporal punishment was reasonable, judges consider the child's age and size, the means used to inflict discipline (e.g., open hand versus fist or belt), the place on the child's body that was hit (buttocks vs. head), how much pain or injury occurred, and whether there was a single questionable incident of excessive punishment or a history of brutality.

In addition to expert medical testimony, proof of physical abuse is accomplished thorough investigation by police officers and/or a CPS worker. Investigators examine the place where the child was injured. Photographs are taken, and the evidence is preserved. Investigators interview any witnesses and the adult suspected of hurting the child. Photographs, including gruesome ones, are admissible in court so long as they help an expert describe injuries. In this context, a picture really is worth a thousand words.

APPLY WHAT YOU HAVE LEARNED

Who Broke the Baby's Arm?

Rick and Melony are the parents of 4-year-old Alice and 7-month-old twins, James and Deanne. Rick and Melony argued. Melony was in the kitchen. Rick was in the living room with the kids. The twins were in a playpen. Melony heard Rick sit down in the recliner. Minutes later, she heard him get up. Then she heard James crying. As Melony ran to the living room, Rick passed her on the way upstairs. Melony entered the living room and noticed that 4-year-old Alice was now in the playpen, holding James's head in her lap. When Melony picked up James, his arm flopped backward at an odd angle.

Melony took James to the hospital, where a doctor determined that James had suffered a spiral fracture of the right humerus caused by a sharp and severe twisting of the arm. The doctor determined that the fracture was likely caused by an adult and was not accidental.

A hospital official called CPS. Social worker John Geist responded to the call and spoke with the doctor. The doctor believed the fracture was caused by abuse. Geist then spoke with Melony, and told her that James would need to be temporarily removed from the home. Melony agreed that all three children would live temporarily with the paternal grandparents.

A week after the children were removed from home and placed with the grandparents, Geist interviewed Rick. Rick denied hurting the baby, and suggested that 4-year-old Alice might have broken James's arm. Shortly after talking to Rick, Geist went to the grandparents' home and talked to Alice, while sitting on the front porch. Geist asked Alice if she remembered her brother getting hurt. Alice said, "Yes." Geist asked if the other baby did it, and Alice said, "No." Geist asked if Melony did it, and Alice said, "No." Geist asked if Alice did it, and Alice said, "No." Geist asked if Rick did it, and Alice got scared, and said, "Yes." Alice told Geist that Rick grabbed the baby's arm and pulled.

Geist arranged for Alice to be evaluated by a psychologist, who interviewed Alice about 2 weeks later. Again, Alice implicated Rick, saying, "Daddy hurt him," and described how Rick was angry and grabbed and yanked the baby's arm.

Rick is charged with child abuse for breaking the baby's arm. Rick denies that he hurt the baby, and argues instead that Alice caused the injury. At Rick's child abuse trial, the prosecutor offers testimony from the physician who diagnosed the broken arm. Is it proper for the doctor to answer the following questions? "What was your diagnosis?" "On what information did you base your diagnosis?" "In your opinion, to a reasonable degree of medical certainty, could a child age 4 cause this kind of injury?" "In your opinion, to a reasonable degree of medical certainty, was the injury the result of accident?"

The prosecutor offers testimony from Geist, the social worker, and the psychologist, both of whom will repeat what Alice told them about the injury. Rick's defense attorney makes hearsay and Confrontation Clause objections to the repetition in court of Alice's hearsay statements. How should the judge rule?—*Commonwealth v. Allshouse,* 36 A.3d 163 (Pa. 2012)

Analysis: Regarding testimony from the physician, a properly qualified doctor should be allowed to answer all of the prosecutor's questions. For a discussion of the so-called "reasonable certainty" standard, see Chapter 9.

Regarding hearsay, Alice's statements to Geist and the psychologist were not exited utterances. Alice's statements to Geist were not for purposes of diagnosis or treatment. Was the statement to the psychologist within the diagnosis or treatment exception? The Pennsylvania Supreme Court did not decide that issue. The Supreme Court ruled that Alice's statements to Geist and the psychologist were admissible under Pennsylvania's residual or child hearsay exception. So, that takes care of the hearsay objection.

How about the objection made by Rick's attorney that Alice's statements to Geist and the psychologist were testimonial, and thus inadmissible under the Confrontation Clause? Rick's attorney argued that there was no emergency when Geist talked to Alice on the front porch, a week following the injury to the baby. He maintained that Geist was acting forensically to gather evidence, thus making Alice's statements to Geist testimonial. The Pennsylvania Supreme Court rejected this position. The court observed that on the very day that Geist interviewed Alice, Rick suggested to Geist that Alice was the culprit. With this information in mind, Geist was confronted with an emergency. All three children were living with their grandparents, and if 4-year-old Alice posed a danger to the babies, Geist needed to get that sorted out as quickly as possible. Because Alice's statements to Geist were in the context of an ongoing emergency, the statements were not testimonial.

But what about Alice's statements to the psychologist? Where those statements testimonial? At that point, there was no longer an emergency.

Arguably, the primary reason the psychologist interviewed Alice was to gather evidence. The Supreme Court ducked the issue. The court ruled that even if Alice's statements to the psychologist were testimonial, allowing the statements in court was not a sufficiently serious mistake to warrant a new trial.

PROOF OF NEGLECT

Neglect occurs when parents or caretakers fail to provide a child with basic food, clothing, shelter, or medical care. No one describes neglect better than psychologist James Garbarino. "Child neglect is a pattern of behavior or a social context that has a hole in the middle where we should find the meeting of basic developmental needs" (Garbarino & Collins, 1999, p. 3). Occasionally, neglect is so severe that it constitutes a crime.

Medical neglect arises when parents refuse to provide their child with essential medical or psychological treatment. When parents refuse recommended treatment, a physician or therapist will endeavor to change their minds. If parents persist in refusing, and the professional believes that treatment is critical, he or she may file a report of medical neglect with CPS. Following an investigation, CPS may commence proceedings in juvenile court, seeking a court order overriding the parents' refusal.

The judge in a medical neglect case balances (1) the right of parents to make medical decisions for their children, (2) the government's interest in the child's well-being, and (3) the child's interests.

Each medical neglect case is unique, and no two balancing processes are the same. Yet, there is a pattern in judicial decisions. If medical treatment is essential to save a child's life, and the treatment is likely to be effective and without serious or painful side effects, the judge is likely to overrule the parents and authorize treatment. On the other hand, if lifesaving treatment is experimental or has a relatively low probability of curing the child's condition, the judge is likely to defer to parents.

In non-life-and-death cases, where treatment is important but not essential to preserve life, it is difficult to predict how judges will rule. The judge considers the seriousness of the medical condition and the likelihood that the proposed treatment will be effective. The result turns on the facts of the case, with the odds favoring the parents.

In many medical neglect cases, the parents' decision to refuse medical care for their child is based on the parents' religious beliefs. Parents have the right to raise their children in a particular religious tradition.

This does not mean, however, that parents have unlimited authority to deny essential medical care to their children in the name of religion. The U.S. Supreme Court observed, "The family itself is not beyond regulation in the public interest, as against a claim of religious liberty. . . . The right to practice religion freely does not include liberty to expose the community or the child to communicable disease or the latter to ill health or death. . . . Parents may be free to become martyrs themselves. But it does not follow they are free, in identical circumstances, to make martyrs of their children" (*Prince v. Massachusetts,* 1944).

PROOF OF CHILD SEXUAL ABUSE

Mental health professionals play a minor role in proving physical abuse. Sexual abuse, by contrast, is ground zero for mental health professionals. Mental health expert testimony that is offered to prove sexual abuse is complex and controversial. I have a particular interest in the subject, and have written about it at length (see, e.g., Myers, 1997, 2010b, 2016).

Sexual abuse is often difficult to prove in court. In *Pennsylvania v. Ritchie* (1987), the U.S. Supreme Court wrote, "Child abuse is one of the most difficult crimes to detect and prosecute, in large measure because there often are no witnesses except the victim" (p. 60). In a similar vein, the California Supreme Court observed in *In re Cindy L.* (1997), "There are particular difficulties with proving child sexual abuse: the frequent lack of physical evidence, the limited verbal and cognitive abilities of child victims, the fact that children are often unable or unwilling to act as witnesses because of the intimidation of the court room setting and the reluctance to testify against their parents" (p. 28).

Unlike physical abuse, wherein the child's injuries often provide powerful evidence, medical evidence is lacking in most sexual abuse cases. According to Lawrence Ricci and Joyce Wientzen (2014), "The physical examination is often normal or otherwise noncontributory to the determination of sexual abuse. In a review of 2,384 children, only 4% had findings diagnostic of sexual abuse" (vol. 2, p. 5).

In most child sexual abuse cases, the child is the most important witness. Some kids are great witnesses; others are not. Some children are too young or too shy to testify in court. Children's hearsay, which was discussed in Chapter 4, plays a key role in child sexual abuse litigation.

Sexual abuse causes stress-related symptoms including nightmares, regression to earlier stages of development (e.g., bedwetting or soiling in toilet-trained children), depression, poor self-esteem, misbehavior at home and at school, somatic problems such as headaches and stomachaches, anxiety, hypervigilance, and fear. Many sexually abused children have some of the symptoms of posttraumatic stress disorder (PTSD). Roughly a third of sexually abused children meet the full diagnostic criteria for PTSD.

For perpetrators of sexual abuse, disclosure often spells disaster, and offenders are at pains to maintain silence. Many children are threatened, some with death. Perpetrators often saddle children with responsibility for maintaining silence—"If you tell, I'll go to jail and your mom and your brothers and sisters won't have a place to live"; "If you tell, social workers will take you away"; "No one will believe you." Some offenders maintain silence by distorting the adult–child relationship—"This is our secret, and we can't tell anyone." Indeed, "Our little secret" is a common mantra among perpetrators.

Stress-related symptoms are not unique to sexual abuse. For instance, witnessing domestic violence causes stress-related symptoms in children. Children who are neglected but not sexually abused often have mental health issues. Family disorganization, poverty, substance/alcohol abuse, and battles over custody are stressful for children. Even children growing up in "normal" homes can be anxious, and some psychological symptoms (e.g., nightmares) are so common among nonmaltreated children that they are considered a normal part of growing up.

Do stress-related symptoms provide evidence of sexual abuse? Controversy swirls around this question. If a symptom were seen *only* in sexually abused children, that symptom would be diagnostic of sexual abuse or, as some say, pathognomic for sexual abuse. Unfortunately, there is no psychological symptom or group of symptoms that are found *only* among sexually abused children. Moreover, there is no psychological syndrome that diagnoses sexual abuse, and there is no psychological test that can tell whether a child was sexually abused.

All the stress-related symptoms observed in sexually abused children are also seen, to a greater or lesser extent, in nonabused children. Thus, the question becomes: Does the presence of psychological symptoms observed in sexually abused *and* nonabused children provide evidence of sexual abuse? In some cases the answer is yes, but arriving at that answer requires an understanding of two issues: (1) How often is the symptom observed in sexually abused *and* nonabused children? and (2) What are the populations of sexually abused and nonabused children?

The more often a symptom is observed in abused children, and the less often it is seen in nonabused children, the greater the potential probative value becomes. However, this conclusion is immediately complicated by the fact that little comparative data are available on the prevalence of various symptoms among abused and nonabused children. Moreover, quite a few sexually abused children have no detectable symptoms.

The fact that a symptom is seen more often in sexually abused than in nonabused children is not enough to conclude that the symptom helps prove abuse. One must also consider the fact that the population of non-abused children is much larger than the population of abused children (see Faust, Bridges, & Ahern, 2009). Even though a symptom is observed more often in sexually abused children, the fact that there are many more nonabused than abused children means that most children with the symptom are nonabused.

Consider the following scenario in the imaginary city of Dillville. Ten thousand female children between 3 and 10 years of age live in Dillville. Twenty percent of Dillville's girls are sexually abused. Thus, there are 2,000 sexually abused 3- to 10-year-old girls in Dillville, and 8,000 nonabused girls. A 5-year-old Dillville girl started wetting the bed at night, and medical reasons for the bed-wetting are ruled out. Sexual abuse causes some toilet-trained children to wet the bed. Does the child's bedwetting tend to prove sexual abuse?

Assume that bedwetting in toilet-trained children is observed in 20% of sexually abused children and in 5% of nonabused children. We would expect to find 400 sexually abused bed wetters among Dillville girls. Yet, because 5% of nonabused children wet the bed, and because there are many more nonabused than abused children, we find an equal number of bed wetters—400—among the nonabused children in Dillville.

Changing the percentages reinforces the conclusion that psychological symptoms seen in abused *as well as* nonabused children provides little evidence of sexual abuse. Suppose that 10% of the sexually abused and 5% of the nonabused girls wet the bed. Now 200 sexually abused girls and 400 nonabused girls wet the bed! A bed wetter is twice as likely to be nonabused as abused!

The Dillville hypothetical situation demonstrates that if all you know about a child is that she wets the bed, she is more likely to be nonabused than abused. David Faust, Ana Bridges, and David Ahern (2009) note, "Given the relative base rates for abused versus non-abused children, it is not at all unrealistic to believe that in various settings many children suspected of having been abused have in fact not been abused, and that the number of non-abused children will sometimes greatly exceed the number of abused children even when screening is performed carefully and competently" (p. 12). Debra Poole and Michele Wolfe (2009) add,

"Behaviors that are typical of a large percentage of nonabused children have little value for determining any individual child's abuse status" (p. 101).

The more stress-related symptoms a child has, the more likely the child has experienced some stress-inducing event. However, sexual abuse is not the only possibility. The statistical impact of population sizes remains.

As mentioned above, up to a third of sexually abused children meet the diagnostic criteria for PTSD. Does a diagnosis of PTSD help prove sexual abuse? The problem is that a diagnosis of PTSD *presupposes* that something traumatic happened. How can you use the diagnosis to prove the trauma, when the diagnosis presupposes the trauma? A diagnosis that assumes trauma occurred cannot prove the trauma. It is reasoning in a circle. The best approach is to eschew the label of PTSD and focus on the child's symptoms. Of course, if these symptoms are also observed in nonabused children—and they are—you are back to the twin issues of symptom frequency in abused and nonabused children and population sizes.

Stress-related symptoms seen in sexually abused and nonabused children say little about sexual abuse. With children younger than 10 or so, however, symptoms of a sexual nature have a stronger connection to sexual knowledge. Sexual knowledge is sometimes rooted in sexual abuse. Particularly concerning symptoms are: (1) aggressive sexuality in young children, (2) imitation by young children of adult sexual acts, and (3) sexual knowledge that is unusual for a child of that age.

Children are not asexual. Yet, developmentally inappropriate sexual knowledge or behavior in a young child indicates sexual knowledge. Consider a 4-year-old who says, "Joey's pee-pee was big and hard, and he made me lick it and white stuff popped out and tasted yucky." This child has seen a pornographic video, has been coached, or has been sexually abused. Pornography is unlikely to be the explanation when a child describes the taste and texture of ejaculate, leaving coaching or abuse as likely explanations. Could a 4-year-old be coached to provide such a graphic description of abuse? I'm no expert, but I doubt it. That leaves sexual abuse. Of course, Joey may not be the abuser. The child might have named the wrong person. Thus, graphic descriptions of sexual abuse from young children can provide evidence of sexual abuse.

In addition to graphic verbal descriptions, behaviors can indicate developmentally unusual sexual knowledge. Such behaviors include attempting to engage in explicit sex acts, inserting objects in the child's or someone else's vagina or anus, initiating French kissing, excessive masturbation, masturbating with an object, and imitating sexual intercourse. One has to rule out benign explanations before attributing behavior to sexual abuse.

Although some sexualized behavior is uncommon in nonabused children, it does occur, reminding us of the conundrum of population sizes. The fact that sexual behavior is more frequent in sexually abused than in nonabused young children does not eliminate the fact that the population of nonabused children is much larger than the population of abused children. Giving proper respect to population sizes and benign alternative explanations, developmentally unusual sexual knowledge can provide evidence of sexual abuse, although great care is needed in the assessment process.

Mental health professionals consider the symptoms just described in making treatment decisions. After all, it is hardly appropriate to treat a child for the effects of sexual abuse if there is no reason to think the child was abused. However, the degree of certainty required to diagnose and treat sexual abuse in the clinic may not be enough to provide expert testimony in court.

Experts on sexual abuse disagree about whether mental health professionals know enough to testify that a child's symptoms and behavior provide evidence of sexual abuse. Melton and Limber (1989) claim, "Under no circumstances should a court admit the opinion of an expert about whether a particular child has been abused" (p. 1230). In a different publication, Melton and his colleagues (2007) argue that mental health professionals cannot reliably detect sexual abuse. "There is no reason to believe that clinicians' skill in determining whether a child has been abused is the product of specialized knowledge" (p. 516). Melton believes that evaluating symptoms observed in abused and nonabused children is a matter of common sense, and that mental health professionals have little to add. Moreover, Melton argues that mental health professionals rely heavily on the child's words to reach conclusions about sexual abuse and, therefore, a diagnosis of sexual abuse is often little more than a thinly veiled opinion that the child told the truth. Judges agree, however, that experts are not permitted to claim that a child was truthful.

Steve Herman (2005) reviewed empirical research discussing the accuracy of clinical judgments about sexual abuse and concluded, along with Melton, that such judgments lack validity. Herman concluded, "Empirical studies and theoretical analyses indicate that the reliability, validity, and accuracy of evaluators' clinical judgments about the validity of uncorroborated allegations of [child sexual abuse] are low" (p.

87). According to Pesisoli, Herman, and Dalbosco Dell'Aglio (2014), "There is mounting scientific evidence that [mental health professionals'] judgments about the veracity of uncorroborated [child sexual abuse] allegations are psychometrically unreliable and low in validity and accuracy" (p. 37). Herman (2009) concluded, "Professionals' informal clinical judgments about the validity of children's reports of sexual abuse are currently too inaccurate to 'make forensic application appropriate.' Because of the high false positive rate, these judgments pose a particularly severe risk of harm and injustice to nonabused children who are the objects of false allegations of abuse and to those who are wrongfully accused" (p. 260).

Faust and colleagues believe that mental health assessments "rest mainly on unverified methods or conjecture that almost certainly at times increase, rather than decrease error. . . . A clinician who claims to have mastered the distinction between sexually abused children and non-abused children via clinical experience almost surely bases the claim on evidence with serious deficiencies and may well be falsely confident" (Faust, Bridges, & Ahern, 2009, p. 4; see also Bridges, Faust, & Ahern, 2009, p. 45).

Contrary to the views of Melton, Herman, Faust, and like-minded experts, are the beliefs of equally well-qualified experts who defend the position that it is possible, in some cases, to determine whether a child's symptoms, behaviors, and disclosures are likely to have resulted from sexual abuse. Kathleen Faller (2003) argues that most clinical experts hold that view. Everson and Faller (2012) write:

> The methodology underlying [comprehensive forensic] evaluations is well designed to address common threats to the diagnostic utility of sexualized behavior in [child sexual abuse] CSA assessments. This methodology includes the use of a broad range of information sources for a comprehensive search for evidence supporting or refuting the allegations, weighing substantive evidence based on the degree of corroboration, the testing of alternative hypotheses, and the construction of a case-specific narrative to account for the available evidence. Such a methodology is also likely to increase the likelihood of a balanced evaluation that emphasizes reducing both false positive and false negative errors. (pp. 66–67)

For my part, I published an article in 2012, titled "'Nobody's Perfect'—Partial Disagreement with Herman, Faust, Bridges, and Ahern," in which I agreed with many of Herman, Faust, Bridges, and Ahern's conclusions, but disagreed rather strenuously with others, some of which

I argued are simply wrong. It seems clear that no end is in sight in the debate over whether professionals are competent to offer an opinion that a child was sexually abused.

Most appellate courts reject mental health testimony stating that a particular child was sexually abused. Some courts are concerned that the opinion too closely resembles testifying to the ultimate legal issue of guilt or innocence. In *State v. Favoccia* (2012), for example, the Connecticut Supreme Court wrote, "Although expert witnesses may testify about the general behavioral characteristics of sexual abuse victims, they cross the line into impermissible vouching and ultimate issue testimony when they opine that a particular complainant has exhibited those general behavioral characteristics."

Although most appellate decisions reject mental health testimony that a child was sexually abused, many courts approve testimony that a child's symptoms are consistent with sexual abuse. Judges are generally comfortable with "consistent with" testimony because it is a step away from the ultimate issue. The expert simply informs the jury that the child's symptoms are consistent with sexual abuse and lets the jury reach its own conclusion.

Despite the tendency of the courts to admit "consistent with" testimony, there are problems with it. First, although the testimony that a child's symptoms are consistent with sexual abuse is not an opinion in so many words that a child was sexually abused, the testimony is offered precisely for that purpose. The testimony invites the following reasoning: Because the child has symptoms consistent with sexual abuse, the child was sexually abused. Thus, "consistent with" testimony is really an opinion regarding whether a child was abused.

"Consistent with" testimony is the functional equivalent of an opinion on abuse. We know, however, that there is controversy over whether mental health professionals can validly make such judgments. "Consistent with" testimony masks the controversy behind the innocuous term "consistent with." One can argue that if testimony in the form of a direct opinion on sexual abuse is excluded because of doubts about validity, the same should be true for testimony that a child's symptoms are "consistent with" sexual abuse.

A second concern about "consistent with" testimony is that many symptoms that are consistent with sexual abuse are also consistent with nonabuse. Nightmares are consistent with sexual abuse, but also with a host of issues that have nothing to do with abuse. In fact, nightmares are consistent with normal child development. Expert testimony that a child's symptoms are consistent with sexual abuse can inflate the probative value of symptoms and mislead the jury.

Finally, "consistent with" testimony masks the twin issues of symptom frequency and population size. When an expert testifies that a child's symptoms are consistent with sexual abuse, the jury takes the testimony as proof the child was sexually abused. The jury is unlikely to appreciate the complexity of symptom frequencies in abused and nonabused children, relative to population size. And jurors are not the only ones in the dark. Many attorneys fail to appreciate these issues, with the result that attorneys often fail to conduct the probing cross-examination needed to expose the weaknesses of "consistent with" testimony.

Given the shortcomings of "consistent with" testimony, such testimony should be excluded from court trials unless the proponent of the testimony addresses two issues during the expert's direct examination. First, the expert should explain *why* symptoms tend to prove sexual abuse. It is not enough for the expert to state that a child's symptoms are consistent with sexual abuse. Second, the expert should explain the impact of symptom frequency and population size on probative value. Only when an explanation of symptom frequency and population size is added to "consistent with" testimony is the jury equipped with the information it needs to give "consistent with" testimony its proper weight. Absent this information, "consistent with" testimony is inherently misleading.

To conclude, expert testimony from mental health professionals that is offered to prove sexual abuse is complex and controversial. If such testimony is allowed, it should be offered only by highly qualified experts. The expert should have a thorough grasp of child development, memory and suggestibility, normal sexual development, the impact of sexual abuse, normal and abnormal psychology, medical evidence of sexual abuse, the process by which children disclose sexual abuse, proper and improper interview methods, prevalence rates of various symptoms in abused and nonabused children, the impact of population size and symptoms frequency, and the strengths and weaknesses of clinical judgment. The expert should be conversant with the debate regarding the validity and reliability of expert testimony offered to prove sexual abuse. Relatively few mental health professionals working with sexually abused children possess this depth of knowledge, and, therefore, should not provide expert testimony that a child was sexually abused or has symptoms consistent with sexual abuse.

Let's turn our attention from the controversy surrounding expert testimony that is offered to prove sexual abuse to a type of mental health testimony that is not controversial, and that is well accepted in court. This testimony is offered to rehabilitate a child's credibility after the child is attacked by a defense attorney.

A common defense strategy in child sexual abuse cases is to undermine the child's credibility by pointing out that the child delayed reporting, gave inconsistent versions of abuse over time, or recanted. This is legitimate impeachment. However, when the defense adopts this strategy, judges generally allow the prosecution to offer expert testimony to rehabilitate the child's credibility. An expert may testify that it is not uncommon for sexually abused children to delay reporting, be inconsistent, or recant. The expert ventures no opinion on whether the child was abused or has symptoms consistent with abuse. Indeed, the expert need never have met the child. All the expert does is summarize the literature on delay, inconsistency, or recantation. The defense attorney can hardly object, since it was his or her attack that invited the expert's testimony.

While we are discussing expert testimony to rehabilitate children's credibility, it is appropriate to mention Roland Summit's (1983) child sexual abuse accommodation syndrome (CSAAS). This maligned and much misunderstood "syndrome" was described by Summit in 1983. His goal was to help mental health professionals understand the psychological dynamics of sexual abuse, particularly incest. Summit explained that many sexually abused children delay reporting. The child feels trapped and struggles to make the best of a bad situation. When disclosure finally comes, it may be halting and piecemeal. Following disclosure, some children feel compelled to recant.

Summit never intended CSAAS as a test for sexual abuse. The syndrome neither detects nor diagnoses sexual abuse. Thus, CSAAS does not provide proof of sexual abuse. Rather, CSAAS assumes abuse occurred and explains how some children respond. Although CSAAS must not be offered as evidence of sexual abuse, the syndrome plays a useful role in rehabilitating children's credibility. Judges generally allow expert testimony on CSAAS to explain why children delay reporting, are inconsistent, and recant (see Myers, 2016). The New York Court of Appeals observed in *People v. Nicholson* (2016), "We have previously held that expert testimony on CSAAS is admissible, like other psychological syndromes, because it helps to explain victim behavior that might be puzzling to the jury" (p. 954). Other courts agree.

Proving child sexual abuse is a complicated business. However, one thing is clear: Mental health and medical professionals are in an ideal position to document the verbal, medical, physical, and behavioral evidence that is needed to protect children in court.

A FINAL CASE STUDY: ALLEGATIONS OF CHILD SEXUAL ABUSE IN FAMILY COURT—SYSTEMIC DYSFUNCTION

This book is largely optimistic about the role of the legal system in responding to interpersonal violence. Of course, the legal system is imperfect. Yet, the system reaches just results most of the time, and clinicians play critical roles in achieving justice. Unfortunately, there is one type of case that, in my judgment, the legal system often handles badly: cases in which allegations of child sexual abuse are made in family court custody litigation. These concluding case studies address this complex and troubling issue, beginning with a true story that typifies such cases. The following story is a long one, but, if you do this difficult work, you no doubt understand that there are seldom short stories, only long, often sad, ones.

Sue grew up in a middle-class suburb. After high school, she attended college, but interrupted her studies to become a flight attendant. Three years later, she quit her job and moved to Hawaii, where she returned to college and worked as a sales representative. In Hawaii, Sue met Roger, who was a medical student. Roger was as handsome as Sue was beautiful. They quickly fell in love. They lived together while Roger finished medical school and began his training as a brain surgeon. Two years later, they married.

When Roger finished his surgical training, the couple moved to a midwestern city, and Roger began practicing medicine. Sue stayed home, and it wasn't long before their first child, Eric, arrived. Two other children followed in quick succession, Brittany and Trent. Sue loved being a full-time mother, and Roger buried himself in his work. Before long, the family was living in a beautiful home and enjoying the affluent lifestyle that comes with a successful medical practice.

The first time Sue noticed something odd about Roger was on a visit to his parents' home. Several of Roger's brothers were there with their children, including a 10-year-old girl. Roger and the 10-year-old were playing badminton in the backyard. The shuttlecock flew into the bushes, and Roger and the girl went looking for it. Sue was standing inside, watching from a window. She saw Roger come up behind the girl, grab her by the shoulder, and push his crotch against her bottom. It only took a moment, and Sue didn't think much of it. She turned away from the window thinking, "That's odd. I wonder why he did that? Oh well, it's probably nothing."

Time went by. Eric, the first born, was a toddler, and Brittany was just 2 months old. One evening, Roger was lying on his back on the couch. The baby was lying on top of him, right over his crotch, and Roger's hand was down the front of her diaper. When Sue entered the room, Roger jerked his hand away. This time, Sue was worried, but she was afraid to ask Roger anything. He had a temper and could fly into a rage.

From the time the children were babies, Roger found ways to press them against his genital area. He didn't hug his children like other fathers; he didn't put his arms around them and hug face to face. At the time, Sue didn't think much of it. Yes, it was odd, it didn't seem quite right, but Sue couldn't bring herself to think that her husband—a doctor and a community leader—could be a pervert.

Roger's sexualized touching of the children continued, but when Eric was 6 and Brittany turned 4, things got worse: The children started touching their father's crotch. One night Sue said, "Roger, why don't you tell the children to stop. It's not right." Roger became furious. "I have my own style," he snarled. "Just shut up!" Sue persisted; they had numerous arguments, but Roger wouldn't stop.

The inappropriate touching was not the only source of friction in the marriage, and Sue and Roger started seeing a marriage counselor. Sue was talking to the counselor by herself one day when she described how Roger touched the children. Sue mentioned a recent episode where Roger had been lying on his side on the couch. He greeted Eric, now 7, by pulling him down onto the couch and positioning the child's bottom tight against his own genitals. Then, Roger lifted his leg over Eric to pull him tighter. The counselor said, "That's sexual abuse. Your husband is sexually abusing your son." Sue was shocked. Sexual abuse? She knew the behavior was odd, but it had gone on so long it seemed almost normal. It was just "my own style," as Roger put it. The counselor said, "I'm scheduled to see Roger tomorrow, and I'll tell him how inappropriate this is." Sue asked if she should call the CPS office, but the counselor said, "No. Getting protective services involved will ruin the family, and all that will happen is Roger will be ordered to see another counselor. I've got some experience with men who do this. Let me talk to him." As Sue drove home, the counselor's words began to sink in: "sexual abuse." The nightmare had begun.

That evening, Sue said nothing, and Roger went to his appointment the next day. When he came home, his face was purple with rage. He hissed between clenched teeth, "I hope it was worth it, telling the counselor those things, because it cost you your marriage." From that moment, Roger was cold and distant. He opened a new bank account in his own name. He started seeing a different counselor and refused to let

Sue talk to the counselor. He talked to a divorce lawyer. When he got angry—which was often—he'd walk up to Sue and hold his thumb and finger a fraction of an inch apart while he seethed, "You're this close to a divorce."

Finally, Sue couldn't stand it anymore. She told Roger she was leaving, but before she was out the door, Roger was begging her to stay. "Don't go, honey. Let's not throw everything away. We can work it out." But Sue was determined. She took the children and moved to a city 2 hours away.

During the separation, the children lived with Sue during the week and visited Roger on weekends. One Sunday afternoon, after Roger returned the kids to Sue's house, he said, "I think I'll take Eric to a movie before I drive home." It was late when Roger dropped Eric off and drove away. The two younger children were already asleep. Sue was getting Eric ready for bed when he said, "Mom, I know what teenagers do on dates." Sue replied, "What, honey?" Eric explained, "Dad told me all about it on the way home from the movie. They take off their clothes and screw." Sue stared in disbelief as her 7-year-old son continued, "Dad showed me how to get a hard-on. See?" Eric put his hand down the front of his pajamas and rubbed his penis. Then he started masturbating. Sue said, "Did your daddy show you that?" Eric replied, "Yeah." Sue removed Eric's hand from his pajamas and gently told him, "Honey, it's not OK to do that in front of other people. Daddy shouldn't have told you that. You're too young. Go to bed now. Mommy loves you." Sue tucked Eric in, gave him a good-night kiss, and turned out the light before she let herself cry. In a daze, she walked to the kitchen and slumped into a chair. Tears fell like rain.

Other disturbing incidents piled up. Eric said his dad and his new girlfriend walked around the house naked. Roger made the children sleep on the floor in his room while he and his girlfriend occupied the bed. When the alarm went off in the morning, Roger and the girlfriend had sex while the children pretended to sleep.

During the separation, Sue was seeing a counselor. She asked if there was anything she could do about her husband's sexual behavior. The children didn't like it and they were confused. The counselor suggested that the children write a letter to their father, but the children were afraid, so they told the counselor the things they didn't like and the counselor wrote the letter. What a sad letter: Two little children pleading with their father to stop touching them inappropriately and to respect their privacy. The letter had a place for Roger to agree by signing his name. He refused.

When Brittany learned that Roger refused to sign the letter, she called him and left a message on his answering machine. Sue was in the next room and she heard her daughter's angry words, "Daddy, I want you to sign that letter. You should sign it 'cause you got off easy in the letter, and you know what I mean." For several months, Sue had suspected Brittany wasn't telling her everything her father did, and Brittany's words—"You got off easy"—confirmed her fear.

Up to this point, Sue hadn't worried much about the little one, Trent. After all, he was barely 3. Yet, following visits to his dad's house, Trent began acting strangely. He started having nightmares and he became afraid of the dark. Over and over again, he pushed his face into his mother's crotch. Sue gently pushed him away, but he persisted. Two or three times, Trent tried to pull Sue's head down to his crotch. He did the same to his big brother, who, in typical big brother fashion, punched him. Then, in the car one day, Sue looked in the rearview mirror to see Trent sitting with his eyes half closed slowly pushing three fingers in and out of his mouth and sucking. Trent never sucked his thumb or fingers. Sue said, "Honey, what are you doing?" Trent removed his fingers and said, "Somebody hurt Trent," but he wouldn't say more.

A week later, Sue was busy getting the kids packed for a weekend visit with Roger. They were leaving after school. Trent walked quietly up to Sue and whispered in her ear, "Somebody go pee-pee in my mouth." Sue asked who, but Trent said, "Nobody." He wouldn't talk about it. Sue took Trent for a drive. Strapped in his car seat, Trent was a captive audience. Sue took a tape recorder. She said, "Remember when you told me somebody went pee-pee in your mouth?" Trent said, "Yes." Sue asked, "Who's been going pee-pee in your mouth?" Trent answered, "Daddy." He said it with such sadness in his little voice that Sue knew he was telling the truth. Trent picked up a small plastic sword and slowly pushed it in and out of his mouth while he made sucking sounds. Then he said, "Me kill Daddy."

Sue drove immediately to the CPS office and asked to speak to a social worker. She had called CPS several times before, but no one there had been of any help. After half an hour, a social worker came out and escorted Trent into a little office with no windows and nothing to make him feel comfortable. Sue was not allowed to go with him. Trent wouldn't say a word, and the social worker told Sue there was nothing that the agency could do. Sue said, "I've got a tape I just made. On the tape, he says what happened. Will you listen to it?" The social worker said she was too busy to listen to the tape, and she started back to her office. Sue followed, saying, "Oh please, it'll just take a minute. Please listen to it." The social worker said, "Alright, leave the tape here. I'll listen to it later. Come back at 4 o'clock this afternoon."

At the appointed hour, Sue returned to the CPS office only to find the social worker gone for the day. Another social worker handed Sue the tape and a note that read, "I didn't have time to listen to the tape. You will have to send the children on the visit." No one else in the office would help her. Sue called her attorney, but the attorney could see no way out of the visit. Sue hid her tears as she drove the children to the man she knew was a child molester.

After Sue dropped the children off at Roger's house, she had 2 hours to think as she drove home. By the time she pulled into her driveway, her mind was made up. Since CPS wouldn't help, she was going to court to protect her children. A divorce was already under way, and she would ask the family court judge for help. The next morning, Sue called her lawyer, who suggested that they seek a judge's order that Roger's visits with the children be supervised by a responsible adult. Sue said, "That's a wonderful idea." She felt relieved and hopeful.

The children had been seeing a counselor since Sue and Roger separated, and the children told the counselor about some of the things that Roger did. In particular, Trent told the counselor how Roger pushed his penis into his mouth and how "white stuff came out." Sue told the counselor she was going to court to get supervised visits, and the counselor said he would testify for her.

The court day arrived. Sue and Roger were there with their attorneys. Sue's lawyer told the judge, "Your honor, we are asking for supervised visits because there is evidence the father sexually abused the children." Roger's lawyer said, "Your honor, Roger absolutely denies these charges. He's a doctor, your honor. He's not the kind of man who would do such a horrible thing. I don't know where this idea of sexual abuse comes from, but it's ridiculous. There is no need for supervised visits." The judge said, "Alright, let's hear from the mother. What do you have to say?" Sue started to tell her story, but the judge cut her off, saying, "I don't have time for all the details. Just tell me the latest thing you say happened." Sue described what Trent said about his father pushing his penis into his mouth. After Sue finished, Trent's counselor testified that he was convinced Trent was sexually abused and that supervised visits were essential. Roger looked pale and worried, but he denied any abuse.

The judge ruled that visits would be supervised until a psychological evaluation was completed. Now the question was, who should supervise the visits? Sue's lawyer suggested someone from the protective services agency in Roger's city. Roger's attorney suggested Roger's housekeeper.

To Sue's amazement, the judge chose the housekeeper, despite the fact that the woman was financially dependent on Roger and, in the housekeeper's own words, "loved Roger like a son."

Sue felt partially vindicated by the judge's decision. It was true the housekeeper wasn't the best choice, but some supervision was better than none. The most important thing was that somebody finally seemed to believe what her children had been saying for so long. Sue was happy, but not for long.

The court hearing frightened Roger. He realized that if Sue could prove sexual abuse, he'd be ruined. Roger decided to go on the attack. In addition to his regular lawyer, Roger hired a $450-an-hour attorney who specialized in defending fathers accused of sexual abuse. This lawyer knew every legal angle, and the first thing he did was file a document in court seeking full custody of the children. Up to that point, Sue and Roger had agreed that Sue should have custody. But the new attorney charged that Sue was unfit, that she made false charges of sexual abuse, and that she was alienating the children. Sue couldn't believe it. "Oh my God, he's trying to take the children!" Sue was in for the fight of her life.

Sue's lawyer devoted more and more time to getting ready for the next court hearing, and before long Sue was paying her attorney nearly $4,000 a month! Roger had plenty of money for his team of lawyers, but Sue was quickly running out of funds. Roger was getting the upper hand.

The judge appointed a psychologist to evaluate the allegations of sexual abuse. The psychologist's report would be the most important evidence in the case. Yet, the psychologist knew very little about sexual abuse. The psychologist interviewed Sue, Roger, and the children and gave them some psychological tests. A week before the critical hearing, Sue looked in her mailbox, and there was the psychologist's report. Sue tore open the envelope. Her eyes raced over the pages, looking for the psychologist's opinion. Finally, at the bottom of the third page, she read, "No credible evidence of child sexual abuse." Her heart sank. No evidence of sexual abuse? What about everything the children had told her! Didn't anybody listen to the children? Didn't anybody care about them? Sue let the report flutter to the floor. She turned to the window and watched her children playing happily outside. The true meaning of what was happening pierced her like a knife. In a week's time, the children could be gone.

It was time for the final custody hearing in court. Sue was the first witness and the hearing started out smoothly. Sue's lawyer asked her what she had seen and what her children had told her. For a while, the judge allowed her to repeat her children's words, but then Roger's attorney interrupted, saying, "Your honor, she should not repeat what the children may have said. It's hearsay and clearly inadmissible." The judge agreed, and Sue was not permitted to repeat any more of what her children had told her about abuse.

When Sue had told as much of the story as the judge allowed, Roger's lawyer started grilling her. He said, "What kind of a mother are you? What kind of mother would invent such a preposterous story? You are just trying to hurt Roger, aren't you? You're trying to get revenge with this little lie about sexual abuse. But it won't work. We know what you're up to. You planted those false ideas in your children's minds to alienate the children from the father who loves them so much. What kind of mother are you?" The attack went on and on.

The children's counselor testified that he believed the children were abused, but Roger's attorney made short work of the counselor's testimony.

The psychologist who conducted the evaluation testified. She said, "I could find no credible evidence of sexual abuse. The children said some things to me, but I couldn't make much out of it. The father does not have the personality to abuse children. The mother, on the other hand, is emotionally high-strung and borders on unstable."

Sue's attorney asked the psychologist, "If Sue is emotional, couldn't that be because she's worried about her children—worried that they are being sexually abused? Wouldn't such fear make any normal, loving mother emotional?" The psychologist said, "I suppose anything is possible."

Finally, Roger testified. He was calm and collected. He denied doing anything inappropriate to the children and said, "The only thing I care about is my children. I'm convinced I can provide a more stable home than their mother can. They will be better off with me." Sue watched the judge's face. As Roger testified, the judge shook his head approvingly.

At the end of the hearing, the judge said, "I will take the case under consideration and issue my decision within a week. In the meantime, the children will live with their father. Court is adjourned." Sue and her attorney walked slowly out of court. Roger was standing in the hall smiling and shaking hands with his attorneys and with the court-appointed psychologist. As Sue walked by, Roger said coldly, "Have the children at my house by 5:00, and don't forget their clothes."

The days of waiting for the judge's decision dragged by. Sue wandered aimlessly through the empty house. The sounds of children's laughter were gone—there was only silence. Sue walked in and out of her children's rooms, holding their toys. She pressed Trent's teddy bear against her cheek and put it down, damp with tears.

Late one morning, the phone rang. Sue picked it up. It was her lawyer. There was a long pause as the attorney struggled to find words. Finally, he said, "Sue, I'm so sorry, so very sorry. The judge ruled against you. Roger will have full custody. The judge thinks you shouldn't even have much visitation. All you will have is one day of visitation a month. And your visitation has to be supervised. I'm so sorry." Sue cried and her lawyer cried with her. Somewhere else, three children must have cried too.

Sue's story is true. Sue lost custody of her children to the man she believed was molesting them. I sat with Sue as she told me her sad tale, just as I've sat with other mothers who believed their children were sexually abused, went to family court for help, and ended up losing them. Indeed, I've talked to so many mothers like Sue that I wrote a book for parents on the dangers of going to family court: *A Mother's Nightmare—Incest: A Practical Legal Guide for Parents and Professionals* (Myers, 1997).

To come to grips with why the struggle to prove sexual abuse went so terribly wrong for Sue, and for mothers like her, let's delve a little deeper into the family court system. Imagine you are standing in the hallway of a family court anywhere in the United States. A small gaggle of lawyers chats in a corner, waiting for the afternoon family law calendar to begin. The clock strikes 1:30 P.M., and courtroom doors swing open. A stream of dour, frightened, and angry litigants trudge in. As the lawyers bid each other adieu, one quips, "Time to listen to more testilying." Colleagues chuckle as they disperse.

Was the lawyer's remark nothing more than the grousing of a cynic, or is "testilying" common in family court? Is it *more* common in family court than elsewhere? There is no way to know. Ask a prosecutor or defense attorney whether witnesses lie in criminal court, and you are likely to be met with a wry smile and the reply, "Obviously, you don't spend much time in criminal court. Of course witnesses lie. It's my job to catch them." I suspect similar sentiments would flow from attorneys in other spheres of practice.

Don't get me wrong. I'm not suggesting that most, or even many, witnesses lie in family court. But it is naïve to think deliberate lying is rare. Some family law litigants are mentally ill, or nearly so, and lying is part and parcel of their tenuous grip on reality. The stakes in family court are so high, especially in child custody cases, that parents sometimes justify lying "for the good of the kids."

Is deliberate lying the only explanation for testimony that falls short of the truth? Hardly. It is amazing to sit in family court and listen to two people who experienced the same event give diametrically opposite versions of what happened. It occurs all the time, and it must drive judges crazy. Are both parties lying? Is one lying and the other telling the truth? Is it possible both are telling the truth—*their* version of the truth? I'm convinced the latter scenario occurs often. Indeed, it is probably more common than intentional testilying. Both parties tell the truth, but vagaries of human memory, coupled with the emotions and motives rife in family court, distort memory. This is hardly news. If there are five witnesses to a car accident, there are likely to be five versions of what happened. Sometimes, witnesses to the same event have remarkably different memories of what transpired. Yet, everyone is telling the truth.

In family court, skepticism about credibility, or concern about testilying, reaches its zenith when one parent accuses the other of child abuse, particularly child sexual abuse. "Skepticism on steroids" is not too strong a term.

Everyone agrees that sexual abuse is serious and that victims must be protected. So why does an accusation of sexual abuse in family court so often meet with disbelief? There are several reasons.

False allegations of sexual abuse occur, and a small body of research suggests that false allegations are more common in family court than elsewhere (see Trocme & Bala, 2005). But what is a "false" allegation? Is a false allegation a deliberate lie? Is it a report of abuse that is made in good faith, but that turns out to be wrong? Frances Sink (1988) observed, "The broadly defined category of 'false allegations' includes almost any situation in which an abuse report cannot be substantiated. The term fails to differentiate situations of intentional falsification from situations of misunderstanding or situations where inadequate information is available to determine the true or false nature of a report" (p. 38).

The term "false" is ambiguous, leads to confusion, and should be avoided. A more accurate term is "fabricated." A fabricated allegation is a lie; a deliberate misstatement of truth. Fabricated reports are distinguishable from Sink's "situations of misunderstanding or situations where inadequate information is available." It is reasonable to blame someone who fabricates a report of abuse and to question the fabricator's fitness as a parent. By contrast, it is unreasonable to blame or doubt the parenting of someone who makes a good faith report that can't be proven, or that is mistaken.

Concern about words like "false" is not trivial. Real injustice flows from failing to distinguish lies from honest mistakes and from labeling both "false." In too many cases, parents who *honestly* suspect sexual abuse, but can't prove it, are labeled "false accusers." Once you are branded a "false accuser," your credibility is destroyed. In case after case, parents who are trying to protect their children end up losing custody because they allege sexual abuse, can't prove it, and are branded a "false accuser."

The scarlet letter—"false accuser"—is often accompanied by the conclusion that the villain is an "alienator" and is probably mentally ill. These added stigmas seem especially likely when the accuser is a woman. One of the ironies of this area of family law is that when a loving parent honestly alleges sexual abuse and is disbelieved, she may take actions that are mislabeled as alienation. She may act irrationally *because* she isn't believed and can't protect her child. For discussion of parental alienation in child custody cases, see Bow, Gould, and Flens (2009) and Myers (2016).

In addition to reports that are fabricated, it is important to understand another kind of report, a report that is best described as a "misperception" report (Hendershot & Bow, 2013; Myers, 1997, 2016). For parents, the initial suspicion of sexual abuse arises in several ways. Often, children disclose what happened. Some children come right out with it. Others drop hints that something is wrong. Some children are too confused, frightened, or young to disclose, and a parent's suspicion is aroused by changes in the child's behavior. Regardless of how the possibility of sexual abuse arises, the parent gets a horrible sinking feeling: "Oh dear God. Could this be true? What should I do?" It is perfectly normal to react emotionally to the thought your child might be sexually abused. Some parents were victims themselves, and the idea that your own child is also a victim often can be devastating. The mind is flooded with thoughts and emotions, including the hope that it isn't true, fear that it is, outrage, doubt about what to do and who to talk to, and desperation to protect the child.

The emotions stirred up by possible sexual abuse have effects that are positive and negative. On the positive side, fear gets the parent started on the road to protection. On the negative side, the emotional reaction that is natural for any loving parent can cloud thinking and cause parents to jump too quickly to conclusions and accusations. The danger of jumping to premature conclusions seems particularly pronounced when parents are embroiled in divorce or custody litigation.

Consider the case of Brenda and Fred, who divorced a year ago after Fred had an affair. The divorce was bitter, with Brenda and Fred fighting over the house, spousal support, and, especially, custody of their 3-year-old daughter, Heather. After a nasty custody trial, Brenda got custody and Fred got weekend parenting time. One Sunday, Fred returned Heather from a visit. The little girl seemed unusually quiet. Brenda gave Heather a bath and noticed Heather's genitals were red and irritated. Brenda asked, "How come you're red down there, honey?" Heather replied, "Owie, cause daddy hurted me." Brenda asked, "What did daddy do?" Heather said, "Finger owie." Alarm bells sounded in Brenda's mind. Heather seemed to be saying that her father hurt her genitals with his finger. Could this be sexual abuse? Brenda got that sinking feeling. She was ready to think the worst of Fred, and she quickly concluded that he sexually abused their daughter. Brenda thought, "That bastard. He'll never do this again. I'll take away his visitation."

The emotions that overwhelmed Brenda were a combination of anger from a bitter divorce and Brenda's understandable reaction to what her daughter said. Brenda jumped quickly to the conclusion that Heather was sexually abused. But did Brenda jump too quickly? Was Brenda's thinking clouded by her feelings after the divorce? Is there an innocent explanation for Heather's redness and "owie" words? If Brenda rushes to family court with accusations of sexual abuse, will she be able to prove it? Once a parent launches the "atomic bomb" of sexual abuse, the parent *has* to prove it—something that is often difficult to do—or be branded a "false accuser." It is nearly impossible to withdraw an unprovable accusation of sexual abuse without looking like a fool or worse.

Would you like to know what happened at Fred's house? Fred gave Heather a bubble bath. He put far too much bubble solution in the tub—the more bubbles the better, right?—and the solution irritated Heather's genitals. Later, Heather told Fred her "privates" hurt. Fred saw the redness and said, "Daddy's sorry you got an owie. We'll make it better with salve." Fred used his finger to apply soothing ointment to Heather's irritated genitals. By the time Fred returned Heather to Brenda, he'd forgotten the whole incident. Brenda misinterpreted what happened. When she saw the genital irritation and heard Heather's words, Brenda's animosity toward Fred kicked in. Sexual abuse was the *only* explanation she could see.

Brenda's case exemplifies a recurring scenario: A well-intentioned parent, trying to do the right thing, *misinterprets* innocent or ambiguous behavior as evidence of sexual abuse. The consequences can be disastrous for the accusing parent if she goes to court with accusations she can't prove. The accused parent will be madder than a hornet, and will accuse the accuser of lying, destroying the parent–child relationship, alienating the child, and so forth. Brenda can try to explain herself, but I don't give her much chance of success.

If a parent who suspects sexual abuse turns to the police or CPS, an investigation may ensue. If the evidence is weak, the case goes no further. If the officer or social worker is knowledgeable, the concerned parent may be reassured that it is unlikely that abuse occurred. If the evidence for abuse is strong, law enforcement officials and CPS may align with the accusing parent.

Often, a parent who suspects abuse visits a hospital, calls the child's pediatrician, or makes an appointment with a therapist. The parent may not want to involve the authorities, at least not yet. However, the parent does not realize that physicians, nurses, and therapists are mandated reporters. When a mandated reporter has a reasonable suspicion—a low threshold—that a child has been abused, he or she *must* report the abuse to law enforcement authorities or CPS.

In many cases, these professionals inform parents of two things. First, as a mandated reporter, the professional will file a report of suspected abuse. Second, the parent should report to CPS or the police.

Because mandated reporters have no discretion over whether to report suspected abuse, many reports are based on weak evidence—little more than a vague suspicion that something is wrong. As for the parent, she reports suspected abuse because a professional *told her to,* but her report is based on the same thin evidence.

Because of the reporting law, weak cases that cannot be proven are reported to CPS and law enforcement authorities. The accusing parent is stuck with the report, and when she can't prove the accusations, she is branded a "false accuser." Her protestation that she was only doing what the professional told her to do falls on deaf ears, and the report is often used against her.

Accusations of sexual abuse are litigated in criminal trials, in juvenile court proceedings to protect children from maltreatment, and in family court. Often, the evidence is weakest in family court. Why? The answer is not hard to find. Prosecutors don't bring criminal charges without strong evidence. Police investigation weeds out weak cases. Because of the screening mechanisms in place in criminal law, cases that *are* charged usually rest on strong evidence. Much the same occurs in juvenile court. CPS social workers, often working with the police, investigate reports of sexual abuse. The agency does not file in juvenile court when the evidence is too weak to stand up in court. In family court, by contrast, there is *no* screening mechanism to eliminate weak cases. A parent who believes her child was abused often feels she has no choice but to seek relief in family court. As a result, many accusations of sexual abuse filed in family court are based on flimsy evidence that would never see the light of day in a criminal or juvenile court.

In addition to the paucity of evidence in many family court sexual abuse cases many parents err by overvaluing their evidence. It is common for parents to believe that their evidence is much stronger than it is.

As for the accused parent, he will mount a spirited defense, beginning with an indignant denial, and then charges that the accuser is lying, seeking an unfair advantage, and alienating the child from the innocent accused. (Note that this defense is the same whether the allegations of abuse are true or untrue.) Often, the accused parent combines denial with a request for full custody.

The accusing parent, especially if she lacks a lawyer, has no understanding of the burden of proof, and that it is her obligation to prove the abuse. When the dust settles, and the judge rules against the accuser, she is usually stunned. She can't believe it. "What about my evidence?" Sadly, some accusing parents conclude the judge is incompetent or corrupt. Usually, the court made the right decision based on the evidence and who had the burden of proof. Yet, the accusing parent is devastated, while the accused is victorious. But that's not the end of it. The vindicated parent is in an excellent position to press the case that custody should be awarded to him, and removed from the vindictive, falsely accusing, lying, alienating, and crazy mother.

No offense to my fellow lawyers, but most attorneys know very little about child sexual abuse, including how to prove it in court and how to effectively cross-examine experts. As an example of where lawyers go astray, consider the initial encounter with a reporting parent. What is the almost knee-jerk reaction of many attorneys when a parent comes to his or her office with suspicions that the other parent sexually abused a child? File an emergency motion to cut off the offending parent's custody or parenting time, right? A seemingly sensible idea, and often the worst possible course of action. Marching prematurely to court, before conducting a thorough assessment of the evidence, can prove disastrous. A lawyer who charges sexual abuse and can't prove it brands the client a false accuser or a fabricator, and it's downhill from there.

Family court is so suspicious of allegations of sexual abuse that some experts believe the court is dysfunctional or broken. What steps can be taken to reform the system? First, all professionals working in family law—be they judges, mediators, or attorneys—need to reboot their credibility meters, and set the needle to neutral. As things stand now, the needle *starts* at, "It's probably a lie." Repositioning the needle to, "It could be true; let's find out," would do wonders.

Family law lawyers need additional training to help them understand the difficulties of proving child sexual abuse and the danger of going to court too quickly so that they can offer wise counsel to terrified clients. Judges, too, need time at the training table. The vast majority of judges are fair, honest, and intelligent. They do their best to decide cases on the evidence and to keep their personal opinions to themselves. Unfortunately, the air is so thick with skepticism about allegations of sexual abuse that judges can't help but absorb some of the doubt.

Anyone who thinks there isn't an element of sexism here either isn't paying attention or has no understanding of history. The vast majority of parents who raise suspicions of sexual abuse are mothers. The over-the-top skepticism is directed at women. There is a long tradition in law and culture of *not* believing women, and of attributing women's claims of sexual abuse to fantasy, vindictiveness, or mental instability. Is history repeating itself?

Before leaving this troublesome issue, permit me to say, I believe family courts get it right most of the time, despite high levels of skepticism. The legal system will never be perfect. I just wish it did a better job with these heartrending cases.

Circling back to our earlier story, whatever happened to Sue and her children? After she lost custody, Sue moved away and tried to start her life anew. She visited her children when she could. Eventually, I lost track of Sue. Her children are grown by now. My hope is that when they got old enough to have a voice of their own, they sought her out. I hope so. Sue didn't deserve what the legal system did to her. Her kids didn't either.

CONCLUSION

The psychotherapist's office has comfortable furniture to put the client at ease. The physician's workplace is the clinic, hospital, or operating room. For a police officer, the office is the patrol car and the street. Social workers ply their trade wherever clients need them. For the lawyer, it is the courtroom. It is there, in the cauldron of the courtroom, that we prove interpersonal violence. It is not surprising that when you think of court, you think first of lawyers and judges. They are the prime movers in that domain. Yet, clinicians must understand that without them, legal professionals would often be at a loss to prove abuse. The capacity to protect victims, and hold perpetrators accountable, truly is a team effort. Without clinicians, the legal system is hobbled.

13

Concluding Thoughts

Readers of this book understand the harm caused by interpersonal violence, abuse, and neglect. Fortunately, our society has created legal and social systems to address these problems. These systems are far from perfect, and many children and adults continue to become victims. Yet, there is no gainsaying the progress that has been achieved. Across the United States, thousands of mental health, social work, medical, and legal professionals devote the full measure of their energy to preventing interpersonal violence, abuse, and neglect, and repairing the damage when prevention fails.

The laboring oar of prevention and repair is pulled by clinicians. In their efforts, clinicians are surrounded by and, one hopes, supported by a dizzying array of laws and legal procedures. The criminal justice system is enormously complicated. Yet, the complexity of criminal law pales in comparison to the breadth and intricacy of the civil justice system, which embraces disparate topics, such as the licensing of clinicians, continuing professional education, confidentiality and privilege (think HIPAA), civil commitment, and family law.

Although many laws support clinicians, candor compels me to admit that the impact of law is so pervasive that, at times, the legal system may act as an impediment rather than as a support. More than one clinician has voiced complaints like, "I spend so much time complying with legal-driven paperwork that I don't have time for my clients!" and "Today, I went to court to testify, and I waited in the hall for 3 hours. Finally, the bailiff came out and told me to come back tomorrow! What a waste of time."

Despite admitting that the requirements of the legal system sometimes make clinical practice more challenging, no one disputes that law is essential. The absence of law would be chaos, and result in exponentially *more* violence, abuse, and neglect. The trick is in finding the right balance, so that the legal system facilitates rather than hinders clinical work. As an exercise in striking the right balance, let's revisit the four cases described in the Preface, beginning with 3-week-old Mary, who froze to death lying on the ground in a homeless camp next to Rachel, her mother, who was in a methamphetamine-induced stupor. How did the system fail Mary? Should Rachel be charged with a crime?

Child protection workers, police officers, and firefighters rescue children like Mary every day. We don't know why Mary wasn't among the rescued. We do know that poverty, mental illness, and substance abuse are rampant, that our society does a pretty pitiful job of addressing these scourges, and that those of us who are lucky enough to be comfortable, sometimes turn a blind eye. One answer here, it seems, is to keep advocating for the financial resources, policies, and legislation required to address pressing social issues like poverty, racism, addiction, homelessness, and hopelessness. We will never rescue every Mary, but if we make measurable progress on social issues, there will be fewer Marys to rescue.

Should Rachel be charged with a crime? Some argue, yes; Rachel killed her baby. She could be charged with involuntary manslaughter based on criminal negligence, or, at a minimum, child endangerment. Were it not for Rachel's irresponsible, not to mention, illegal conduct, Mary would be alive. Others say, what good will it do to put Rachel in jail? Hasn't she suffered enough? Why not offer her drug treatment, housing, job training, and the possibility of a meaningful future? She is going to suffer guilt the rest of her life. Is society advanced by locking her up?

Next, recall Rita, who came to the United States from Mexico to attend college, and entered into a tumultuous, sometimes violent relationship with Sam, a veteran suffering from PTSD and mild TBI. When their baby Jasmine was born, Sam showed little interest in her. Shortly after that, immigration authorities told Rita that her student visa was expired, and she had to return to Mexico or be deported. Rita returned to Mexico with the child. Once there, she made it difficult for Sam to find her. Eventually, Sam got treatment for his PTSD, finished college, and matured. After 2 years of searching, he managed to find Rita and their daughter. What can Sam do? What should Rita do? What is best for Jasmine?

This case falls into the domain of family law, with added elements of international law and, possibly, criminal law. On the criminal side, states have laws against parental kidnapping. It is possible Rita could be charged with kidnapping her own child. Turning to international law, Mexico, the United States, and many other nations are parties to the Hague Convention on the Civil Aspects of International Child Abduction. This treaty encourages judges to return children from one country to another when a child has been wrongfully removed by a parent. Sam may want to avail himself of the Hague Convention, though doing so is complicated, and may require simultaneous litigation in Mexico and in the United States. Finally, this is a child custody case, and so ought to be resolved through the family court systems here and in Mexico. If Sam cannot get the child returned to the United States, he will need to decide whether to seek custody in a Mexican family court. If the child is returned, or Rita comes back voluntarily, custody can be determined here.

Two issues are noteworthy about this case. First, the law in this and similar cases is extremely complicated. Second, how many parents can afford to pay the legal costs involved in international children custody litigation? A case like this takes many attorney hours, and Sam may need to hire attorneys in both countries.

In the United States, people charged with a crime have a constitutional right to an attorney. If they cannot afford an attorney, the court appoints a public defender. We have all heard stories of overworked and underpaid public defenders. There is a cynical cartoon in which an attorney asks a new client, "How much justice can you afford?" Most public defenders *are* overworked. Yet, in my nearly four decades teaching law students, I've seen countless budding lawyers who are hungry to defend the downtrodden, the poor, and the wrongfully accused. When I go to court, I see these former students, now seasoned public defenders, still committed to equal justice. Our criminal justice system has many flaws, but at least the United States makes an effort to provide lawyers to those who cannot afford to pay.

In most civil cases, including family law and child custody, there is no constitutional right to an attorney. Those who cannot afford an attorney simply go without one. Many attorneys offer free or low cost advice when they can, but attorneys have to make a living, and attorneys pay their staff and themselves by billing clients who can afford to pay. In many communities across the country, more than 70% of family law litigants lack legal representation. Can Sam and Rita afford the attorney time—on both sides of the border—that is needed to do what is best for their child? If they can't, what are the odds that they will successfully traverse the legal labyrinth alone?

As mentioned in the Preface, Priya is a psychotherapist whose former client, Ted, stalked her. Ted asked Priya out on a date, which Priya declined. When Ted would not abandon his desire for a social relationship, Priya terminated therapy. Nevertheless, Ted persisted. One Saturday morning, Priya saw Ted sitting in his parked car near her home, 40 miles from her office.

Priya should consult an attorney. Most attorneys, however, know little about stalking, restraining orders, and related matters. The best place to start is probably the local domestic violence center. Priya may also want to talk to a prosecutor or a police officer.

If Priya came to me for legal advice, I would examine the facts of her case in light of the legal requirements for a stalking restraining order. Every state has criminal and civil laws against stalking. Although a civil restraining order is "only a piece of paper," it is a powerful document. If Priya obtains a restraining order, Ted may finally desist, although there is no guarantee. Still, if the restraining order is in place, a police officer may feel comfortable intervening and arresting Ted.

But are the facts of Priya's case sufficient to convince a judge to grant a restraining order? Stalking statutes generally require proof of a credible threat. Ted didn't threaten Priya, did he? His conduct is scary, but is it threatening? A restraining order imposes substantial burdens on the restrained person, and judges do not issue such orders lightly. Some judges would read a veiled threat into Ted's behavior. Other judges would not. Priya needs a thorough assessment of the likelihood she could obtain a restraining order. The best place to get such advice is from a domestic violence organization or an attorney experienced in such matters. The last thing she wants is to seek a restraining order, and be denied. Ted would view a denial as a victory over Priya, and possibly a green light to continue and even intensify his obnoxious, and possibly dangerous, conduct.

Then there is 90-year-old John, a widower who became involved with Mary Sue when she offered to help John around the house. Mary Sue also paid John's bills, and paid *herself* out of John's monthly Social Security check. Eventually she helped him to draft a will giving all his property to her, and nothing to his family.

The most common form of elder abuse is financial abuse. A family member or "new friend" robs the elder blind, often under the ruse of helping. On the other hand, competent older persons have the right to do what they want with their property. In this situation, it may be wise to call an adult protective services agency so that an impartial professional can assess the situation. A clinician can evaluate John's decision-making capacity.

These four cases illustrate a theme that pervades this book. Time and again, the solutions to complex issues of interpersonal violence, abuse, and neglect lie in coordinated efforts between clinical and legal professionals. Indeed, that is the moral of the story: Our best work for victims happens when we work together.

Our legal journey is at an end. I hope portions of the book interested you, and that you didn't need more than a few double-shot espressos to get through it. Law can be tedious (just ask my law students). My hope is that you will find some of the information useful in your important clinical work, and that it will boost your confidence when you or your clients find yourselves interacting with our legal system. I leave you with a line from a song by David Haas: *We are called to act with justice.*

References

Adams v. State, 435 S.W.3d 520 (Ark. Ct. App. 2014).

Addington v. Texas, 441 U.S. 418 (1979).

Adoptive Couple v. Baby Girl, 133 S. Ct. 2552 (2013).

Alphin v. Alphin, 219 S.W.3d 160, 165 (Ark. 2005).

Amato, P. R. (2010). Research on divorce: Continuing trends and new developments. *Journal of Marriage and Family, 72*, 650–666.

American Academy of Psychiatry and the Law. (2005). *Ethics guidelines for the practice of forensic psychiatry*. Bloomfield, CT: Author.

American Bar Association. (2016). *Model rules of professional conduct*. Chicago: Author.

American Medical Association. (2007). Ethics opinion 5.05—Confidentiality. Retrieved from *www.ama-assn.org/go/code*.

American Nurses Association. (2015). *Code of ethics for nurses with interpretive statements*. Silver Spring, MD: Author.

American Psychiatric Association. (2012). *Position statement on assessing the risk of violence*. Washington, DC: Author.

American Psychiatric Association. (2013). *Diagnostic and statistical manual of mental disorders* (5th ed.). Arlington, VA: Author.

American Psychiatric Association. (2014). *Position statement on the insanity defense*. Washington, DC: Author.

American Psychiatric Association. (2015). *Commentary on ethics in practice*. Washington, DC: Author.

American Psychological Association. (2010a). *Ethical Principles of psychologists and code of conduct*. Washington, DC: Author.

American Psychological Association. (2010b). Guidelines for child custody evaluations in family law proceedings. *American Psychologist, 65*, 863–867.

American Psychological Association. (2013). Specialty guidelines for forensic psychology. *American Psychologist, 68*, 7–19.

American Psychological Association Committee on Legal Issues. (2016). Strategies for private practitioners coping with subpoenas or compelled testimony for client/patient records or test data or test materials. *Professional Psychology, Research and Practice*, *47*, 1–11.

Amundsen, A. J. (2015). Balancing the court's parens patriae obligation and the psychologist–patient privilege in custody disputes. *Journal of the American Academy of Matrimonial Lawyers, 28,* 1–23.

Ankenbrandt v. Richards, 504 U.S. 689 (1992).

Association of Family and Conciliation Courts. (2006). *Model standards of practice for child custody evaluation.* Madison, WI: Author.

Bachman v. Bradley, 91 A.2d 379 (Pa. Super. 1952).

Baker, D. C., & Bufka, L. F. (2011). Preparing for the telehealth world: Navigating legal, regulatory, reimbursement, and ethical issues in an electronic age. *Professional Psychology, Research and Practice, 42,* 405–411.

Barclay v. Campbell, 704 S.W.2d 8 (Tex. 1986).

Barsky, A. E. (2012). *Clinicians in court: A guide to subpoenas, depositions, testifying, and everything else you need to know* (2nd ed.). New York: Guilford Press.

Bartholet, E. (1999). *Nobody's children: Abuse and neglect, foster drift, and the adoption alternative.* Boston: Beacon Press.

Bartholet, E. (2015). Differential response: A dangerous experiment in child welfare. *Florida State University Law Review, 42,* 573–644.

Batson v. Kentucky, 476 U.S. 79 (1986).

Bersoff, D. N. (2014). Protecting victims of violent patients while protecting confidentiality. *American Psychologist, 69,* 461–467.

Berzin, S. C. (2008). Difficulties in the transition to adulthood: Using propensity scoring to understand what makes foster youth vulnerable. *Social Service Review, 82,* 171–196.

Boldt, R. C. (2015). The "voluntary" inpatient treatment of adults under guardianship. *Villanova Law Review, 60,* 1–58.

Bow, J. N., Gould, J. W., & Flen, J. R. (2009). Examining parental alienation in child custody cases: A survey of mental health and legal professionals. *The American Journal of Family Therapy, 37,* 127–145.

Bradford, G. F. (2001). Dissecting Missouri's requirement of "reasonable medical certainty." *Missouri Bar Journal, 57,* 136–142.

Brady v. Maryland, 373 U.S. 83 (1963).

Bridges, A. J., Faust, D., & Ahern, D. C. (2009). Methods for the identification of sexually abused children: Reframing the clinician's task and recognizing its disparity with research on indicators. In K. Kuehnle & M. Connell (Eds.), *The evaluation of child sexual abuse allegations: A comprehensive guide to assessment and testimony* (pp. 21–47). Hoboken, NJ: Wiley.

Brodsky, S. L. (1999) *The expert witness: More maxims and guidelines for testifying in court.* Washington, DC: American Psychological Association.

Brown v. Board of Education, 347 U.S. 483 (1954).

Bush v. State, 809 So.2d 107 (Fla. Ct. App. 2002).

Caldwell v. Chauvin, 464 S.W.3d 139 (Ky. 2015).

Campbell v. Thomas, 897 N.Y.S.2d 460 (A.D. 2010).

Capers, B. (2010). The unintentional rapist. *Washington Law Review, 87,* 1345–1395.

Chadwick, D. L. (1990). Preparation for court testimony in child abuse cases. *Pediatric Clinics of North America, 37,* 955–970.

Chase v. State, 171 So. 3d 463 (Miss. 2015).
Cherlin, A. J. (2010). Demographic trends in the United States: A review of research in the 2000s. *Journal of Marriage and Family, 72*, 403–419.
Child Welfare Information Gateway. (2014, November). *Differential response to reports of child abuse and neglect.* (Issue Brief.) Washington, DC: Children's Bureau.
Clark v. Arizona, 548 U.S. 735 (2006).
Clausen, J. A. (2014). Making the case for a model mental health advance directive statute. *Yale Journal of Health Policy, Law, and Ethics, 14*, 1–65.
Cole v. Panos, 128 A.D.3d 880 (N.Y. 2015).
Collier v. Harris, 261 P.3d 397 (Alaska 2011).
Commonwealth v. DiPadova, 951 N.E.2d 891 (Mass. 2011).
Comstock v. McCrary, 273 F.3d 693 (6th Cir. 2002).
Conservatorship of Pamela J., 133 Cal. App. 4th 807 (2005).
Cooney v. Rossiter, 583 F.3d 967 (7th Cir. 2009).
Cooper v. Aaron, 358 U.S. 1 (1958).
Cooper v. Takeda Pharmaceuticals America, Inc., 191 Cal. Rptr. 3d 67 (2015).
Courtney, M. E., Dworsky, A., Cusick, G. R., Keller, T., Havicek, J., & Bost, N. (2005). *Midwest evaluation of the adult functioning of former foster youth: Outcomes at age 19.* (Chapin Hall Working Paper.) Chicago: Chapin Hall Center for Children at the University of Chicago.
Crawford v. Washington, 541 U.S. 36 (2004).
Daubert v. Merrell Dow Pharmaceuticals, Inc., 509 U.S. 579 (1993).
David D. v. Luzio, 802 N.Y.S.2d 233 (A.D. 2013).
Deasy v. United States, 99 F.3d 354 (10th Cir. 1996),
Deen v. Pounds, 718 S.E.2d 68 (Ga. App. 2011).
Detention of New, 21 N.E.3d 406, 409 (Ill. 2014).
Devereaux, R. L., & Gottlieb, M. C. (2012). Record keeping in the cloud: Ethical considerations. *Professional Psychology, Research and Practice, 43*, 627–632.
Diehl v. Danuloff, 618 N.W.2d 83 (Mich Ct. App. 2000).
Disciplinary Counsel v. Bunstine, 995 N.E.2d 184 (Ohio 2013).
Dixon v. United States, 548 U.S. 1 (2006).
Dunnigan v. Silva, 916 So. 2d 1166 (La. Ct. App. 2005).
Durham v. United States 214 F.2d 862 (D.C. Cir. 1954).
Dusky v. United States, 362 U.S. 402 (1960).
Edwards, G. (2014). Doing their duty: An empirical analysis of the unintended effect of *Tarasoff v. Regents* on homicidal activity. *Journal of Law and Economics, 57*, 321–345.
Elija W. v. Superior Court, 216 Cal. App. 4th 140, 153 (2013).
Elledge v. Williamson, 132 So. 3d 432 (La. Ct. App. 2014).
Everson, M. D., & Faller, K. C. (2012). Base rates, multiple indicators, and comprehensive forensic assessments: Why sexualized behavior still counts in forensic child sexual abuse evaluations, *Journal of Child Sexual Abuse, 21*, 5–71.
Ex Parte Milteer, 571 So. 2d 998 (Ala. 1990).
Expose v. Thad Wilderson & Associates, 863 N.W.2d 95 (Minn. Ct. App. 2015).

Faller, K. C. (2003). *Understanding and assessing child sexual maltreatment* (2nd ed.). Thousand Oaks, CA: Sage.

Farrell L. v. Superior Court, 203 Cal. App. 3d 521 (1988).

Faust, D., Bridges, A. J., & Ahern, D. C. (2009). Methods for the identification of sexually abused children: Suggestions for clinical work and research. In K. Kuehnle & M. Connell (Eds.), *The evaluation of child sexual abuse allegations: A comprehensive guide to assessment and testimony* (pp. 49–66). Hoboken, NJ: Wiley.

Faust v. Pesses, 164 So. 3d 920 (La. Ct. App. 2015).

Foster v. Chatman, 136 S. Ct. 1737 (2016).

Fox, A., Frasch, K., & Berrick, J. D. (2007). *Listening to children in foster care.* Berkeley: Child Welfare Research Center, University of California, Berkeley.

Fradella, H. F. (2007) *From insanity to diminished capacity: Mental illness and criminal excuse in contemporary American law.* Bethesda, MD: Academica Press.

Frye v. United States, 293 F. 1013 (D.C. 1923).

Gagon v. Lemoyne Sleeper Co., 2009 WestLaw 1324141 (M.D. Pa. 2009).

Garbarino, J., & Collins, C. C. (1999). Child neglect: The family with a hole in the middle. In H. Dubowitz (Ed.), *Neglected children: Research, practice and policy* (pp. 1–23). Thousand Oaks, CA: Sage.

Gates v. Texas Department of Protective and Regulatory Services, 537 F.3d 404 (5th Cir. 2008).

Gelles, R. (1996). *The book of David: How preserving families can cost children's lives.* New York: Basic Books.

Gelman, S. (1984). Mental hospital drugs, professionalism and the constitution. *Georgetown Law Journal, 72,* 1725–1784.

Gracy v. Eaker, 837 So. 2d 348 (Fla. 2002).

Gutheil, T. G. (2013). *The mental health professional in court: A survival guide.* Washington, DC: American Psychiatric Publishing.

Guy, L. S., Douglas, K. S, & Hart, S. D. (2015). Risk assessment and communication. In B. L. Cutler & P. A. Zapf (Eds.), *APA handbook of forensic psychology* (Vol. 1, pp. 35–86). Washington, DC: American Psychological Association.

Haar v. Ulwelling, 154 P.3d 67 (N.M. Ct. App. 2007).

Hafemeister, T. L. (2003). Financial abuse of the elderly in domestic settings. In R. J. Bonnie & R. B. Wallace (Eds.), *Elder mistreatment: Abuse, neglect, and exploitation in an aging America* (pp. 382–445). Washington, DC: National Academies Press.

Haney-Caron, E., & Heilbrun, K. (2014). Lesbian and gay parents and determination of child custody: The changing legal landscape and implications for policy and practice. *Psychology of Sexual Orientation, 1,* 19–29.

Harrison v. Roitman, 362 P.3d 1138 (Nev. 2015).

Hart, H. L. A. (1968). *Punishment and responsibility: Essays in the philosophy of law.* New York: Oxford University Press.

Hart, H., & McNaughton, J. (1958). Evidence and inference in the law. *Daedalus, 87,* 40–64.

Hathcock v. Barnes, 25 P.3d 295 (Okla. Civil App. 2001).

Heisterkamp v. Pacheco, 47 N.E.3d 1192 (Ill. Ct. App. 2016).

Hendershot, L., & Bow, J. N. (2013). Investigating sexual abuse allegations in child custody disputes. *American Journal of Forensic Psychology, 31,* 37–52.

Herman, S. (2005). Improving decision making in forensic child sexual abuse evaluations. *Law and Human Behavior, 29,* 87–120.

Herman, S. (2009). Forensic child sexual abuse evaluations: Accuracy, ethics, and admissibility. In K. Kuehnle & M. Connell (Eds.), *The evaluation of child sexual abuse allegations: A comprehensive guide to assessment and testimony* (pp. 247–266). Hoboken, NJ: Wiley.

Hicks v. State, 6 So. 3d 1099 (Miss. Ct. App. 2009).

Huey, S. R. (2015). Tarasoff's catch-22. *American Psychologist, 70,* 284–285.

Illinois v. Gates, 462 U.S. 213 (1983).

In the Matter of A.A.,885 A.2d 974 (N.J. Super. 2005)).

In re A.J., 27 So. 3d 247 (La. 2009).

In re A.M., 856 N.W.2d 365 (Iowa 2014).

In re Cindy L., 17 Cal. 4th 15 (1997).

In re Clergy Cases, 188 Cal. App. 4th 1224 (2010).

In re Detention of Thorell, 72 P.3d 708, 724 (Wash. 2003).

In re Gault, 387 U.S. 1 (1967).

In re Jonathan C., 2015 WL 10038653 (N.Y. Family Ct. 2015).

In re L.M., 186 P.3d 164 (Kan. 2008).

In re P.W., 364 P.3d 891 (Colo. 2016).

In re R.K.L., 2016 WL 2957932 (Colo. Ct. App. 2016).

In re R.V., 61 Cal. 4th 181 (2015).

In re Z.K. (201 Cal. App. 4th 51 (2011).

INS v. Delgado, 466 U.S. 210, 217 (1984).

Jackson v. United States, 76 A.3d 920 (D.C. 2013).

Jacoves v. United Merchandizing Corp., 9 Cal. App. 4th 88 (1992).

Johnson v. Rogers Memorial Hospital, 700 N.W.2d 27 (Wis. 2005).

Johnson v. State, 452 S.W.3d 398 (Tex. Ct. App. 2014).

Jones, C. (2014). A new age of eyewitness identification evidence in light of modern scientific research: Why state v. Henderson does not significantly alter the management of eyewitness identification evidence. *Rutgers Law Journal, 44,* 511–545.

Jussab, F., & Murphy, H. (2015). "I just can't, I am frightened for my safety, I don't know how to work with her": Practitioners' experiences of client violence and recommendations for future practice. *Professional Psychology, Research and Practice, 46,* 287–297.

J.S. v. Berla, 456 S.W.3d 19 (Ky. Ct. App. 2015).

Kansas v. Crane, 534 U.S. 407 (2002).

Kansas v. Hendricks, 521 U.S. 346 (1997).

Kim, H. S. (2011). Consequences of parental divorce for child development *American Sociological Review, 76,* 487–511.

Kinsella v. Kinsella, 696 A.2d 556 (N.J. 1997).

Kirchmeyer v. Phillips, 245 Cal. App. 4th 1394 (2016).

Kivisto, A. J., Berman, A., Watson, M., Gruber, D., & Paul H. (2015). North

American psychologists' experiences of stalking, threatening, and harassing behavior: A survey of ABPP diplomats. *Professional Psychology, Research and Practice, 46,* 277–286.

Knapp, S., Handelsman, M. M., Gottlieb, M. C., & VandeCreek, L. D. (2013). The dark side of professional ethics. *Professional Psychology, Research and Practice, 44,* 371–377.

Knapp, S. J., & VandeCreek, L. D. (2002). *Practical ethics for psychologists: A positive approach.* Washington, DC: American Psychological Association.

Koch v. Cox, 489 F.3d 384 (D.C. Cir. 2007).

Kockelman v. Segal, 61 Cal. App. 4th 491 (1998).

Kohn, N. A. (2012). Elder (in)justice: A critique of the criminalization of elder abuse, *American Criminal Law Review, 49,* 1–29.

Komlodi v. Picciano, 89 A.3d 1234 (N.J. 2014).

Koocher, G. P., & Daniel, J. H. (2012). Treating children and adolescents. In S. J. Knapp, M. G. Gottlieb, M. M. Handlesman, & L. D. VandeCreek (Eds.), *APA handbook of ethics in psychology* (Vol. 2, pp. 3–14). Washington, DC: American Psychological Association.

Kozlovski v. Altapointe Health Systems, Inc., 2015 WL 1877656 (Ala. 2015).

Kuehnle, K. & Connell, M. (Eds.). (2009). *The evaluation of child sexual abuse allegations: A comprehensive guide to assessment and testimony.* Hoboken, NJ: Wiley.

Kumho Tire Company, Ltd. v. Carmichael, 526 U.S. 137 (1999).

LaFave, W. R., Israel, J. H., King, N. J., & Kerr, O. S. (2015). *Criminal procedure* (4th ed.). Eagan, MN: West Publishing.

L.A.N. v. L.M.B., 292 P.3d 942 (Colo. 2013).

Landeros v. Flood, 17 Cal. 3d 399 (1976).

Leon v. Ohio Board of Psychology, 590 N.E.2d 1223, 1226 (Ohio 1992).

L.L. v. Medical Protective Company, 362 N.W.2d 174 (1984).

Lewin, J. L. (1998). The genesis and evolution of legal uncertainty about "reasonable medical certainty." *Maryland Law Review 57,* 380–504.

Lincoln, A. (1953). Notes for a law lecture. In R. D. Basler (Ed.), *The collected works of Abraham Lincoln* (Vol. 2, p. 82). New Brunswick, NJ: Rutgers University Press. (Original work published 1850)

Logerquist v. McVey, 1 P.3d 113 (Ariz. 2000),

Loving v. Virginia, 388 U.S. 1 (1967).

Lustgarten, S. D. (2015). Emerging ethical threats to client privacy in cloud communication and data storage. *Professional Psychology, Research and Practice, 46,* 154–160.

Lyon, T. D. (2014). Interviewing children. *Annual Review of Law and Social Science, 10,* 73–89.

Lyon, T. D., & Saywitz, K. J. (1999). Young maltreated children's competence to take the oath. *Applied Developmental Science, 3* 16–27.

Manela v. Superior Court, 177 Cal. App. 4th 1139 (2009).

Marriage of Brown and Yana, 37 Cal. 4th 947 (2006).

Marriage of Davenport, 194 Cal. App. 4th 1507 (2011).

Marshall v. Klebanov, 902 A.2d 873, 879 (N.J. 2006).

McKeiver v. Pennsylvania, 403 U.S. 528 (1971).

McKenzie v. State, 670 S.E.2d 158 (Ga. Ct. App. 2008).

McLaughlin, J. L., & Kan, L. Y. (2014). Test usage in four common types of forensic mental health assessment. *Professional Psychology, Research and Practice, 45,* 128–135.

McNally v. Bredemann, 30 N.E.3d 557 (Ill. Ct. App. 2015).

Melton, G. B., & Limber, L. (1989). Psychologists' involvement in cases of child maltreatment. *American Psychologist, 44,* 1225–1233.

Melton, G. B., Petrila, P., Poythress, N. G., & Slobogin, C. (2007). *Psychological evaluations for the courts: A handbook for mental health professionals and lawyers* (3rd ed.). New York: Guilford Press.

Mental Health Commitment of James H., 2015 West Law 3476936 (Wis. Ct. App. 2015).

Midgett v. State, 729 S.W.2d 410 (Ark. Ct. App. 1987).

Miller v. Harbaugh, 698 F.3d 956 (7th Cir. 2012).

Miller-Jenkins v. Miller-Jenkins, 12 A.3d 768 (Vt. 2010).

Minow, M. (1993). All in the family and in all families: Membership, loving and owing. *West Virginia Law Review, 95,* 275–332.

Mississippi Band of Choctaw Indians v. Holyfield, 490 U.S. 30 (1989).

M.M. v. L.M., 55 A.3d 1167 (Pa. Super. 2012).

Monahan, J. (2008). Limiting therapist exposure to *Tarasoff* liability: Guidelines for risk containment. In D. N. Bershoff (Ed.), *Ethical conflicts in psychology* (4th ed., pp. 180–186). Washington, DC: American Psychological Association.

Monahan, J., Bonnie, R. J., Appelbaum, P. S., Hyde, P. S., Steadman, H. J., & Swartz, M. S. (2001). Mandated community treatment: Beyond outpatient commitment. *Psychiatric Services, 52,* 1198–1205.

Montana v. Egelhoff, 518 U.S. 37 (1996).

Moses v. State, 39 S.W.3d 458 (Ark. Ct. App. 2001).

M'Naghten, 8 Eng. Rep. 718 (1843).

Mueller, C. B., & Kirkpatrick, L. C. (2012). *Evidence* (5th ed.). New York: Wolters Kluwer Law and Business.

Myers, J. E. B. (1997). *A mother's nightmare—incest: A practical legal guide for parents and professionals.* Thousand Oaks, CA: Sage.

Myers, J. E. B. (2004). *A history of child protection in America.* Xlibris.

Myers, J. E. B. (2006). *Child protection in America: Past, present and future.* New York: Oxford University Press.

Myers, J. E. B. (2010a). Expert testimony in child sexual abuse litigation: Consensus and confusion. *U.C. Davis Journal of Juvenile Law and Policy, 14,* 1–57.

Myers, J. E. B. (2010b). *The history of child protection in America.* Sacramento, CA: University of the Pacific.

Myers, J. E. B. (2012). "Nobody's perfect: Partial disagreement with Herman, Faust, Bridges, and Ahern. *Journal of Child Sexual Abuse, 21,* 203–209.

Myers, J. E. B. (2014a). California's eavesdropping law endangers victims of domestic violence. *Journal of Information Technology and Privacy Law, 31,* 57–68.

Myers, J. E. B. (2014b). "I won't pay child support, but I insist on visitation":

Should visitation and child support be linked? *McGeorge Law Review, 45*, 695–705.

Myers, J. E. B. (2016). *Myers on evidence of interpersonal violence: Child maltreatment, intimate partner violence, rape, stalking and elder abuse* (6th ed.). New York: Wolters Kluwer Law and Business.

Myers v. Alaska Psychiatric Institute, 138 P.3d 238 (2006).

Nadler v. Superior Court, 255 Cal. App. 2d 523 (1967).

Nagy, T. F. (2011). *Essential ethics for psychologists: A primer for understanding and mastering core issues*. Washington, DC: American Psychological Association.

National Association of Social Workers. (2008). Code of ethics. Retrieved from *www.socialworkers.org/pubs/code.*

National Conference of Commissioners on Uniform State Laws. (2009) *Collaborative Law Act.*

Neuman v. State, 773 S.E.2d 716 (Ga. 2015).

Obergefell v. Hodges, 135 S. Ct. 2584 (2015).

Ohio v. Clark, 135 S. Ct. 2173 (2015).

Pachowitz v. LeDoux, 666 N.W.2d 88 (Wis. Ct. App. 2003).

Palmore v. Sidoti, 466 U.S. 429 (1984).

Parham v. J.R., 442 U.S. 584 (1979).

Park v. Kovachevich, 982 N.Y.S.2d 75, 81 (A.D. 2014).

Parry, J. (2009). *Criminal mental health and disability law, evidence and testimony*. Washington, DC: American Bar Association.

Patel, S. H., & Choate, L. H. (2014). Conducting child custody evaluations: Best practices for mental health counselors who are court-appointed as child custody evaluators. *Journal of Mental Health Counseling, 36*, 18–30.

Pedeferri v. Seidner Enterprises, 216 Cal. App. 4th 359 (2013).

Pennsylvania v. Ritchie, 480 U.S. 39 (1987).

People v. Acosta, 338 P.3d 472 (Colo. Ct. App. 2014).

People v. Chatman, 38 Cal. 4th 344, 384 (2006).

People v. Cross, 114 P.3d 1 (Colo. Ct. App. 2004), *reversed on other grounds*, 127 P.3d 71 (Colo. 2006).

People v. Clark, 432 N.W.2d 173 (Mich. Ct. App. 1988).

People v. Davis, 208 P.3d 78 (Cal. 2009).

People v. DeHoyos, 57 Cal. 4th 79, 123 (2013).

People v. Gilmore, 653 N.E.2d 58 (Ill. Ct. App.1995)

People v. Gonzales, 56 Cal. 4th 353 (2013).

People v. Kailey, 333 P.3d 89, 91 (Colo. 2014).

People v. Mills, 55 Cal. 4th 663 (2012).

People v. Nicholson, 2016 WL 633925 (N.Y. 2016).

People v. Richter, 977 N.E.2d 1257 (Ill. Ct. App. 2012).

People v. Rivera, 25 N.Y.3d 256 (2015).

People v. Sullivan, 53 P.3d 1181 (Colo. Ct. App. 2002).

People v. Superior Court, 18 Cal. 4th 667 (1998).

People v. Wetmore, 22 Cal. 3d 318 (1978).

Perez v. Oakland County, 466 F.3d 416 (6th Cir. 2006).

Perlin, M. (2008). *Mental disability Law: Civil and criminal* (2nd ed.). Los Angeles: LexisNexis.

Pesisoli, C., Herman, S., & Dalbosco Dell'Aglio, D. (2014). Child sexual abuse research knowledge among child abuse professionals and laypersons. *Child Abuse and Neglect, 40,* 36–47.

Petric v. People, 2014 WestLaw 5284572 (V.I. 2014).

Pomerance, B. (2015). Finding the middle ground on a slippery slope: Balancing autonomy and protection in mandatory reporting of elder abuse. *Marquette Benefits and Social Welfare Law Review, 16,* 439–492.

Poole, D. A., & Wolfe, M. A. (2009). Child development: Normative sexual and nonsexual behaviors that may be confused with symptoms of sexual abuse. In K. Kuehnle & M. Connell (Eds.), *The evaluation of child sexual abuse allegations: A Comprehensive guide to assessment and testimony* (pp. 101–128). Hoboken, NJ: Wiley.

Poythress, N. G. (1982). Concerning reform in expert testimony: An open letter from a practicing psychologist, *Law and Human Behavior, 6,* 39–43.

Prince v. Massachusetts, 321 U.S. 158 (1944).

Prink v. Rockefeller Center, Inc., 48 N.Y.2d 309 (1979).

P.T. v. Richard Hall Community Mental Health Care Center, 837 A.2d 427 (N.J. App. Div. 2000).

Reed v. Pieper, 713 S.E.2d 309 (S.C. Ct. App. 2011).

R.D. v. P.M., 202 Cal. App. 4th 181 (2011).

Reid, J. H. (1959). Next steps: Action called for—recommendations. In H. S. Mass & R. E. Engler, Jr. *Children in need of parents* (pp. 378–397). New York: Columbia University Press.

Ricci, L. R., & Wientzen, J. (2014). Sexual abuse: Overview. In D. L. Chadwick, A. P. Giardina, R. Alexander, J. D. Thackerray, & D. Esernio-Jenssen (Eds.), *Chadwick's child maltreatment* (Vol. 2, pp. 1–17). Florissant, MO: STM Learning.

Riley v. California, 134 S. Ct. 2473 (2014).

Robinson, P. H. (1984). *Criminal law defenses.* Eagan, MN: West Publishing.

Robinson, P. H., Kussmaul, M. G., Stoddard, C. M., Rudyak I., & Kuersten, A. (2015).The American criminal code: General defenses. *Journal of Legal Analysis, 7,* 37.

Roe v. Roe, 324 S.E.2d 691 (Va. 1985).

Roe v. Wade, 410 U.S. 113 (1973).

Rost v. State Board of Psychology, 659 A.2d 626 (Pa. Commonwealth Court 1995).

Satterfield v. State, 33 N.E.3d 344 (Ind. 2015).

Saywitz, K. J., & Camparo, L. B. (2014). *Evidence-based child forensic interviewing: The developmental narrative elaboration interview.* New York: Oxford University Press.

Sell v. United States, 539 U.S. 166 (2003),

Sepulveda v. Aviles, 762 N.Y.S.2d 358 (A.D. 2003).

Sheetz, B. M. (2007). Note. The choice to limit choice: using psychiatric advance directives to manage the effects of mental illness and support self-responsibility. *University of Michigan Journal of Law Reform, 40,* 401, 403.

Sink, F. (1988). Studies of true and false allegations: A critical review. In E. B. Nicholson & J. Bulkley (Eds.), *Sexual abuse allegations in custody and visitation cases* (pp. 37–47). Washington, DC: American Bar Association.
Slater, L. K., & Finck, K. R. (2012). *Social work practice and the law.* New York: Springer.
Smith, C. (2015). The conundrum of family reunification: A theoretical, legal, and practical approach to reunification services for parents with mental disabilities. *Stanford Law and Policy Review, 26,* 307–348.
Squeo v. Norwalk Hospital Association, 113 A.3d 932 (Conn. 2015).
Stahl, P. M., & Martin, L. (2013). An historical look at child custody evaluations and the influence of the AFCC. *Family Court Review, 51,* 42–47.
State Department of Hospitals v. Superior Court, 61 Cal. 4th 339 (2015).
State v. Anderson, 851 N.W.2d 760 (Wis. 2014).
State v. Andring, 342 N.W.2d 128 (Minn. 1984).
State v. Coats, 3 N.E.3d 528 (Ind. 2014).
State v. DeLeon, 319 P.3d 463 (Hawai'i 2014).
State v. Douglas, 671 S.E.2d 606 (S.C. 2009).
State v. Duran, 343 P.3d 207 (N.M. Ct. App. 2014).
State v. Favoccia, 51 A.3d 1002, 1009 (Conn. 2012).
State v. Gardner, 616 A.2d 1124 (R.I. 1992).
State v. Gordon, 952 S.W.2d 817 (Tenn. 1997).
State v. Higginbotham, 790 So.2d 648 (La. Ct. App. 2001).
State v. Kucharski 866 N.W.2d 697 (Wis. 2015).
State v. Norman, 366 S.E.2d 586 (N.C. Ct. App. 1988), *reversed,* 378 S.E.2d 8 (N.C. 1989).
State v. Singleton, 48 A.3d 285 (N.J. 2012).
State v. Timmendequas, 737 A.2d 55 (N.J. 1999).
State v. Tyler, 867 N.W.2d 136 (Iowa 2015).
State v. Whittaker, 650 S.E.2d 216 (W. Va. 2007).
State v. Willis, 87 P.3d 1164 (2004).
Sugarman v. Board of Registration in Medicine, 662 N.E.2d 1020 (Mass. 1996).
Summit, R. C. (1983). The child sexual abuse accommodation syndrome. *Child Abuse and Neglect, 7,* 177–193.
Tarasoff v. Regents of the University of California, 17 Cal. 3d 425 (1976).
Terry v. Ohio, 392 U.S. 1 (1968).
Thapar v. Zezulka, 994 S.W.3d 635 (Tex. 1999).
Trocme, N. & Bala, N. (2005). False allegations of abuse and neglect when parents separate. *Child Abuse and Neglect, 29,* 1333–1345.
Troxel v. Granville, 530 U.S. 57 (2000).
Trudrung v. Trudrung, 686 F. Supp. 2d 570 (M.D. N.C. 2010).
United States v. Auster, 517 F.3d 312 (5th Cir. 2008).
United States v. Babarinde, 2015 WL 5158972 (D. D.C. 2015).
United States v. Brawner, 471 F.2d 969 (D.C. Cir. 1972).
United States v. Ewing, 494 F.3d 607 (7th Cir. 2007).
United States Fidelity and Guaranty Co. v. Guenther, 281 U.S. 34 (1930).
United States v. Hayes, 227 F.3d 578 (6th Cir. 2000).
United States v. McDonald, 73 M.J. 426 (C.A.A.F. 2014).

Varela, J. G., & Conroy, M. A. (2012). Professional competencies in forensic psychology. *Professional Psychology: Research and Practice, 43*, 410–421.

Walden Behavioral Care v. K.I., 27 N.E.3d 1244 (Mass. 2015).

Wallis v. Spencer, 202 F.3d 1136 (9th Cir. 2000).

Weiss, R. A., & Rosenfeld, B. (2012). Navigating cross-cultural issues in forensic assessment: Recommendations for practice. *Professional Psychology: Research and Practice, 43*, 234–240.

Wigmore, J. H. (1974). *Evidence in trials at common law* (4th ed.). Boston: Little, Brown. (Original work published 1904)

Williams v. State, 970 So. 2d 727 (Miss. Ct. App. 2007).

Wood, D. (2016, March 22). Nurse pleads guilty to HIPAA violation. *Nursing News*. Available at *www.americanmobile.com/nursezone/nursing-news/Nurse-Pleads-Guilty-to-HIPAA-Violation*.

Zeranski, L., & Halgin, R. P. (2011). Ethical issues in elder abuse reporting: A professional psychologist's guide. *Professional Psychology: Research and Practice, 42*, 294–300.

Zumbach, J., & Koglin, U. (2015). Psychological evaluations in family law proceedings: A systematic review of the contemporary literature. *Professional Psychology: Research and Practice, 46*, 221–234.

Zur, O. (2007). Boundaries in psychotherapy: Ethical and clinical explorations. Washington, DC: American Psychological Association.

Index

Abandonment, 243
Adoption, 120
Advance directive, 137–138
Adversary system, 12–15, 88, 146
Aliention, 272
Annulment, 88–89
Arrest, 55–56
Attack on interview, 183

B

Battered child syndrome, 250
Boundaries. *See* Ethics and malpractice
Burden of proof, 165–166

C

Court-appointed special advocate (CASA), 118
Certiorari, writ, 11
Child abduction, 6
Child abuse
  battered child syndrome, 250
  child protective services. *See* Child protective services
  corporal punishment, 116, 250
  juvenile court, 116–125
  medical neglect, 253–254
  neglect, 116–117, 253–254
  physical abuse, 116, 250–253
  proof of neglect in court, 250–253
  proof of sexual abuse in court, 254–262
  proof of physical abuse in court, 250–253
  psychological abuse, 116
  sexual abuse, 116, 254–262
  shaken baby syndrome, 116, 250
Child custody. *See* Custody of children
Child protective services
  differential response, 111–112
  emergency removal, 107–108
  exigent circumstances, 108
  family preservation, 110
  federal leadership, 109–112
  foster care, 109
  immunity, 109
  juvenile court, 116–125
  reasonable efforts, 109–110
  reporting laws, 109
Child sexual abuse accommodation syndrome, 262
Child witness, 144
Closing argument, 64
Commitment to hospital
  advance directives, 137–138
  children, commitment of, 133–134
  dangerousness, 129–131
  gravely disabled, 130
  insanity defense, 46
  intellectual disability, 133

Commitment to hospital (*continued*)
outpatient commitment, 131–132
periodic review of commitment, 132–133
refuse treatment, 132
risk assessment, 130–131, 135
sex offender commitment, 134–135
short-term commitment, 128–129
voluntary hospitalization, 136–137
Common law, 11
Competence
stand trial, 60–61
testify, competence to, 143–144
transfer property, 33
undue influence, 33
Competence to stand trial, 60–61
Confessions, 59–60
Confidentiality and privileged communications
alcohol and drug treatment records, 210
attorney–client privilege, 214
child abuse cases, 215
child abuse reporting, 210
children and adolescents, 208–209, 215
clergy–penitent privilege, 215
complaint against professional, 217
confidentiality defined, 204
couple therapy, 219–220
court ordered treatment, 218
dangerous patient, 217, 222, 235, 237–242
differences between confidentiality and privilege, 211–212
disclosure of confidential and privileged information, 220–224, 233–234
domestic violence cases, 215
court ordered disclosure, 209
emergencies, 223
ethics codes, 205–206
evaluation, 217–218
family therapy, 219–220
forensic evaluation, 217–218
forfeiture of privilege, 215–216
group therapy, 219–220
HIPAA, 204, 207–210, 222–223
patient–litigant exception, 216, 225
psychotherapist–client privilege, 203, 212–213
physician–patient privilege, 204, 213–214
privacy, right to, 205
privileges, 210–211
protective order, 224
psychotherapy notes, 209
records, confidentiality of, 207–210
reporting law, 217, 222
sources of confidentiality, 205–206
spousal privileges, 214–215
subpoenas, 3, 203, 209, 211–213, 219, 223
suicide, 234–237
taking client records to court, 224
Tarasoff duty to warn, 222, 238–239
waiver, 215–216
Confrontation Clause. *See* Hearsay
Consistent with sexual abuse, 183–184, 193–201
Corporal punishment, 250
Courts
federal courts, 6
juvenile court, 112–125
U.S. Supreme Court, 6, 9–10
Criminal law
actus reus, 22–23, 35
defenses, 35–41
diminished capacity, 50
insanity defense, 37–39, 43–51
intent, 23–24, 35
intentional, 23–24
intoxication, 38–39, 50–51
justification, 24
knowing, 23–24
malice, 23
manslaughter, 21, 24–26
mental illness, 37–38
mens rea, 22–24, 35–36, 38, 46
murder, 23–25
negligent, 23
rape, 28–29
reckless, 23

self-defense, 39–41, 52
stalking, 29–31
statutory rape, 29
Cross-examination. *See* Testifying
Custody of children
alienation, 272
best interest of the child, 93
education, 93–95
evaluation, 93–96, 228
gay and lesbian parents, 96–97
history, 91
immunity for court-appointed custody evaluator, 245
impact of divorce on children, 91
legal custody, 92
military, 101
modification, 98–99
move-away cases, 100– 101
physical custody, 92
psychological records, 216
privilege, 216
race, 97–98
recommendations, 95
sexual abuse, allegations of, 263–276
sexual conduct, 97
temporary, 98
visitation, 103–104

D

Dangerous patient, 217, 222, 235, 237–242, 245–246
Dangerous patient exception to confidentiality. *See* Confidentiality and privilege
Daubert, 167–169, 250
Delinquency, 112–115
Diagnostic and Statistical Manual of Mental Disorders, ix
Diminished capacity, 50–51
Direct examination. *See* Testifying
Discovery, 61–62
Divorce, 88–89, 91–92
Domestic violence. *See* Intimate partner violence
Dual relations. *See* Ethics and malpractice

E

Elder abuse, 32–34, 280–281
Equal protection, 7–10
Ethics and malpractice
abandonment, 243
boundaries, 228–230
civil rights violations, 244–245
clinical versus forensic practice, 228
dangerous patient, 222, 237–242
discharge decision, 235–236
disclosure of confidential or privileged matters, 233–234
dual relations, 229–230
duty of care, 227, 234–237
ending therapy, 243
forensic practice, 218, 228–229
immunity, 235, 244–245
informed consent, 232–233
release of confidential client information, 217, 221
malpractice defined, 226
multiple relationships, 22, 228
negligence, 226
psychotherapy, malpractice claims, 227
reasonable person standard, 22
reporting maltreatment, duty to, 243–244
sex with client, 229, 231
standard of care, 226–227
suicide, 234–237
Tarasoff, 222, 237–242
tardive dyskinesia, 232
unauthorized disclosure of confidential information, 221
Evaluation
child custody, 93–96
competence to stand trial, 60–61, 228
confidentiality and privilege, 217–218
immunity for court-appointed evaluators, 245
informed consent, 232–233
insanity defense, 46–47
sexual abuse, 254–262

Expert testimony
bases of expert testimony, 162–163
child physical abuse, 250–253
credibility, opinion on, 184
cross-examination, 171–192
Daubert, 167–169
direct examination, 170–171
eyewitness, 36
forensic interviews, 182–183
Frye, 167–169
hypothetical question, 159, 170, 172
immunity for court-appointed experts, 245
insanity defense, 47–50
lay witness compared, 158–160
learned treatises, 192–201
novel scientific evidence, 167–169
objectivity, 170
opinion, 159, 170
preparation, 169
qualifications, 161–162
reasonable certainty, 164–167, 252
review of client records prior to testifying, 224
scientific evidence, 167–169
sexual abuse, 3
taking client records to court, 224
types, 3–4
ultimate issues, 163–164

F

Family law, 12–13
Federal government
child protection, 109–112
limited powers, 4
Necessary and Proper Clause, 5
separation of powers, 5, 8
spending power, 5–6
Supremacy Clause, 7–8, 10
U.S. Constitution, 4
Financial exploitation, 33
Forensic practice. *See* Ethics and malpractice
Foster care, 119–123
Foundation, 179–180, 195
Frye, 167–169, 250

G

Guardianship, 120, 233
Guilty but mentally ill, 51

H

Hague Convention on the Civil Aspects of International Child Abduction, 6–7, 102–103
Hearsay
admissions, 75
child hearsay exception, 74–75
Confrontation Clause, 75–81, 252
defined, 68
excited utterance exception, 71–72, 83, 249
expert testimony based on, 162
importance of hearsay, 32
medical diagnosis or treatment exception, 73–74, 83, 250
party admissions, 75
prior inconsistent statements, 75
residual exception, 74–75, 250, 252
HIPAA. *See* Confidentiality and privilege

I

"Illegitimate" child, 90
Immunity, 96, 109, 244–245
Impeachment. *See* Testifying
Indian Child Welfare Act, 124
Informed consent, 230, 232–233
Insanity defense, 37–39, 43–51
Intentional, 23–24, 29
Interstate Compact on the Placement of Children, 124–125
Interviews, 174, 184
Intimate partner violence
crime, 31–32
proof in court, 249–250
recantation, 31
self-defense, 40–41, 52
Violence Against Women Act, 6
Intoxication, 38–39, 50–51
Irresistible impulse, 45

J

Jurisdiction
 child custody, 101–102
 divorce, 89
Jury trial, 13, 62, 63, 113, 118
Juvenile court
 abuse and neglect, 116–125
 court-appointed special advocate, 118
 delinquency, 112–115
 foster care, 119–123
 status offenses, 115–116
 termination of parental rights, 118–120

L

Law
 common law, 11
 defined, 3
 federal law, 5–6
 jury trial, 13
 ordinances, 8–9
 regulations, 6, 8
 sources, 4–5
 statutes, 5, 11
Learned treatises, 192–201

M

Malice aforethought, 25–26
Malpractice. *See* Ethics and malpractice
Manslaughter, 21, 24–26
Medical neglect, 253–254
Medication
 informed consent, 232
 restore to competence to stand trial, 61
Mental illness, 37–38, 42–51
Miranda warnings, 56–58
Mistake of fact, 37
M'Naghten, 43–51
Multiple relationships. *See* Ethics and malpractice
Murder, 23–25, 38, 51

N

Neglect. *See* Child abuse
Negligence, 21, 23, 26, 238
Novel scientific evidence, 167–169

O

Opening statement, 63

P

Parentage, 90
Parental rights, 107–109
Parental Kidnapping Prevention Act (PKPA), 101–102
Patient–litigant exception to privilege. *See* Confidentiality and privilege
Penetration, 28, 38
Plea bargaining, 62, 113, 117
Posttraumatic stress disorder, 257
Premeditation, 25, 51
Prior inconsistent statements, 31, 75, 147
Privileged communications. *See* Confidentiality and privilege
Probable cause, 55, 58
Punishment, 64–65

R

Rape, 28–29, 40, 163
Rape shield statute, 28
Reasonable certainty, 164–167
Reasonable person, 21–22, 55–56, 243
Reasonable suspicion, 56
Reckless, 23
Regulations, 6, 8
Reporting duty, 3, 109, 116, 210, 217, 222, 228, 243–244, 274

S

Search and seizure
 car searches, 59
 consent, 59
 exclusionary rule, 59
 exigent circumstances, 59
 plain view, 59
 search incident to arrest, 58–59
Self-defense, 39–41
Sentencing, 64–65
Service Members Civil Relief Act, 101

Sex offender commitment, 134–135
Sex with client. *See* Ethics and malpractice
Sexual abuse/assault
  alienation, 272
  allegations of sexual abuse in family court, 263–276
  child sexual abuse accommodation syndrome, 262
  consistent with sexual abuse, 183–184, 193–201, 260–261
  defined, 116
  expert testimony, 3, 171, 193–201, 260–262
  fabricated allegations, 271
  misperception, 273–274
  rehabilitation of child's credibility, 262
  proof in court, 254–262
  rape, 28–29
Shaken baby syndrome, 116, 250
Soldiers and Sailors Relief Act, 101
Stalking, 29–31, 246
State and local government, 8–9
Statute of limitations, 51
Statutory rape, 29
Status offenses, 115–116
Stop and frisk, 56
Subpoenas. *See* Confidentiality and privilege
Suicide, 22, 234–237
Supreme Court, 6, 9–11

T

Tarasoff duty to warn, 222, 237–242
Termination of parental rights, 118–120
Terry stop, 56
Testilying, 270–271
Testifying
  bias, 148, 152–153
  child's credibility, 262
  competence to testify, 143–144
  contradiction, 147–148
  control the witness, 150, 153–154
  conviction used to impeach, 148
  cross-examination, 146, 171–192
  direct examination, 144–145, 170–171
  impeachment, 146–149
  leading questions, 150, 155
  learned treatises, 192–193
  lies to impeach, 148
  memory, 148
  narrative, 145, 155
  objection, 145, 154–156
  opportunity to observe, 148–149, 151
  prior inconsistent statements, 147
  redirect examination, 144, 146, 150, 153, 183, 201
  testifying not necessarily forensic practice, 228
  ultimate issues, 163–164
Trial, 63–64, 118
Trier of fact, 13, 62–63

U

Ultimate issues, 48–50, 95, 163–164, 260
Undue influence, 33
Uniform Child Custody Jurisdiction and Enforcement Act (UCCJEA), 101–102
U.S. Constitution, 4, 6–8, 205–207

V

Visitation, 103–104